D0467875

The Official Guidebook Of CHINA

The Official Guidebook Of
CHINA

Edited by China Travel and Tourism Press

Edition Authorized by
China International Travel Service

Sunshine
Books

Published by
Sunshine Books, an imprint of
Child & Henry Publishing Pty Ltd.
9 Clearview Place, Brookvale, NSW, Australia, 2100

First Edition, 1982
Sunshine Books Edition, 1985, 1986
© China Travel and Tourism Press, Beijing, 1982, 1985

Designed by Irene Friedman

Printed in the United States of America

National Library of Australia Card Number and
ISBN 0 86777 185 2

PREFACE

In preparing THE OFFICIAL GUIDEBOOK OF CHINA for publication in English, much thought was given to how best this Guidebook could aid the traveler prior to and during a visit to the People's Republic of China. When one visits a foreign country there are often many adjustments to be made as a result of the differences one encounters. Unfamiliar language and currency, differences in lifestyle and cuisine--in fact, almost all aspects of daily life take on new meanings and require certain adjustments. In gathering information for this volume, special efforts were made to take into account the differences one might expect to encounter while traveling in China. This Guidebook brings together all the information the traveler needs to fully prepare and truly enjoy the trip.

THE OFFICIAL GUIDEBOOK OF CHINA is designed both for "armchair" browsing and quick reference. The Table of Contents is very complete and should be helpful in locating information quickly. The three major cities most often visited by tourists--Beijing (Peking), Guangzhou (Canton), and Shanghai (Shanghai)--are each given special sections. Other places which are readily accessible to travelers are grouped in alphabetical order. An extensive Appendix has been designed to consolidate the most frequently used information. Thus, the various charts, addresses, conversion tables, menus, and other reference material is in one place and can be used both to plan your visit and to assist you while you are in China. The Appendix provides a convenient source for the information you most likely will want at your fingertips.

Throughout the Guidebook you will note two spellings for Chinese names and places. The first variation shown is the Pinyin spelling which, since 1958, has been the official phonetic alphabet of China. During your visit you will see Pinyin on the various signs throughout the country. The second spelling, shown in parenthesis, is the Wade-Giles system which is more familiar to English-speaking travelers. One of the best examples to show you the difference is the name of China's capital city. In Pinyin it is called Beijing but it is better known to the Western world as Peking which is the Wade-Giles spelling. At the end of the Table of Contents the cities and regions covered in this Guidebook are listed in both Pinyin and Wade-Giles so that you can more easily recognize the places you will be visiting. Note: When adopting Pinyin not all names have been changed. Shanghai is the same in both spelling systems. When this variation occurs the name is shown twice, i.e., Shanghai (Shanghai).

China is an exciting and fascinating country. Hopefully this Guidebook will convey the unique qualities of excitement and mystery that have captivated the traveler to China since the days of Marco Polo.

TABLE OF CONTENTS

Section 1
Introduction To China

Page

Introduction..21

Capital..22

Climate...22

Oceans..22

Rivers...23

Lakes..23

Islands..23

Harbors...24

Topography...24

Natural Resources/Agriculture..25

History..25

Language..28

Government...29

Section 2
Visitor's Information

General Information..33

Visas...36

Quarantine..36

Customs Regulations..36

Clothing..38

Hotels/Hotel Service..39

Medical Services..40

Telephones..41

Telegrams/Cables...42

Postal Services..43

Miscellaneous Services..43

Chinese Currency...43

Foreign Exchange Certificates 44

Renminbi (Chinese) Traveler's Checks...............................45

Foreign Currency, Bills and
  Traveler's Checks...46

Credit Cards...46

Air Service..47

Railroads (Inter-city Transportation)...............................50

Intra-city Transportation...51

Shopping...51

Chinese Cuisine..53

Chopsticks..56

Wines and Liquors...57

Arts and Crafts..57

Entertainment...60

Special Native Products..62

Freshwater Fish..66

Birds/Animals of China..66

Section 3
Main Tourist Cities

*Beijing (Peking)..71

   Places of Interest..74

   Shopping...102

   Hotels..105

   Restaurants...109

*Guangzhou (Canton)..112

   Places of Interest..115

   Shopping...123

   Hotels..124

   Restaurants...127

*Shanghai (Shanghai)...130

   Places of Interest..134

   Shopping...141

	Page
Hotels	141
Restaurants	145

*Denotes City Map Included

Section 4
Other Places To Visit

	Page
Anshan (Anshan)	149
Baotou (Paotow)	150
*Changchun (Changchun)	151
Changjiang (Yangtze River) Gorges	152
*Changsha (Changsha)	154
Chengde (Chengteh)	158
*Chengdu (Chengtu)	159
Chongqing (Chungking)	161
*Dalian (Talien)	164
Datong (Tatung)	166
Dazu County (Tatzu County)	167
Emei Shan (Mount Omei)	167
Foshan (Foshan)	169
Fushun (Fushun)	173
Fuzhou (Foochow)	174
*Guilin (Kweilin)	176
Handan (Hantan)	179
*Hangzhou (Hangchow)	180
*Harbin (Harbin)	185
*Hefei (Hofei)	188
*Hohhot (Huhehot)	189
Huang Shan (Yellow Mountain)	193
Hua Shan (Huashan Mountain)	195
Jiayuguan Pass (Chiayukuan Pass)	196
Jilin (Kirin)	197
Jinggang Shan (Chingkang Mountain)	198
*Jinan (Tsinan)	199
Jingdezhen (Chingtehchen)	202
Jinghong (Chinghung)	203
Jiuhua Shan (Nine Flowers Mountain)	206

Jiujiang (Chiuchiang) 207

Jiuquan (Chiuchuan) 208

Kaifeng (Kaifeng) 209

*Kunming (Kunming) 211

*Lanzhou (Lanchow) 214

Leshan (Leshan) 216

Lhasa (Lhasa) 217

Lianyun Gang (Lienyun Harbor) 218

Liuzhou (Liuchow) 219

*Luoyang (Loyang) 220

Lu Shan (Lushan Mountains
or Mount Lushan) 222

Mogan Shan (Mokan Mountain) 225

Mogao Grottoes (Mokao Grottoes) 225

*Nanchang (Nanchang) 226

*Nanjing (Nanking) 228

*Nanning (Nanning) 234

Ningbo (Ningpo) 237

Qingdao (Tsingtao) 238

Qinhuangdao (Chinhuangtao) 240

Quanzhou (Chuanchow) 241

Qufu (Chufu) 242

Shaoshan (Shaoshan) 243

*Shenyang (Shenyang) 247

Shenzhen (Shumchun) 248

*Shijiazhuang (Shihchiachuang) 250

Shilin (Stone Forest) 251

*Suzhou (Soochow) 252

Tai Shan (Taishan Mountain) 255

*Taiyuan (Taiyuan) 259

*Tianjin (Tientsin) 261

Turpan County (Turfan County) 264

*Ürümqi (Ürümchi) 265

*Wuhan (Wuhan) 267

*Wuxi (Wuhsi) 270

Xiamen (Amoy) 273

*Xi'an (Sian) 275

Xingzi County (Hsingtsu County).................................280

Xuzhou (Hsuchow)...281

Yan'an (Yenan)..282

Yangshuo (Yangshuo)..283

Yangzhou (Yangchow)...284

Yantai (Yentai)..286

Yichang (Ichang) 287

Yixing (Yihsing)..288

Yueyang (Yoyang)...291

Zhangzhou (Changchow) 292

*Zhengzhou (Chengchow)...293

Zhenjiang (Chenchiang)..295

Zhuoxian County (Chohsien County)..............................297

Zunhua (Tsunhua)..298

Section 5
Appendix

Helpful Hints... 303

China International Travel Service
    Branches and Addresses.. 307

Air Route Map.. 309

Railway Map... 310

Distances Between Main Tourist Cities
    By Rail.. 311

Time Differences.. 313

Temperature Chart.. 314

Rainfall Chart... 316

Credit Card Acceptance.. 317

Hotels 318

Friendship Stores and Sailor's Clubs
    and Addresses... 320

Major Arts and Crafts Department
    Stores and Addresses.. 321

	Page
Major Antique Stores and Address	322
Foreign Currency, Traveler's Checks, and International Bank Drafts Accepted	324
Money Conversion Chart	326
Postage Costs	327
Weights and Measures, Table of	327
Chinese Dynasties	328
Holidays	330
Useful Phrases	332
Wines and Liquors	335
Banquets — Sample Menus	339
100 Most Popular Chinese Dishes	347

Index 351

List of City Maps

Beijing (Peking)	73
Guangzhou (Canton)	113
Shanghai (Shanghai)	132
Changchun (Changchun)	151
Changsha (Changsha)	155
Chengdu (Chengtu)	159
Dalian (Talien)	164
Guilin (Kweilin)	177
Hangzhou (Hangchow)	181
Harbin (Harbin)	185
Hefei (Hofei)	188
Hohhot (Huhehot)	190
Jinan (Tsinan)	199
Kunming (Kunming)	211
Lanzhou (Lanchow)	214
Luoyang (Loyang)	220
Nanchang (Nanchang)	227

Nanjing (Nanking).. 229

Nanning (Nanning)... 235

Shenyang (Shenyang)... 248

Shijiazhuang (Shihchiachuang).. 250

Suzhou (Soochow)... 252

Taiyuan (Taiyuan).. 258

Tianjin (Tientsin)... 263

Urumqi (Urumchi)... 267

Wuhan (Wuhan)... 269

Wuxi (Wuhsi).. 270

Xi'an (Sian).. 275

Zhengzhou (Chengchow).. 293

Cities covered in Sections 3 and 4 are alphabetized by Pinyin (the official Chinese phonetic alphabet) with the better-known Wade-Giles spelling in parenthesis. For ease in reference the following is an alphabetical listing by the Wade-Giles method of spelling (with Pinyin also shown) of the cities and regions covered in this Guidebook

Wade-Giles	**Pinyin**
Amoy	Xiamen
Anshan	Anshan
Canton	Guangzhou
Changchow	Zhangzhou
Changchun	Changchun
Chenchiang	Zhenjiang
Chengchow	Zhengzhou

Wade-Giles	Pinyin
Chengteh	Chengde
Chengtu	Chengdu
Chiayukuan Pass	Jiayuguan Pass
Chinghung	Jinghong
Chingkang Mountain	Jinggang Shan
Chingtehchen	Jingdezhen
Chinhuangtao	Qinhuangdao
Chiuchiang	Jiujiang
Chiuchuan	Jiuquan
Chohsien County	Zhuoxian County
Chuanchow	Quanzhou
Chufu	Qufu
Chungking	Chongqing
Foochow	Fuzhou
Foshan	Foshan
Fushun	Fushun
Hangchow	Hangzhou
Hantan	Handan
Harbin	Harbin
Hofei	Hefei
Hsingtsu County	Xingzi County
Hsuchow	Xuzhou
Huashan Mountain	Hua Shan
Huhehot	Hohhot
Ichang	Yichang
Kaifeng	Kaifeng
Kirin	Jilin
Kunming	Kunming
Kweilin	Guilin
Lhasa	Lhasa
Lanchow	Lanzhou
Leshan	Leshan
Lienyun Harbor	Lianyun Gang
Liuchow	Liuzhou
Loyang	Luoyang
Lushan Mountains	Lu Shan
Mokan Mountains	Mogan Shan
Mokao Grottoes	Mogao Grottoes
Mount Omei	Emei Shan
Nanchang	Nanchang
Nanking	Nanjing

Wade-Giles	Pinyin
Nanning	Nanning
Nine Flowers Mountain	Jiuhua Shan
Ningpo	Ningbo
Paotow	Baotou
Peking	Beijing
Shanghai	Shanghai
Shaohsing	Shaoxing
Shaoshan	Shaoshan
Shenyang	Shenyang
Shihchiachuang	Shijiazhuang
Shumchun	Shenzhen
Sian	Xi'an
Soochow	Suzhou
Stone Forest	Shilin
Taishan Mountain	Tai Shan
Taiyuan	Taiyuan
Talien	Dalian
Tatung	Datong
Tatzu County	Dazu County
Tientsin	Tianjin
Tsinan	Jinan
Tsingtao	Qingdao
Tsunhua	Zunhua
Turfan County	Turpan County
Ürümchi	Ürümqi
Wuhan	Wuhan
Wuhsi	Wuxi
Yangchow	Yangzhou
Yangshuo	Yangshuo
Yangtze River	Changjiang
Yellow Mountain	Huang Shan
Yellow River	Huang He
Yenan	Yan'an
Yentai	Yantai
Yihsing	Yixing
Yoyang	Yueyang

1. Introduction To China

Jade Screen Tower, Anhui

The People's Republic of China, with a recorded history of four thousand years, is the birthplace of four major inventions: the compass, papermaking, movable-type printing, and gunpowder, all significant contributions to world civilization. Situated in the eastern part of Asia, on the west coast of the Pacific Ocean, China is the third largest nation in area in the world after the U.S.S.R. and Canada. With a population of over 900 million, China is the most populous country in the world comprising a quarter of the earth's population.

China's land boundaries measure over 12,000 mi. (20,000 km.) in length with a coastline of over 11,178 mi. (18,000 km.). From east to west it measures over 3,000 mi. (5,000 km.) and from north to south, over 3,300 mi. (5,500 km.). On its border with Nepal lies the world's highest peak, Qomolangma Feng (Mount Jolmo Lungma), more popularly known in the West as Mount Everest.

A vast country with a great variety of natural scenery, China has a wide range of climates, rich natural resources, plentiful forests, and fertile soil. Composed of twenty-two provinces, five autonomous regions, and three municipalities (altogether over two thousand counties), it is a multi-national country. The Han nationality makes up about ninety-four percent of the total population; the remaining six percent consists of more than fifty minority nationalities.

Capital

Beijing (Peking), China's political, economic, and cultural center, is at the northwest edge of Huabei Pingyuan (North China Plain). It covers an area of 6,870 sq. mi. (17,800 sq. km.) and has a population of 8.5 million people. Beijing has been the capital for over eight hundred years and has numerous historical sites, such as the magnificent Forbidden City, the Summer Palace, the Ming Tombs, and the imposing Great Wall.

Climate

China has a variety of climates covering the tropical, subtropical, temperate, and high frigid zones, with the majority of the areas in the temperate zone. The climate from north to south differs greatly with a temperature difference of over thirty degrees between Guangzhou (Canton) and Harbin (Harbin). While the north is covered with snow in the midst of winter, the inhabitants of Hainan Dao (Hainan Island) in the south start spring planting. In fact, the growing season in the south lasts almost throughout the year providing two, and at times, three crops compared to the one-crop season of the north.

The annual rainfall varies significantly from relatively light precipitation in the northwest to monsoon-like conditions in the southeast. Annual precipitation averages above 59 in. (1,500 mm.) in the southeast and decreases gradually across China to below 2 in. (50 mm.) yearly in the northwest. (See Average Rainfall Chart in Appendix.)

Oceans

To the east of China's mainland lie the Bo Hai (Pohai Sea), the Huang Hai (Yellow Sea), and the Dong Hai (East China

Sea), and to the south the Nan Hai (South China Sea). While the Bo Hai is a gulf, the other three are adjacent to the Pacific Ocean.

Rivers

China has a large number of rivers (over 1,500) crisscrossing and interlocking with each other. The major rivers are the Changjiang (Yangtze River), the Huang He (Yellow River), the Zhu Jiang (Pearl River), the Heilong Jiang (Heilung River), the Yarlung Zangbo Jiang (Yalu Tsangpo River), the Huai He (Huaiho River), and the Hai He (Haiho River). Changjiang is China's largest, extending to 3,828 mi. (6,380 km.). Its abundant waters and favorable navigation systems, along with the rich soil and plentiful growth of its river valleys, sustain 250 million inhabitants. The Changjiang is the world's third longest river after the Amazon and the Nile. The Huang He, China's second largest, is the birthplace of China's history and the cradle of Chinese civilization.

Lakes

The vast Chinese landscape is dotted with lakes. Those of a fair size number around 370. Among its fresh-water lakes are the Poyang (Poyang), the Dongting (Tungting), the Hongze Hu (Hungtse), and the Tai Hu (Taihu). Among China's salt lakes, the Qinghai Hu (Chinghai Lake) is the largest.

Islands

There are over five thousand islands, including Dongsha (Tungsha), Xisha (Hsisha), Zhongsha (Chungsha), and Nansha (Nansha), which are in Nan Hai (South China Sea). Taiwan Sheng (Taiwan Province), is China's largest island, with Hainan Dao (Hainan Island) next in size. These two islands are rich in resources and are commonly termed the Chinese "Treasure Islands."

Harbors

Along the meandering coastline famous ports include Shanghai (Shanghai), Tianjin (Tientsin), Dalian (Talien), Qingdao (Tsingtao), Lianyun (Lienyun), and Huangpu (Whampoa) as well as Jilung (Keelung) and Gaoxiong (Kaohsiung) of Taiwan Sheng.

Topography

China's varied terrain ranges from the high plateaus in the west to the flatlands in the east. Mountains account for thirty-three percent of the country's total area with the balance divided: twenty-six percent plateaus, nineteen percent basins, twelve percent plains, and ten percent hills. Among China's famous high mountain ranges are the Himalaya Shan (Himalayas), the Altay Shan (Altai Mountains), the Tian Shan (Tienshan Mountains), and the Kunlun Shan (Kunlun Mountains). On the China-Nepal border is the 29,198 ft. (8,848 m.) Qomolangma Feng (Mount Jolmo Lungma [Mount Everest]),

Cloud Sea of Huang Shan, Anhui

the world's highest peak. The Qing Zang Gaoyuan (Chinghai-Tibet Plateau) with an average elevation of over 13,200 ft. (4,000 m.) is known as "The Roof of the World." At the foot of the Tian Shan is the Turpan Pendi (Turfan Depression or Basin), China's lowest area. At the lowest point of this basin the floor is 508 ft. (154 m.) below sea level.

Natural Resources/Agriculture
Chief among the mineral resources are coal, iron, petroleum, copper, aluminum, tungsten, antimony, tin, molybdenum, manganese, lead, zinc, and mercury.

Cotton is China's major industrial crop. The south is abundant in the production of rice; the northeast produces soybean, sorghum, and wheat. The north and west are known for wheat, millet, and corn. Among China's other notable agricultural products are potatoes, sugar beets, sugar cane, tobacco, and tea.

History
In 1964 archaeological discoveries made in Lantian Xian (Lantien County), Shaanxi Sheng (Shensi Province), showed primitive men living and working along the Huang He (Yellow River) as far back as 600 thousand years ago. About 400 to 500 thousand years ago, the "Peking Man" inhabited caves in the area of Zhoukoudian (Choukoutien), approximately 29 mi. (48 km.) southwest of Beijing.

To appreciate the historical span of China one must think of its great age, nearly four thousand years of continuous, recorded history. The first recorded dynasty, that of the Xia (Hsia) Dynasty, lasted from 2205-1766 B.C. followed by the Shang (Shang) and Zhou (Chou) Dynasties, 1766-770 B.C. which correspond to the Bronze Age. It was a period of hunting and warfare in which the cultivation of livestock was of far greater importance than agricultural development.

The Spring and Autumn Period which followed, 770-476 B.C., saw the rise of agriculture, the creation of city-states and the establishment of the first codes of justice and taxation. The further development of centralization continued during the Warring States era which corresponded to the Iron Age, 476-221 B.C. The size of towns grew as did commerce and a middle class began to appear.

Between 221-206 B.C. the idea of an empire was introduced by the Qin (Chin) Dynasty whose founder was known as the first emperor. He expanded the size of his empire by war and diplomacy, established a system of roads laid out in a star pattern emanating from his capital, and restructured the walls of the fortified cities. In order to afford them collective protection, he constructed the Great Wall by linking up individual fortifications with new wall construction to keep out invading nomads. The emperor's methods were sound but his rule was harsh and his dynasty was a short one. However, he was survived not only by the Great Wall but by the concept of a single, unifying ruler of the kingdom.

From B.C. 206 to A.D. 220 the Han (Han) Dynasty at first presided over the continued prosperity and expansion of China. It was during this period that paper was invented. There then developed great wealthy families who tended to draw away from the central authority of the emperor. Eventually some of the regions did split away from central authority and the unity of the kingdom was broken and exposed to attacks by northern nomads.

For the next 370 years China was again mostly a collection of warring states. The Three Kingdoms Period, 220-265 A.D., broke China into three major states. From 265-420 A.D. the Jin (Tsin) Dynasty was in control, followed by the Southern and Northern Dynasties, 420-589 A.D.

Under the Sui (Sui) and the Tang (Tang) Dynasties, 581-907 A.D., the central power of the empire was restored and arts and commerce flourished. In artistic and temporal power the country reached a high point. The brief Five Dynasties and Ten Kingdoms Period (907-960 A.D.), saw a step back from political centralization, but great advances in manufacturing. It was during this time that paper money made an appearance and printing began to appear. This somewhat fractured time was replaced by the Song (Sung) Dynasty, 960-1280 A.D., which presided over a shift in political emphasis from the north to southern China where the new capital was established and the encouragement of a great development in the artistic life of the country. Chinese inventions during this period included gunpowder, the magnetic compass, and movable type for printing. Unfortunately expansion in the arts was not matched by similar development in military skills and the dynasty was ended by Genghis Khan's successful campaigns.

The Yuan (Yuan) Dynasty, 1280-1368 A.D., showed the country considerably weakened but with an increasing trade to the West. It was in this period that Marco Polo and Christian missionaries visited China, bringing with them western ideas, and at the same time took back some of China's developments, such as printing and gunpowder.

During the long period of the Ming (Ming) Dynasty, 1368-1644 A.D., China reasserted its control over the north by repelling invaders and restoring the Great Wall. But by the time of the last of the Ming emperors, internal dissension had undercut the power of the throne and the country was again

Memorial Hall of Chairman Mao Zedong, Beijing

subjected to a Manchu invasion. At this time the last dynasty, that of the Qing (Ching), was established, 1644-1911 A.D. The size of the population grew enormously, rising to about 430 million by the middle of the nineteenth century.

After the Opium War of 1840, China was reduced to a semi-feudal and semi-colonial country. A nation rich in revolutionary tradition, the Chinese people repeatedly revolted against foreign imperial aggression and feudal oppression. The Communist Party of China was founded July 1, 1921. After twenty-eight years of armed struggle under the leadership of the Chinese Communist Party and Chairman Mao, the new democratic revolution was won.

The People's Republic of China was founded on October 1, 1949. At present, in its effort to change China's backwardness, the entire nation, under the leadership of the Chinese Communisty Party has shifted its emphasis to concentrate on the modernization of China.

Language

Pinyin — Chinese Phonetic Alphabet

The State Council of the People's Republic of China in 1958 adopted the Chinese Phonetic Alphabet System (Pinyin) for romanizing Chinese names and places. Beginning on January 1, 1979, all translated texts of Chinese diplomatic documents and Chinese magazines published in foreign languages have utilized the new Pinyin System of spelling Chinese names and places.

It is an important change that replaces various and differing spelling systems, including the Wade-Giles (English) and Lessing (German), and will end the confusion that has existed for a long time in romanizing Chinese. Essentially the system reflects the Beijing (Peking) dialect in pronunciation.

This book adopts the Pinyin spelling system which is beginning to appear on signs, posters and titles of newspapers throughout China. For ease in reference, the first time that the name of a place or person appears in Pinyin in this Guidebook, it will be followed by the Wade-Giles spelling in parenthesis, as the Wade-Giles system is still better known in most English-speaking countries.

According to the Chinese Phonetic Alphabet System names of the late Chairman Mao, Premier Zhou (Chou En-Lai) and Chairman Zhu (Chu) are spelled:

     Mao Zedong   Zhou Enlai   Zhu De

The name of the country will remain as it is now known in languages using the Roman alphabet: China in English, Chine in French, China in German, etc. Chinese geographical names

in principle, will be spelled out according to the Chinese phonetic alphabet. But universal terms, such as province, city, autonomous region, river, lake, sea, road, street, and port should be translated according to their meanings. Names and places in publications and on tourist maps should also be translated to their specific meanings.

Government

The President and the Vice President of the People's Republic of China are elected by the National People's Congress. The National People's Congress is the highest organ of state power with each term of office lasting five years. The NPC is comprised of elected deputies from each of China's provinces. One deputy represents a minimum of 400,000 people, with each province having a minimum of ten deputies.

The Standing Committee of the National People's Congress is elected by the deputies of the NPC. Comprised of a Chairman and several Vice Chairmen, the Standing Committee acts as a full-time branch of the NPC.

The State Council is the Central People's Government. It is also the executive branch of the National People's Congress, to whom it is responsible and accountable.

All citizens are eligible to vote once they have reached the age of eighteen; they are also eligible to stand for election. Women enjoy equal rights with men in all phases of political, cultural, social, and family life.

2. Visitor's Information

Foreigners who have been approved to visit China may choose an itinerary prepared by LÜXINGSHE. The Chinese authorities declared recently that foreigners may visit 28 cities and one county without travel permits.

Following is a list of these 29 places: Beijing, Tianjin, Shanghai, Qinhuangdao, Taiyuan, Shenyang, Changchun, Harbin, Nanjing, Suzhou, Wuxi, Hangzhou, Jinan, Qiangdao, Zhengzhou, Kaifeng, Luoyang, Wuhan, Changsha, Guangzhou, Foshan, Zhaoqing, Nanning, Guilin, Xi'an, Chengdu, Chongqing, Kunming, and Lunan county (Stone Forest).

Foreigners are still required to obtain travel permits for visiting other places.

Travel permits required for the places to be visited can be obtained after the tourists have entered China by applying to the authorities concerned or asking the local LÜXINGSHE to do it for them.

Most famous inhabitants at Beijing Zoo

General Information

Tour groups and individuals traveling to China will be hosted by the China International Travel Service (Lüxingshe) during their stay in China. Although you will already have your own "tour leader" with you since your departure point, once entering China CITS will assign your group a national guide, who will remain with the group during its entire visit. In addition, at each different city, a city guide will also join your tour. Both Lüxingshe guides will speak Chinese and English and will be there to answer questions, co-ordinate your previously-planned activities, and insure everything goes smoothly.

Chinese embassies and consulates, foreign friendship associations, or travel agencies who have established business relations with Lüxingshe should be contacted to plan your trip to China. They, in turn, will contact the CITS head office to arrange the particulars of your trip. To facilitate consideration of all traveling services, the following information will be requested beforehand: number of companions, full name, nationality, age, sex, occupation, whether accompanied by spouse, cities you would like to visit, special interests, (i.e., schools, museums, factories), duration of stay, dates of visit and ports of entry and exit, means of transportation, and language(s) spoken.

When all matters concerning your trip to China have been agreed upon with Lüxingshe's Head Office, you will be advised. Although you will have a planned itinerary for your en-

注意：以墨水或打字机填写清楚，空白处不敷应用时，可另纸填写。
Note: Please write clearly with pen and ink or typewriter.
Use separate piece of paper if blank space is insufficient.

外 国 人 入 境 过 境 申 请 表
ALIEN'S APPLICATION FORM
FOR ENTRY OR TRANSIT VISAS

姓　名（标明姓氏）
Name in full
(In block letters &
underline the surname)

像　片

Photo

国　籍（如曾变更，请说明）
Nationality (state change, if any)

性别　　　　　出生年月日、地点
Sex　　　　　Date & place of birth

会 何 种 语 言
Languages known to applicant

宗教信仰、党派
Religion & political party

护 照
Passport

种　类
type

号　码
number

发照日期
date of issue

发照机关
issued by

有 效 期 至
valid until

现在职业及工作处所
Present occupation & place of work

现 在 住 址
Present address

电 话 号 码
telephone No.

曾于何时何地何机关作何事
Previous occupation (give post, name of organization, place and time)

曾否来过中国（如曾，说明：时间、居留地点及事由）
Ever been in China? (if so, state place, time and purpose of stay)

在 华 亲 友 Relatives and friends in China:

姓　名 Name	国　籍 Nationality	现在职业及工作处所 Present occupation and place of work	住　址 Address	与申请人的关系 Relationship to applicant

34

来中国事由和目的地
Purpose of journey and destination in China _____

拟在中国停留时间
Intended duration of stay in China _____

在中国的旅行路线和交通工具
Itinerary of travel and means of transport in China. _____

_____

入境日期、地点、从何处搭乘何种交通工具到中国
Date and port of entry into China, where from and by what means of transport _____

出境日期、地点、搭乘何种交通工具
Date and port of exit from China, and by what means of transport _____

离中国后前往何国？是否已获该国入境许可？
What country will you proceed to after leaving China? Whether entry permit to that country has been obtained? _____

_____

同行眷属（说明姓名、性别、年龄、国籍及与申请人的关系）
Accompanying family members (name, sex, age, nationality and relationship to applicant)

_____

_____

_____

填 写 日 期   申请人签名
Date of application _____   Signature _____

备   考
Remarks _____

_____

_____

此栏由签证机关填写 To be filled by the visa officer

已于   年   月   日发给   签证。

tire trip, unforeseen circumstances can cause last-minute changes once you arrive in China.

Visas

In addition to a passport, visitors must hold valid visas issued by the Chinese authorities prior to departure. The "Alien's Application Form For Entry or Transit Visas" is a two-sided sheet (see pages 34 and 35). It must be submitted in triplicate (including three recent photographs) either to your travel agent or direct to the Chinese embassy or consulate. See also p. 32.

Quarantine

No inoculations are necessary for Americans, but those entering through Hong Kong should check at the time of their departure if any are necessary. Passengers from newly-declared epidemic areas are required to show appropriate inoculation certificates. It would be wise to check what the current regulations are when your trip dates have been confirmed. Your family doctor may suggest shots for your own protection although not necessarily required by law.

Customs Regulations

Entry

Tourists must fill out a "Baggage Declaration for Passengers" (see sample on page 37). This declaration form may be obtained from various sources including incoming flights and ships as well as some travel agents. All baggage must be submitted for customs inspection.

Personal belongings will be released duty free including food, two bottles of liquor, and two cartons of cigarettes to be consumed during the trip. Wrist watches, radios, tape recorders, cameras, miniature calculators, and movie cameras, for example, may be brought in for personal use but cannot be sold or transferred to others and must be brought out of China.

Gifts for relatives or friends in China, or articles carried on behalf of others, should also be declared. Travelers carrying these articles have to go through special procedures at customs.

Visitors can bring in an unlimited amount of foreign currency and RMB (Chinese) traveler's checks, and the unspent

1001-页

中 国 海 关
Customs of China
旅 客 行 李 申 报 单
Baggage Declaration for Passengers

N. B.

1. Arms, ammunition, narcotics, poisonous drugs, radio transmitters and receivers, plants and seeds must be declared and handed to the Customs to be dealt with according to regulations.

2. Gifts and samples carried in should be declared by filling in the blanks of this declaration.

3. Passengers carrying out of China foreign currencies, bills and cheques other than the remaining amount of those carried in while entering are requested to present certificates issued by the Bank of China.

4. Among the articles declared by the passenger those marked "Δ" by the Customs must be taken out of the country by the passenger on leaving.

5. This declaration, after being duly stamped by the Customs, is to be retained by the passenger and submitted to the Customs for examination at the time of exit or entry. The lost of the declaration or any alterations made on it may be considered breaking the regulations.

Name in full _____

Nationality _____

From/to _____

Hand baggage _____ pieces; Registered baggage _____ pieces.

_____ pieces of unaccompanied baggage are to arrive

at/to be shipped from _____

Descriptions	Entry declaration	Exit declaration
Jewelry		
Antiques		

Signature _____ Date _____

Remarks (To be filled in by the Customs)

Descriptions	Quan-tity		
Wrist watches			
Cameras			
Cinecameras			
TV sets			
Recorders (including multipurpose combination sets)			

portion can be taken out.

Bringing in the following articles is prohibited:

1. Arms, ammunition, and explosives of all kinds;
2. Radio transmitters-receivers and principal parts;
3. Renminbi (Chinese currency);
4. Manuscripts, printed matter, films, photographs, gramophone records, cinematographic films, loaded tapes and video-tapes, etc., which are detrimental to China's politics, economy, culture, and ethics;

37

5. Poisonous drugs, habit-forming drugs, and opium, morphine, heroin, etc.;
6. Animals, plants, and products thereof infected with or carrying germs and insect pests;
7. Unsanitary foodstuffs and germ-carrying foodstuffs from infected areas; and
8. Other articles, the import of which is prohibited by State Regulations.

Exit

On leaving China, tourists must again submit the Baggage Declaration for Passengers for customs inspection (see page 37).

Items purchased in China with RMB converted from foreign currencies may be taken out or mailed out of the country after presenting receipts for customs inspection. In cities where a Customs Office does not exist, this can be arranged through the local Friendship Store.

As of February 1, 1980, the Congress of the United States granted to China "most favored nation" status. Duty is imposed on articles brought into the U.S. as follows:

first $300.00	Duty Free
$301.00 -$900.00	10% of cost
$901.00 and up	Percentage is based on particular commodity*

*Percentages vary from 10% on up.

A few items can be brought back "duty free" regardless of total cost. In this category are: antiques over 100 years old and oil paintings or "art" done solely by hand (however, the frames would have duty imposed on them). Proof of the age of the antique (red authenticating seal) or proof of the originality of the art will be required.

Note: Ivory is not allowed into the United States.

Clothing

Most of China's territory lies in the North Temperate Zone. Although the climate differs from region to region, it is suitable for traveling all year round. On the whole it is temperate and humid in the southeast and central south, and rather dry in the north and northeast.

In the Appendix we have listed the average temperatures for the main tourist areas. These should be consulted when your trip dates are known. In spring (March through May) and autumn (September through November), light clothes, such as jackets and sweaters, are appropriate in most of the areas. In summer bring light dresses or slacks for women, and short-sleeve shirts and slacks or shorts for men. Jeans are acceptable for both men and women in China.

A warm overcoat is needed outdoors in the winter. During this season it is suggested you plan to wear several layers of clothing rather than one bulky, very heavy coat. A raincoat will come in handy at the turn of spring and in summer and autumn, when rainfall is frequent.

Most important: *bring comfortable walking shoes.*

Hotels/Hotel Services

The branches and sub-branches of Luxingshe arrange hotel accommodations for visitors and your hotel will offer a full range of services and facilities.

The hotel rooms can generally be divided into three categories: special, regular, and economy. Special suites of two or three rooms are available in some hotels; this is termed the special classification. Regular and economy categories are one room each. All have private bathroom facilities. For package tours Lüxingshe provides hotel rooms in accordance with agreed upon accommodations. Transit travelers and foreign-

Peking Hotel, Beijing

ers residing in China may make hotel reservations directly with the hotels themselves or through CITS.

In the hotels there are restaurants where both Chinese and Western meals are served for foreign tourists. Each morning a thermos bottle of hot water and a carafe of preboiled water will be brought to your hotel room. The construction of the thermos is such that the water will stay hot all day.

Most hotels provide the following services: postal, telegraph, telephone, cable, foreign exchange, and gift shops. Some also offer hair-dressing salons for men and women. Tourists may go to the service desk for laundry, film developing, newspapers and magazines, current adapters, and other services. Note: 220 volts is the standard electrical current in all hotels in China.

Readily available in most hotels are Chinese stamps, especially low-value stamps. Stamps are prominently displayed and even come in specially-prepared packets, although it is not necessary to buy them that way. Stamps are duty free; it is not necessary to declare them.

Also available in some of the hotels are Kodak color film (usually 16 mm, 35 mm, and 110), U.S. and English cigarettes as well as whiskey, scotch, bourbon, French champagne, and wines (even California wine). You must purchase these items with the special currency recently created for use by foreign visitors especially for products that China must import for the convenience of its foreign visitors.

See Appendix for listing of hotels in main tourist cities. Refer also to sections on specific cities.

Medical Services

Should you require medical care while in China, advise your Lüxingshe guide, your hotel, or contact the local CITS office (see listing in Appendix). Either a doctor will be called or you will be taken to the nearest hospital.

There is no shortage of doctors with formal training in Western medical procedures in the cities you will visit, so there is no cause for alarm.

Telephones

Rooms in hotels and most guest houses are equipped with

telephones. The following are the various kinds of calls that are available to travelers:

Intra-city Calls

Service is free in hotels. When using outside pay phones, each call is RMB 0.04.

Domestic Long-distance Calls

There are two kinds of domestic long-distance calls, regular and urgent. Travelers can make a call by using the hotel room phone, registering the call through the operator, or by filling

长 途 电 话 挂 号 单	
Booking Ticket of Long Distance Telephone Call	
编号 No.＿＿＿＿＿	日期 Date ＿＿＿＿
请 用 中 文 或 英 文 正 楷 填 写 Please write in Chinese or in English in block letters	
受话国名及城市名 Destination (city and country)	
受话电话号码或单位 Telephone No. or organiza- tion of called party	
受 话 人 姓 名 Name of called party	
发 话 人 姓 名 Name of caller	
发话人房间号码 Room No. of caller	
受 付 或 发 付 Collect or paid call	
予定通话时间 Wanted duration	
以下由工作人员填写 Following will be filled by Operator	
挂 号 时 刻		代 号	
话 毕 时 刻		备 注：	
始 话 时 刻			
计 费 分 钟 数			
话 价		代 号	

out the "long distance call register slip" at the hotel service desk. See page 41.

International Calls

There are two kinds, regular and urgent. Registration procedure is the same as the domestic long-distance calls. Calls are charged according to the length of the call with the basic unit charge being three minutes. Each additional minute will be charged accordingly.

When you make a long-distance call, be prepared to pay for it almost immediately. If you make an overseas call from your hotel room, you can bill it to your ITU Credit Card. However, this service is only available to those who have made prior arrangements.

Telegrams/Cables

There are various types available: domestic, regular and ex-

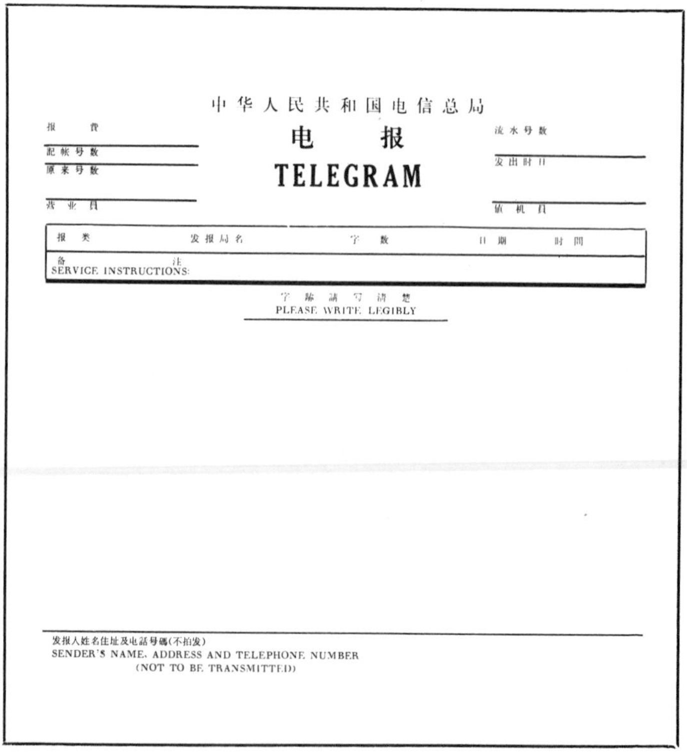

中 华 人 民 共 和 国 电 信 总 局

报　费

起 账 号 数

原 来 号 数

营 业 员

电　报

TELEGRAM

流 水 号 数

发 出 时 日

填 机 员

报　类　　　发 报 局 名　　　字　数　　　日 期　　时 间

备　　注
SERVICE INSTRUCTIONS:

字 迹 请 写 清 楚
PLEASE WRITE LEGIBLY

发报人姓名住址及电话号码(不拍发)
SENDER'S NAME, ADDRESS AND TELEPHONE NUMBER
(NOT TO BE TRANSMITTED)

press; international, regular and express; international photo telegraphic service; and international telex.

When sending a domestic or international cable or an international telex, telegram forms issued by the Ministry of Posts and Telecommunications of China must be used. See illustration page 42.

Cables and telegrams are charged by the word, with a minimum charge in each category. The photo telegraphic service is charged by the size of the photo to be transmitted; this service is not available in all cities. International telex rates are charged by the actual number of minutes used.

Postal Services

Hotels and guest houses have postal service desks that sell stamps, envelopes, stationery, and postcards. Postal service in China is very convenient and efficient.

Letters and postcards mailed via air mail take five to ten days to get to their destination outside of China. Material sent ocean freight, although much cheaper, will take much longer to arrive.

Miscellaneous Services

If a problem develops and your national or city Lüxingshe guide is not readily available, contact the local branch office of CITS. In the Appendix we give the addresses and telephone numbers of the local CITS offices.

Chinese Currency

Chinese currency is called Renminbi (RMB) and is issued by the People's Bank of China.

The basic unit of RMB is the Yuan and the subsidiary units are the Jiao and Fen. One Yuan is about $.50 in United States currency. A Yuan is divided into 10 Jiao and a Jiao is equal to 10 Fen. Yuan and Jiao are issued in notes and Fen in coins. Yuan notes are in denominations of 1, 2, 5, and 10; Jiao notes are in denominations of 1, 2, and 5; and Fen coins are in denominations of 1, 2 and 5. The amount of Renminbi one thousand two hundred and thirty-four Yuan, five Jiao, and six Fen would be expressed RMB ¥ 1,234.56

Foreign Exchange Certificates

Foreign visitors, diplomats, Overseas Chinese and Chinese from Hong Kong and Macao must use Foreign Exchange Certificates instead of RMB in places that serve foreigners only, such as the Friendship Stores, hotels and foreign trade centers. The Foreign Exchange Certificates are also to be used for payment of plane fares, through-train or ship fares to Hong Kong and Macao, and international telecommunications charges and parcel post.

Foreign Exchange Certificates come in seven demoninations — 100 Yuan, 50 Yuan, 10 Yuan, 5 Yuan, 1 Yuan, 5 Jiao and 1 Jiao. Visitors may convert the certificates into foreign currency when they leave China, or may take them in and out of China as they please.

Renminbi may not be taken out of the country. Before leaving China, the visitor must convert all Renminbi into foreign currency.

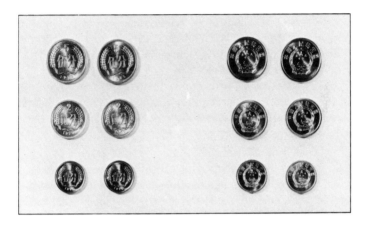

Renminbi (Chinese) Traveler's Checks (RMB T/C)

For the convenience of travelers the Bank of China sells Chinese traveler's checks in its Hong Kong branch and in some of its agencies and subsidiaries in Hong Kong and Macao. At present RMB T/C are also being sold at the Bank of China in Beijing, Guangzhou, Shanghai, and Tianjin. See illustration on page 46 for examples of RMB T/C.

There is no limit to the amount of RMB T/C allowed into the country. They can be easily cashed at various offices of the Bank of China and other exchange counters. All travelers, foreign guests, foreign organizations, and foreign nationals stationed in China (excluding foreign residents) may pay directly in RMB T/C when purchasing tickets, goods at designated stores, shops at the Guangzhou (Canton) Chinese Export Fair, Sailor's Clubs, arts and crafts department stores, antique stores, as well as hotels, restaurants, international airports, and international railroad stations.

Foreign Currency, Bills and Traveler's Checks

No limit is set on the amount of foreign currency and bills which may be brought into China. However, the traveler must immediately on landing declare to customs the amount of foreign currency and bills as well as all traveler's checks he has brought with him when filling out the Baggage Declaration for Passengers (see page 37). Details must be entered in a column under the heading of foreign currency/bills/traveler's checks with a separate line used for each country. After being checked and endorsed by customs, this Declaration Form is to be kept by the traveler as a certificate as it will be needed at the end of your trip.

During your stay in China, the foreign currency, and traveler's checks brought in should not be transferred, used for making payment, or given away as gifts. Whenever the need arises the traveler may, against the Declaration Form, have his foreign currency or traveler's checks exchanged for RMB, and/or Foreign Exchange Certificates.

In China currencies from seventeen countries and regions, including the American and Canadian dollar and the British pound, as well as sixty-seven kinds of traveler's checks and international bank drafts, may be exchanged into RMB. Among the traveler's checks accepted are American Express, Bank of America, Thomas Cook & Sons, and the Royal Bank of Canada. See Appendix for a complete listing of acceptable traveler's checks.

Credit Cards

In general, credit cards are gaining more acceptance in China for use by foreign visitors. *Federal Card* is accepted at several locations in Beijing, Tianjin, Nanjing, Guangzhou (Canton), Hangzhou, Shanghai, Fuzhou, Hankou, and Kunming. *Visa* is accepted at several locations in Guangzhou, Beijing, Shanghai, Tianjin, and Hangzhou. **MasterCard** is accepted at several locations in Shanghai, Guangzhou, Hangzhou, Beijing, and Nanjing. **American Express** is accepted at several locations in

Guangzhou and Shanghai. ***Diners Club*** can be used at several locations in Shanghai and Guangzhou.

Negotiations are underway to allow credit cards at additional locations throughout China. (See Appendix for a list of locations in each city which accept one or more credit cards.)

Note: A surcharge is usually added for credit card purchases.

New International Airport Terminal, Beijing

Air Service

The Civil Aviation Administration of China (CAAC) has one hundred and sixty-six domestic air routes at the present time, connecting more than eighty cities, with their routes totaling over 113 thousand miles (190 thousand km.). CAAC international routes reach many countries in Asia, Europe, America, and Africa.

In addition to the CAAC flights, many foreign airlines fly into the major cities of China. A map of CAAC routes can be found in the Appendix.

Reconfirmation of Reservation

If a passenger breaks his journey for more than seventy-two hours at any point on the international service of CAAC, he is required to reconfirm his intention of using the continuing or return space reserved at least seventy-two hours before flight departure. Failure to reconfirm will result in the cancellation of the space reserved. This provision does not apply to CAAC flights when all legs of the trip are within Europe.

Tickets

CAAC booking offices issue tickets for all domestic flights. Foreign travelers and overseas Chinese should have in their possession all necessary travel documents when picking up their tickets. Tickets are not transferable and should not be mutilated or altered.

47

Ticket Validity

Domestic tickets are valid for ninety days and international tickets are valid for one year, both from the date of commencement of travel. Fixed-date tickets will be accepted only for the date and flight entered on the ticket.

Children's Fares

A child under twelve years of age must travel in the company of an adult passenger. An infant under two, not occupying a separate seat, will be charged at ten percent of the adult fare. Any more than one infant per adult passenger and all children between two and twelve years of age are charged at fifty percent of the adult fare and may occupy separate seats. Children twelve years of age or older will be charged full adult fare.

Health Requirements

Passengers suffering from a serious illness must possess a doctor's certificate and, with the agreement of CAAC officials, can then make reservations and obtain their tickets. Newborn babies under ten days old and women passengers passing the stage of thirty-five weeks of pregnancy are generally not allowed on board CAAC flights

Cancellation

If passengers on domestic flights apply for cancellation of a ticket two hours before the scheduled departure time, each ticket is charged RMB ¥4.00 (US $2.00). Should the face value of the ticket be under RMB ¥20.00 (US $10.00), a cancellation fee of RMB ¥1.00 (US $.50) will be assessed. If the request for cancellation is not made two hours before the schedule departure time, a charge of twenty percent of the ticket fare will be collected as the cancellation fee. No cancellation fee is charged on infant tickets which were purchased at ten percent of the full fare. Full refund will be made to passengers holding international tickets if cancellation is made before the airport check-in time.

No Show

If a passenger holding a domestic air service ticket fails to appear for a scheduled flight, the ticket will be voided and no refund will be granted. If a passenger holding an international ticket fails to appear for a scheduled flight, a no-show charge will be assessed at twenty-five percent of the applicable one-way fare for the portions not flown or to the first point of stopover exceeding six hours' duration. The no-show charge will not be more than RMB ¥130.00 (US $65.00) and will not be less than RMB ¥10.00 ($5.00).

Check-in Time
Passengers are requested to be at the airport at the time designated by CAAC. Tickets and personal documents are required for check-in procedures.

Airport Fee
Effective January 1, 1980, an airport fee of RMB ¥ 10.00 was levied on all international flight passengers departing Beijing, Shanghai and Guangzhou on CAAC or foreign aircraft. Holders of diplomatic passports, transit passengers and children under 12 are exempt.

Baggage
For each domestic and international passenger paying full or half the adult fare, the free baggage allowance is 66 lbs. (30 ks.) for first class, 44 lbs. (20 ks.) for economy class. Hand baggage is limited to 11 lbs. (5 ks.). Children paying only ten

percent of the full fare are not given free baggage allowance. Excess weight over the free-baggage limit is charged according to the standard rates stipulated in the tariff effective at the time of your trip. Excess baggage can only be carried with the availability of space on the same flight.

Each passenger may carry on one piece of hand luggage, an overcoat, an umbrella or walking stick, a reasonable amount of reading material for the flight, infant's food for consumption en route, infant's portable carrier, and a fully collapsible invalid's wheelchair.

Railroads (Inter-city Transportation)

The major means of inter-city transportation in China is the railway system which links up all major cities and tourist centers. International train service is available twice a week between Beijing and Pyongyang, and twice a week between Beijing and Ulan Bator, and Moscow. Express train service is available every day from Beijing to Guangzhou (Canton) which joins the train service in Hong Kong.

Trains are comfortable and clean. Tea and other refreshments are offered at a moderate price and at regular intervals during your journey.

Tickets

There are three kinds of domestic train tickets with two price levels for each:

regular fare:	soft or hard seats
express fare:	regular or special
sleeping-coach fare:	soft or hard berths

A lost ticket has to be replaced at the traveler's expense. Substitute tickets can be purchased at the railroad station or directly from the conductor. When the traveler finds the original ticket, he may get a partial refund by presenting both the original and substitute ticket before leaving the train station.

Passengers should follow the date, train number, seat number or compartment number specified on the ticket. In the event that the passenger cannot meet the specified schedule, he may apply once for an alternative train within the valid period of his ticket. When a later train is required, the application must be submitted no later than two hours after the original departure time. No time alternative is allowed for a berth ticket.

Children's Fares

Children's fare (regular and express) is one quarter of the adult fare. A child qualifies for the reduced fare if his height is between 3 ft. 3 in.-4 ft. 3 in. (1 and 1.3 m.). Children taller than this will be charged the regular adult fare.

Distances

For charts showing shortest distances between cities via rail, in both miles and kilometers, see Appendix.

Intra-city Transportation

In all the major tourist cities there are bus and cable car routes leading to scenic and cultural points of interest. These are easily accessible.

Taxi service is also available. Travelers can get a taxi through the local travel agency, hotel service desk, or, if you speak Chinese, by calling the taxi company directly. Taxi fares are charged according to the cab model and mileage driven. Drivers will not accept tips.

Shopping

In general, stores in China are open from 9:00 AM to 7:00 PM. For the convenience of visitors and overseas Chinese, foreign exchange counters are set up in business areas, at airports, railway stations, and hotels. Travelers should retain receipts for all their purchases to facilitate clearing customs upon departure.

As pricing structures are set by the State, the cost of an item will not vary by much from store to store or city to city. A word of advice, if you see something you want, buy it. You may see the item again, but you may not.

Friendship Stores and Sailor's Clubs

For the purpose of providing convenient shopping and services to visitors and foreign guests, China has set up Friendship Stores in cities where foreign embassies are located and at places where sightseers frequently visit. In port cities, there are Sailor's Clubs which provide food supplies, maintenance materials, and articles for daily use to ships and sailors.

Both these facilities provide various kinds of quality merchandise, such as traditional Chinese handicrafts, jewelry, jade and ivory carvings, fabrics, liquors, cigarettes, and candies. Also available are fresh and preserved fruits, assorted delicacies, cosmetics, stationery, and clothing.

Friendship Stores offer products not available in local stores, i.e., expensive silks and jewelry. Sales personnel speak foreign languages beautifully, and, in most cases, provide facilities for packing and sending items to your home once customs regulations have been provided for.

General Department Stores

Friendship Stores are open only to foreign visitors and overseas Chinese. The Chinese people cannot buy products at Friendship Stores but use instead the General Department Stores. Be sure to visit one. Not only will you see where the Chinese themselves shop, but these stores also offer a large variety of reasonably-priced silks and brocades and other everyday items not on sale in Friendship Stores, such as posters, work clothes, and books. Inexpensive souvenirs available are Army caps and sweatshirts.

Arts and Crafts Department Stores

Arts and crafts department stores specialize in the sale of traditional Chinese handicrafts. They carry all kinds of colorful and delicate products, including artistic works intended for display in homes or offices and handicrafts for both practical use and decoration.

The arts and crafts department stores assist local workshops in developing new designs as well as in the practical matters of improving quality and packaging. Many craft items come with an explanation that describes the characteristics and the background of the product so that the visitor can make a considered selection.

A comprehensive list of the arts and crafts department stores is shown in the Appendix.

Antique Stores

China, with its long history and cultural traditions, has a great quantity of antiques. In order to meet the needs of academic research and the understandable demand of antique collectors, shops specializing in these original items and authorized reproductions have been set up in major Chinese cities and visitors centers.

Without exception antiques over one hundred years old carry a red authenticating wax seal on the object itself or on the price tag. Be sure to get the necessary receipt when you make your purchase in order to avoid having to pay a customs duty.

The main artifacts and reproductions to be found in these antique stores are pottery and porcelain from a variety of dynasties, ivory and jade carvings, Chinese calligraphy, classical paintings, and stone rubbings. Also available are jade jewelry, exquisite embroidery, stone, wood and bamboo carvings, and assorted decorative items. All travelers are invited to visit and shop at these stores of which there is a listing of major ones in the Appendix.

Chinese Cuisine

Until recently Chinese food available in the West was basically Guangdong (Cantonese). In too many cases what was termed "Chinese food" was in reality an "American inter-

Entrance to Fang Shan Restaurant, Bei Hai Park, Beijing

pretation" and can only be called a poor substitute for what is truly a superb culinary achievement.

Colorful, varied, savory, complex — all are words used to define true Chinese cuisine. With its long history, it is part of the rich cultural legacy of the Chinese nation.

According to a recent survey there are no less than 5,000 varieties of dishes available throughout China. Many of the restaurants in the main tourist cities are not only skilled in preparing dishes with distinct local flavors, but are also adept at preparing a variety of dishes from other localities as well. This will enable the traveler to sample many different cuisines even if his trip does not provide the opportunity of visiting all the regions.

Chinese cuisine can be broken into four major, regional categories:

Northern Cuisine — Beijing (Peking), sometimes termed Mandarin, and Shandong (Shantung)

Southern Cuisine — Guangdong (Cantonese)

Eastern Cuisine — Shanghai and Jiangzhe

Western Cuisine — Sichuan (Szechuan and Hunan)

Northern Cuisine

Beijing (Peking) cooking is characterized by its exquisite selection of materials, fine cutting, and pure seasonings. It is rich, but not greasy; light, but not skimpy. Skilled in preparing delicacies of every kind, there are no less than thirty cooking methods employed. More prominent are: roasting, quick-fry, stir-fry, sauteing with thick gravy, and braising (stews).

The best-known specialties are: Beijing (Peking) roast duck, rinsed mutton in Mongolian hotpot, assorted barbecue meats Mongolian style, the Imperial Palace Cuisine (sometimes termed Mandarin), and Tan-style cuisine.

Shandong (Shantung) cuisine can be recognized by its light and mellow tastes with emphasis on aroma, freshness, crisp-

ness, and tenderness. Dishes are often served in a clear or creamy soup.

Bird's Nest (or Swallow's Nest) Soup, a specialty of Shandong cooking, is often the first course in a banquet and is praised by all who have tasted it. The famous sweet and sour Huang He (Yellow River) carp, singed on the outside but tender inside, is truly tantalizing.

Southern Cuisine

Guangdong (Cantonese) cuisine comes from Guangzhou (Canton) and uses a great variety of vegetables prepared with a minimum amount of cooking time and an exact degree of heat so that their fresh, tender taste, as well as their vitamins, are preserved.

The area's varied crops provide a wide selection of vegetables and a great range of styles. Guangdong cuisine is the most varied of all the Chinese cuisines and dishes are refreshing, light, crisp, and colorful.

Famous for its novel and exotic style is the well-known snake dish, Dragons Duel Tiger, which combines the gamy taste of wildcat braised with snakemeat. Roast suckling pig and assorted meat shreds braised with shark's fins are among its other delights.

Eastern Cuisine

Shanghai cuisine is typically rich, sweet, and colorful with freshly-picked ingredients. As Shanghai is close to the ocean, surrounded by lakes and streams, fish and shellfish are abundant throughout the year. Cultivated fields in the suburbs provide fresh vegetables year round. Basic flavorings are salty, pickled, sweet, and sour. Traditionally Shanghai cuisine is known for its skillful preparation of seafoods.

Jiangzhe (Jiangsu and Zhejiang) cuisine varies with the season. Meticulously prepared (boiled, stewed, braised, and simmered), the cuisine specializes in poultry and seafoods. Dishes are cooked in their own juices thus preserving their original flavor. Some of the more widely-known dishes are simmered chicken Hangzhou-style, steamed shad from Nanjing, and chicken soup Shaoxin-style.

Western Cuisine

Sichuan (Szechuan and Hunan) cuisine is easily recognizable. The heavily spicy and peppery tastes, invariably a part of this cooking method, leave one with a vivid impression. Sichuan is characteristically sour, sweet, peppery, spicy, bitter, fragrant, and salty. Some visitors call it Chinese-Mexican food. Among its specialities are young chicken with hot pepper, fish in spicy bean sauce, and the nutritious bear's paw braised in brown sauce. Other favorites are Longjing abalone, duck slices rinsed in hotpot, and the crispy and delicious roast pig.

See Appendix for sample menus. Refer also to the restaurant sections in the main tourist cities.

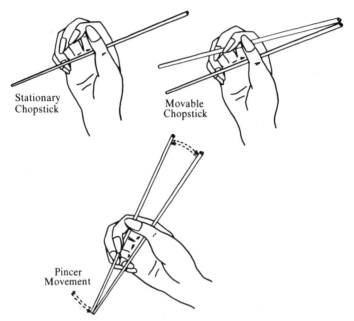

Stationary Chopstick

Movable Chopstick

Pincer Movement

Chopsticks

In China soup is eaten with a spoon, selected foods are picked up in the fingers, but ordinarily food is eaten with a pair of chopsticks.

Chopsticks are thin, rounded, slightly-tapered strips of lacquered bamboo about a foot long. On special occasions chopsticks made of ivory or ebony may be used, but ordinarily one encounters bamboo chopsticks. It is by no means obligatory that visitors use them since knives and forks are readily supplied, but for those who would like to try them, the following suggestions may prove useful.

Chopsticks are held in the fork hand, side by side between the thumb and the forefinger. The one closest to your body stays immobile and rests on the side of the first joint of the ring finger. The moving chopstick is the lead one, which is opened and closed like pincers by the opening and closing of the forefinger and middle finger, which support it. Just think of them as representing the thumb and forefinger when you ordinarily pick something up and you will quickly grasp the action of chopsticks. See illustration.

The shorter the length of the chopsticks, the better your control over them. Therefore novices might request shorter chopsticks until they have mastered their use.

Wines and Liquors

As far back as four thousand years ago winemaking was already widespread in China. Archaeological excavations uncovered a variety of ceramic wine vessels dating back to the Longshan culture. Yeast fermentation, a traditional technique, coupled with contemporary technology, have produced a variety of beverages available today. Chinese brandies are quite good; Chinese wines range from very sweet to dry white.

In 1979 China's National Wine Tasting Committee created an honor roll of "Eighteen Most Appreciated Drinks in China." Best known of these eighteen are the potent Mao Tai Chiew (Mao Tai) and China's Tsingtao-beer.

For the complete list of the Eighteen Most Appreciated Drinks and a brief description of each, see the Appendix.

Arts and Crafts

Chinese art began before recorded history. Bronze castings, decorated pottery, and carved wood and ivory date back prior to the Shang Dynasty (1766-1122 B.C.). Since the founding of the new China, guided by Chairman Mao's policy on art and literature, "Let a hundred flowers blossom; weed through the old to bring forth the new," Chinese arts and crafts have seen a surge of new development, wider subject matter, and greater variety in method of presentation. Today China's arts and

crafts cover over a dozen categories, including painting, sculpture, pottery, embroidery, carving, textile printing and dyeing, carpet weaving, knitting, and the folk art of making papercuts.

Painting has been an art form in China for more than 2,000 years. The simple but finely drawn lines for which traditional Chinese painting is famous can also be found on decorated pottery and lacquerware of the Han Dynasty (B.C. 206-A.D. 220). These ink or watercolor paintings were done mostly with birds, flowers, the aristocracy, and peaceful landscapes as their most popular subjects. Chinese painting varied very little through the ages until the first half of the twentieth century when oil painting and woodcuts became prominent. By the 1970's Chinese painting had undergone a radical change. Modern techniques employ bold brush strokes and many hues of color, a striking contrast to the muted colors and simple lines of the old, traditional style. Although birds and flowers are still used as themes, modern art portrays such subjects as revolution, sports, planting and harvesting, and construction.

Sculpture is China's oldest art form. Chinese sculptors produced many beautiful statues and temple decorations inspired by Buddhism and other religions. Clay sculpture is still alive today throughout China.

Workers affixing embroidery to skullcaps, Xinjiang Uygur Zizhiqu

Pottery craftsmanship in China dates back hundreds of years with porcelain one of its outstanding inventions. The definition for porcelain is pottery that is translucent and vitrified, known as "china" because it was first discovered by the Chinese as early as the fourteenth century. Jingdezhen (Chingtehchen), with its long history of porcelain production, is known as "the capital of porcelain." The most famous variety is eggshell china, reputed to be "thin as paper, resonant as chimes, white as jade, and clear as a mirror."

Embroidery has developed into four major types or schools, most famous of which is the renowned double-sided embroidery of Suzhou (Soochow). The technique used (neat stitching and graceful patterns) and the refined choices of color are so exquisite that one cannot tell the back from the front.

Paper-cuts, also called paper carvings or window flowers, are known and loved throughout China. It is a Chinese folk art with a long history. A creation of the working people, paper-cuts were originally used on windowpanes as decorations during festivals, holidays, or on other festive occasions. They are also used to decorate gift packages and as patterns for embroidery. Paper-cuts are made with scissors or knives. With a good pair of scissors, the skilled artist easily turns out flowers, fruits, and animals, symmetrical or chain patterns, and less sophisticated human figures. With a knife one can produce more intricate patterns and more elaborate scenes, including minute details of facial features.

59

Different parts of China have developed their own artistic style. Some are cut from paper of one color, either by creating the design and eliminating the background/nonessential parts, leaving only the outlines of the principal figures (Yang), or the reverse, cutting out the principal figures or their outlines and retaining the background (Yin). Some paper-cuts are painted, some are a combination of cutting and pasting different colored paper, and some are even made from a thin sheet of copper. Finished paper-cuts are intricate and exquisite. You will note that Chinese paper-cuts have been used on the opening pages of the various sections of this Guidebook, and have been placed as spot illustrations throughout the book.

Entertainment

There are varied forms of entertainment in China including opera, ballet, and the theater. In most cases your tour's itinerary will include your attending at least one, if not more, of these cultural activities.

Opera is performed beautifully throughout China, but the Peking (Beijing) Opera is famous throughout the world. The Opera combines song, dance, acrobatics, and pantomime to brilliant advantage. Unlike most Western operas, no stage sets and very few stage props are used. Instead, the productions depend upon music, make-up and magnificent, intricately made costumes to set the tone.

Workers inspecting theatrical costumes at Beijing costume factory

Originally, operatic roles were all filled by men, with female impersonators playing the feminine parts. In the early half of the twentieth century women began to appear as themselves in opera performances. Female participation can also be seen in the orchestra, traditionally an all-male band of musicians. If you have never attended an opera before, it would be wise to ask your Lüxingshe guide to secure a synopsis of the opera you are going to see ahead of time to enhance your enjoyment of the evening.

Ballet as it is performed in China has fused Chinese folk dancing, military movements, and Western ballet techniques. The themes are revolutionary. Well-known Western ballets such as Swan Lake are also performed. Both Beijing (Peking) and Shanghai have ballet schools. In the last twenty years China has developed several magnificent productions of her own.

Theater is perhaps the chief form of entertainment in China. Historically it served not only as a form of relaxation and enjoyment but also as a means of conveying political messages. This is still true in modern theater. From an audience of only the elite when it began, today's theater is now attended by all. Amateur drama clubs are also prevalent throughout the country in addition to the many professional companies. Themes are varied with historical events being used frequently as backgrounds for the dramas.

61

Other forms of entertainment in China include puppet theaters, the circus, and acrobatic performances, all of which the traveler will find quite enjoyable. Local movie houses and cinemas can be found throughout the country featuring films of Chinese origin, although a few show Western and Japanese films. Chinese film-making runs the gamut: full-length feature films, scientific films, cartoons, documentaries, and newsreels.

Special Native Products

Silk

China was the first country to raise silk worms and to reel silk from cocoons. More than four thousand years ago the Chinese weavers already possessed the know-how to make clothing from silk cocoons. By 100 B.C. the cultivation of silk was flourishing and the ancient Greeks referred to China as Seres, meaning the country of silk. In 166 A.D. the Roman Empire sent a special envoy to China to buy silk. At that time the road from Xi'an (Sian) via middle and western Asia to the eastern harbors of the Mediterranean was called "The Silk Road." Approximately 4,347 mi. (7,000 km.) long, it was the longest and one of the most important trade routes of antiquity.

Currently China produces over one thousand kinds of silks and satins including pure silk, tussah silk, mulberry silk, rayon satin, as well as synthetic silks and satins. In China silk is still made on traditional, manually-operated spinning wheels. Whether it is the pure silks (light, soft, elastic, colorful, and comfortable to wear), the gorgeous silver- and gold-threaded brocades, or the unique oak-grown tussah silks (absorbent, chemically resistant, providing good insulation), the variety of the colors and designs available are ever-changing and constantly increasing. Apparel made from Chinese silks and satins has always enjoyed great prestige on the international market.

Tea

China was one of the first countries to grow and process tea leaves. As early as 2000 B.C. tea leaves were taken as medicines. By 303 B.C. tea was used as a daily beverage. Written records from the sixth century A.D. show evidence that the exportation of tea had already begun.

Tea has been a traditional Chinese export and is known for

its high quality and variety. The types available vary according to the soil in which it grows, the season in which the leaves are picked, and the way the leaves are processed. Each type has its own distinctive qualities. The five major types are: black tea, green tea, scented tea, Wulong (Oolong) tea, and Bai tea. Recent pharmaceutical studies indicate that the pigments in tea leaves contain multiple vitamins, tannin, oils, and other components. This combination is used to stimulate the nerve centers, quicken metabolism, and aid muscle, heart, kidney, and digestive functions.

Black Tea (Fermented Tea) is rich and mellow in taste. Oxidation after fermentation gives the tea a dark, glossy shine with a reddish color. Famous black teas include Qimen (Keemun), Yunnan, and Yinde.

Green Tea (Non-fermented Tea) has a sweet smelling fragrance and delicate, refreshing taste. The excellence of its quality is matched only by its varieties. Among the best known are Longjing (Lungching), Biluochun, Maofeng, and Guapian.

Scented Tea (Flower Tea) is made by adding flower petals to choice green tea leaves. The heavy fragrance of fresh flowers (usually jasmine or magnolia) is blended into the aromatic tea leaves so that the two compliment each other. Scented teas are named after the flowers used: Jasmin, Magnolia, Zhulan, Daidaihua, and Shaddock (Pomelo).

Wulong (Oolong) Tea (Semi-fermented Tea) is treated in a unique, traditional way giving the tea a long-lasting fragrance, mellow taste, and a lingering sweetness on the palate. Famous

brands are Wuyi, Narcissus, Qizhong, Dahongpao, and Tieguanyin.

Bai Tea (White Tea) is a special kind of tea, neither fermented nor treated. The two varieties are Yinzhenbaihao and White Peony.

Ginseng

Ginseng is a medicinal herb known for its nutritious values and curative effects. China was one of the first countries to discover and use it. Since ancient times ginseng has been used as a strengthening and enriching tonic for clinical purposes. Containing various chemical elements (panaxic glucoside and panaxic acid) as well as vitamins, the ginseng root and its derivatives are used to stimulate the heart, regulate blood pressure, lower blood sugar, and help metabolism. It also has proven effective for poor memory, anemia, diabetes, insomnia, poor eyesight, and certain intestinal diseases. There are literally scores of medicines which use the ginseng as their main ingredient which are sold both within China and abroad.

Pilose (Deer) Antler

Pilose antler is a rare animal medicine and a superior traditional nutrient. Ancient Chinese medical texts record at least a two-thousand-year history of its use. It is the tender horn of male deer before it is ossified. Rich in proteins, hormones, vitamins, phosphate, calcium, and magnesium, years of experience in medical treatment have proven that pilose antler stimulates body growth and development, the growth of blood producing vessels, as well as increasing one's resistance to dis-

eases. Currently scores of medicines in the form of tinctures, pills, ointments, and powders are made from pilose antlers.

Mink

The mink belongs to the genus Mustela. They are a rare fur-bearing animal with the white sable ranking as the most precious. The rich, glossy pelt is smooth, soft, and highly valued for its beauty, warmth, and lightness. It is used for making top-grade fur coats which are in great demand particularly on the international market.

Beijing Preserved Fruit

Preserved or candied fruit has been a traditional product of Beijing (Peking) for over one thousand years. Beijing's fame as a maker of preserved fruit stems from its history. As the capital of China, monarchs from many dynasties enjoyed these delicious sweets as their daily food. They are processed from selected fresh fruits such as apricots, peaches, pears, dates, apples, and crabapples. After the skin and stones are removed, they are thoroughly cleaned and cut to the required size. After being soaked in different densities of sugar syrup, they are brought to a boil twice. Left to soak in the sugar syrup for twenty-four to forty-eight hours, they are then dried.

These preserved fruits not only retain their original flavor and color, but they have the unique quality of an oriental food, that is, the lingering sweetness remains on the palate long afterward. Besides being tasty, these preserved fruits contain minerals, vitamin C, and fruit acid which laboratory tests and practical experience indicate are effective in preventing and treating some diseases. Travelers to Beijing often like to take back several varieties as gifts to friends and relatives.

Hami Melons and Seedless White Grapes of Xinjiang

At the beginning of the Qing Dynasty (1644-1911 A.D.) a feudal lord in Xinjiang (Sinkiang) by the name of Hami sent loads of melons each year as a tribute to the Manchu court in Beijing. Thereafter the melon became known as the Hami melon. The fruit is large in size, weighing between 6 and 22 lbs. (3 to 10 kilos) and is mellow tasting. It has a delightful fragrance and is extremely juicy, with a high percentage of sugar (12% to 14%).

The seedless white grapes of Xinjiang have a skin that is so thin that when ripe, it is almost transparent. They are plump, juicy, and fragrant, with a sugar content of 20%. The internationally famous Xinjiang seedless white raisins are processed from this strain.

Both the melons and the grapes owe their excellent qualities to the favorable natural environment. They grow abundantly at the foot of the Tian Shan (Tienshan Mountains) in the center of the Turpan Pendi (Turfan Basin). The area has hot summer days with long hours of intense sunlight and sparse rainfall. During the day the ground level temperature is so very high one can literally cook an egg on it. The very hot daytime temperature drops radically after sunset. This temperature differential favors the accumulation of sugar in the fruit and accounts for the special qualities of the melons and the grapes.

Litchi (Lychee)

In the past the fruit of the litchi was used by feudal kings as a tributary item to the emperor's court. To keep them fresh, special courier stations were built for the transport of the perishable fruit.

The litchi is an evergreen tree grown mainly in Guangdong, Guangxi, and Fujian. The fruit of the tree is called the litchi nut. It is a single-seed fruit surrounded by semi-transparent, jelly-like pulp filled with sweet, milky, white juice. This luscious fruit is delicate and sweet with a slight touch of tartness. Litchi nuts contain glucose and a great number of vitamins and proteins giving it a high nutritional value. It is found to have a beneficial effect on such illnesses as dehydration, nervousness, thirst, and fatigue. Fresh litchi nuts are available from April to August and dried litchi nuts are available all year round.

Freshwater Fish

China's freshwater fish resources are ranked one of the best in the world. Among the more than seven hundred varieties are freshwater crabs (considered the best in the world), small carp or sand perch, shad, salmon, and shrimp.

Birds/Animals of China

China's vast territory constitutes one-fifteenth of the world's land area and its wildlife includes 1,160 known species of birds, accounting for one eighth of the world's species, and

Street vendors selling Hami melons, Xinjiang Uygur Zizhiqu

400 species of animals, comprising one ninth of the world's total.

Among the animals known for their scientific value in the study of ancient geography and climate are the giant panda, the white-lipped deer, the golden-haired monkey, the white-finned porpoise, and the brown-eared pheasant, all unique to China. The most remarkable and the most well-known of the group is the giant panda. According to fossil studies, giant pandas proliferated about two million years ago and can be traced in many provinces south of the Changjiang (Yangtze River). Violent climactic changes caused other animals of this class to gradually become extinct leaving the giant panda as the only surviving animal of its kind, successfully producing

67

their off-spring generation after generation. As a result they have come to be called "living fossils" and are of priceless value in the study of paleogeography and paleontology.

Other noteworthy animals of China, which are also found in other countries, but in restricted areas and in limited numbers, include the beautifully coated Manchurian tiger, the red-crowned crane, the long-armed apes (Gibbons) that inhabit the deep jungles in Yunnan and on Hainan Dao (Hainan Island).

3. Main Tourist Cities

Sweeping curves of the Great Wall, Badaling

Beijing (PEKING)

Beijing is the capital of the People's Republic of China and one of the country's three municipalities under direct central authority. To the northwest stands a chain of lofty mountains with the Great Wall snaking through its peaks and to the southeast lies a broad expanse of rolling plain. Situated in the north of Hebei Sheng (Hopei Province), Beijing covers an area of 6,870 sq. mi. (17,000 sq. km.) with a population totaling over 8.5 million people.

Beijing is a city with a long history. In 1929 the first fragment of a skull of what was later termed "Peking Man" was uncovered 29 mi. (48 km.) southwest of the City, verifying civilization at Beijing goes back 400 to 500 thousand years. Over the centuries the City has had many names, serving as China's capital off and on throughout history. The Great Wall, one of the world's most famous sites, was constructed during the Qin (Chin) Dynasty, 221-206 B.C., to protect the capital against invaders. Early in the tenth century Beijing lost some of its stature when the northern conquerors called it Nan Jing (Southern Capital) to distinguish it from their new capital which had been established north in Manchuria. In the twelfth century it was renamed Zhong Du (Central Capital) and enlarged in three directions.

In the thirteenth century fighting destroyed most of Zhong Du. Kubla Khan called the new city he established nearby Da Du (Great Capital). At the beginning of the Ming Dynasty,

1368 A.D., Nanjing (Nanking) became China's capital until the early 1400's when the capital was again moved back to Beijing. During this dynasty the Great Wall was restored.

Beijing remained the capital for almost seven centuries and was witness to many historical events, one of the most famous of which is called the "May 4th Movement." On May 4, 1919, over 300,000 people demonstrated in Tian An Men Square. This demonstration, organized by students from Beijing University, was staged to protest their displeasure with the current government. This movement has been called by many as the beginning of China's search of independence.

In 1928 the political seat was moved to Nanjing (Nanking). But Beijing was restored to its former stature as China's capital when on October 1, 1949, Chairman Mao raised the red flag of China from Tian An Men Sqaure, the inaugural ceremony signifying the founding of the People's Republic of China.

Prior to 1949 industry was almost non-existent in Beijing. Rapid industrial growth has converted it to one of China's major industrial centers. Principal industries are agricultural machinery, machine tools, electronics, textiles, and oil refining. Agriculture is also an important phase of life in the capital with many communes in the outlying areas supplying the city with fruits and vegetables, such as sweet potatoes, beans, lotus roots, and Chinese cabbage.

Beijing is well known as a cultural center and as the home of the famous "Peking Opera." Traditional arts and crafts still flourish including ivory sculpture, jade carving, carpets, embroidery, cloisonné, and lacquerware. Beijing also boasts many theaters and movie houses, China's largest library, and many colleges and universities, including Beijing University, founded in 1898, and Qinghua (Tsinghua) University, famous for its scientific and technical research.

New and old stand side by side along Beijing's avenues, which are flat and wide. Nowhere is this more striking than at the southern extremity of Tian An Men Square. Here the walls that once surrounded the Imperial City have been replaced by an underground subway and a broad avenue of fourteen- to sixteen-story apartment houses. Standing majestically over this scene, as it has since the fifteenth century, is the beautifully restored Qian Men Gate.

As one moves further from Tian An Men, the ceremonial

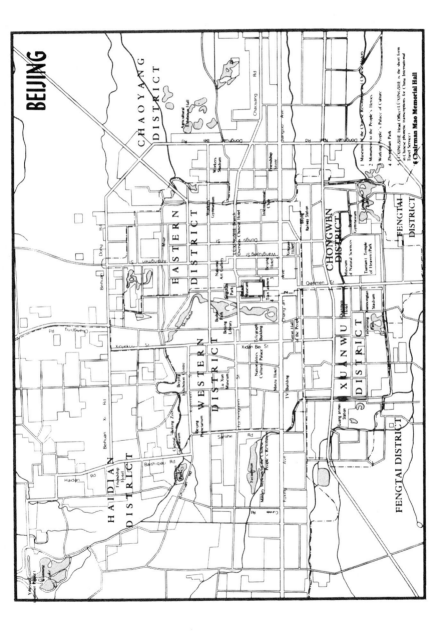

center of the City, one encounters the ebb and flow of customary life in the neighboring residential and business areas. Large city blocks of one-story grey stone and brick houses, which have not changed appreciably in hundreds of years, give way to shopping areas, business offices, and modern apartment construction. And everywhere one looks at any hour of the day will be vast numbers of people on their bicycles going to and from work or school.

PLACES OF INTEREST

Tian An Men Square

Occupying over 98 acres (39.7 ha.), this historic square, also called the Gate of Heavenly Peace Square, lies in the heart of Beijing. It was from here that the establishment of the People's Republic of China was proclaimed.

Tian An Men Gate, Entrance to the Forbidden City

The Square derives its name from the gate on the north side (Tian An Men Gate), and is the largest public square in the world. Reviewing stands have been built at the north end of the Square to accomodate twenty thousand spectators.

To the east of the Square you will find the Museum of the Chinese Revolution and the Museum of Chinese History, and to the west, the Great Hall of the People. At the south end is the Chairman Mao Memorial Hall and to the north, the Forbidden City.

Great Hall of the People
This building, on the west side of the Square, covers an area of 560,000 sq. ft. (51,520 sq. m.). At one time called the National People's Congress Building, it is the home of the NPC when it is in session. Other important political meetings as well as interviews with foreign diplomats are held here.

Comprised of many rooms and reception areas, it has an auditorium-cum-theater large enough to seat 10,000 people. Its banquet hall has a capacity of 5,000 people, and it was here that Richard Nixon, the first American President to visit the People's Republic of China, was honored with a banquet. The Great Hall has been opened recently to visits by tourists.

Museum of Chinese History and Museum of the Chinese Revolution
On the east side of the Square, directly across from the Great Hall of the People, you will find these museums housed in one building. The Museum of Chinese History, in the right wing, begins with primitive man (500,000 B.C.) and traces China's development up to 1840. The Museum of the Chinese Revolution, in the left wing, covers China's history since the Opium War of 1840 to the present, with particular emphasis on revolution and the establishment of socialism.

Monument to the People's Heroes
A lofty, granite obelisk 118 ft. (36 m.) high, this Monument is in the middle of the Square. Built to honor the heroes who died in the cause of the revolution, its base contains ten bas-relief carvings depicting various revolutionary events. Inscriptions on this monument are in the handwriting of Chairman Mao and Premier Zhou (Chou En-lai).

Memorial Hall of Chairman Mao
Opened in 1977 this imposing building is a tribute to Chairman Mao (1893-1976). Erected between the Monument to the People's Heroes and Qian Men Gate, the twin roofs of this building are supported by majestic granite pillars. The materials for this Memorial Hall were gathered from all over China and construction took only ten months to complete.

In the first room there is a commemorative statue of Mao sculptured out of white marble. The second room, called the Chamber of Reverence, contains the remains of Chairman Mao preserved in a crystal coffin. People from all parts of China come here to pay their respects. In the final room of this mausoleum you will find a sample of Mao's calligraphy inscribed on a large marble screen. As you leave the Memorial Hall you will have a good view of Qian Men Gate from the rear terrace.

Although the Memorial Hall is open to the public, visiting hours are restricted. When you arrive in Beijing be sure to check the current schedule of days and hours the Hall is open so you won't be disappointed and miss seeing it.

Qian Men Gate

At the rear of the Memorial Hall of Chairman Mao, on the southern edge of Tian An Men Square, one will find Qian Men Gate. Originally the Imperial City was protected by nine gates of which Qian Men is one of the few remaining. Constructed in the fifteenth century, this Gate was recently restored.

As a protective measure the nine original gates were designed with two doors or gates and space in between (sometimes referred to as double gates). If a hostile force managed to get through the outer or first door, a small enclosure or courtyard would still have to be crossed to get to the inner or second door which led into the City. Towers were strategically placed over these inner doors to allow almost perfect aim at the enemy trapped below.

One should not confuse the terms Imperial City and Forbidden City (Imperial Palace). The Imperial City as it existed many years ago covered an area which encompassed not only the land where the Forbidden City is today, but also Tian An Men Square and acres and acres of surrounding areas. Anyone who worked in the Imperial Palace lived within the walls of the Imperial City. Much of the original wall has been torn down and is now part of urban Beijing. Qian Men Gate is one of the last vestiges marking the old Imperial City's boundaries.

Tian An Men Gate

Tian An Men Gate is an immense stone structure painted red.

Old and new: subway entrance next to Qian Men Gate,
Tian An Men Square

Also called the Gate of Heavenly Peace, the moat that runs through the Imperial Palace continues along at the foot of the Gate. Five marble bridges span this moat, each leading to one of the five passages you must take to go through the Gate.

As you walk towards the Gate, centered on the front wall, is Chairman Mao's portrait. Flanking his portrait, in Chinese characters, are two inscriptions: on the western (left) side, "Long live the People's Republic of China;" on the eastern (right) side, "Long live the great unity of the peoples of the world."

For centuries the passages through the Gate remained closed. Opened only on great ceremonial occasions, the center passageway was always reserved for the emperor. Kept closed until the early part of the twentieth century, the Gate is now open and provides an impressive entrance to the Imperial Palace and its surrounding grounds.

The Forbidden City

The name Forbidden City is a term used by Westerners to refer to the Imperial Palace. It is actually the Imperial Palace and the surrounding grounds. The meaning of "Forbidden City" dates back to the time, prior to the 1911 Revolution, when entrance into the Palace grounds through Tian An Men Gate was forbidden to ordinary people.

FORBIDDEN CITY

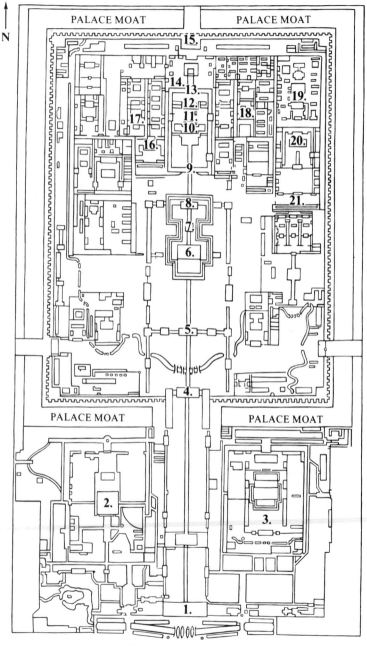

TIAN AN MEN SQUARE

KEY TO SITE PLAN OF FORBIDDEN CITY

1. Tian An Men Gate
2. Zhongshan Park
3. Working People's Cultural Palace
4. Meridian Gate
5. Gate of Supreme Harmony
6. Hall of Supreme Harmony
7. Hall of Complete Harmony
8. Hall of Preserving Harmony
9. Gate of Heavenly Purity
10. Palace of Heavenly Purity
11. Hall of Union
12. Palace of Earthly Tranquillity
13. Gate of Earthly Tranquillity
14. Imperial Garden
15. Gate of Divine Prowess
16. Hall of Mental Cultivation
17. Six Western Palaces
18. Six Eastern Palaces
19. East Outer Section
20. Hall of Paintings
21. Nine Dragon Screen

The Imperial Palace

Built in the early fifteenth century (1406-1420 A.D.), it is also called the Palace Museum or the Old Palace. As you pass through Tian An Men Gate you will enter a walled courtyard. Although you cannot see them, on either side of this courtyard are many gardens and halls. Of particular interest if you have time might be the Imperial Ancestral Temple, which is to the right, and the Sun Yat-Sen Park, on the left.

Covering an area of 175 acres (72 ha.), the Palace is enclosed by walls over 35 ft. (10.4 m.) high and surrounded by a moat 57 yd. (52 m.) wide. Today this moat is still full of water. Four watchtowers are placed, one at each corner. Used as the imperial palace by both the Ming and Qing Dynasties (1368-1911 A.D.), it is the largest and most complete group of ancient buildings standing in China.

The halls and palaces which comprise the Imperial Palace are all built of wood and brick. With a total of over nine thousand rooms, most of the Palace has undergone some reconstruction to repair damage caused by fire and other ravages of time during the long years of its history. Throughout you will find typical masterpieces of ancient Chinese architecture. Two notable examples are the ingeniously constructed watchtowers and the magnificent Hall of Supreme Harmony.

To further insure the Imperial Palace would be given special protection, in 1961 the Chinese government decreed that the entire area be considered one of China's "most important historical sites."

The Palace Museum, with four gates, has its main entrance to the south, known as the Meridian Gate. This is the gate you will approach as you continue along the cobbled roadway from Tian An Men. The Imperial Palace is divided into two ceremonial areas: the Outer Palace and the Inner Court. Through the Meridian Gate and across the Golden Water Bridge, one comes to the Gate of Supreme Harmony, the main gate of the Outer Palace. The main buildings in the Outer Palace are the Hall of Supreme Harmony, the Hall of Complete Harmony, and the Hall of Preserving Harmony.

Hall of Supreme Harmony

Over the years this building was used for major ceremonies and state affairs, such as accessions of new emperors, celebration of New Year, winter solstice, and the promulgation of Imperial edicts. Three flights of stairs lead to the upper terrace, the staircase in the center being the one which the emperor's throne was carried up. Bronze incense burners, storks, and tortoises (symbols of longevity) flank the staircases. Both the emperor's original throne in the center of the Hall and the screen inside the Hall are carved from wood. Each of the high

Gate of Supreme Harmony, Imperial Palace

pillars (60 ft. or 13.8 m.) is made out of a single piece of timber.

Hall of Complete Harmony

Also referred to as the Hall of Perfect Harmony. Before going to supervise major ceremonies, the emperor received homage from his close ministers in this Hall. The worshipping address

Throne in Hall of Preserving Harmony, Imperial Palace

to be read out at the sacrificial ceremonies held in the Temple of Heaven and elsewhere had to be brought here for the emperor to go over beforehand. The two sedan chairs on display in this Hall date back to the Qing Dynasty and were used by the emperor as transport within the Palace.

Hall of Preserving Harmony

"Palace Examinations," the highest level of civil service examinations, took place here in feudal times. In the Qing Dynasty banquets were given in this Hall by the emperor in honor of the princes and ministers from minority nationalities.

The carved marble ramp behind the Hall, weighing some 250 tons, is the largest stone carving in the Imperial Palace. This huge stone block was moved here in the winter by sliding it over an ice path formed by pouring water onto the road to freeze. To provide enough water, wells were sunk along the way in advance.

Further on from the marble ramp one continues along into the Inner Court. Entering the Gate of Heavenly Purity, you then see the three main buildings in the Inner Court: The Palace of Heavenly Purity, the Hall of Union, and the Palace of Earthly Tranquility. These three buildings are built in very much the same architectural style as the three in the Outer Palace.

Palace of Heavenly Purity
The largest of the three buildings, the emperors used to live and handle government affairs in this Hall. After 1901 Dowager Empress Ci Xi received foreign envoys here on many occasions.

Hall of Union
Ceremonies conferring titles on empresses or celebrating empresses' birthdays took place here. In the Hall twenty-five Imperial seals made of jade are kept. The chiming clock and the clepsydra, an ancient water-clock, were both made in the Qing Dynasty.

Palace of Earthly Tranquillity
The Ming empresses used to live in this Palace which was turned into a shrine for worshipping gods in the Qing Dynasty. The small room to the right was used as a bridal chamber for Qing emperors.

Imperial Garden
The Gate of Earthly Tranquillity leads from the Inner Court into the Imperial Garden. It was here where the emperors, empresses, and the Imperial concubines spent their leisure hours, strolling round and enjoying the scenery. Beyond the Imperial Garden stands the Gate of Divine Prowess, the northern entrance to the Imperial Palace.

Hall of Mental Cultivation
This Hall is reached through the right-side gate of the Inner Court. From the time of Emperor Yong Zheng (1723-1736 A.D.), the Qing emperors moved their residence to this Hall

Bronze tortoise, Imperial Palace

and also used it as an office. In its eastern chamber Dowager Empress Ci Xi took charge of state affairs "behind a screen." A screen was placed between the front and back thrones, with the child emperor sitting in front and Ci Xi behind the screen. After the 1911 Revolution the Qing court still occupied the Inner Court and the deposed Emperor Puyi lived here until 1924 when he was driven out of the Palace by the army under General Feng Yuxiang.

Six Western Palaces
Going through the back gate you will find after a few turns along the way, the Six Western Palaces, which were the living quarters for the Ming and Qing empresses and Imperial concubines. On display in these palaces are all sorts of antiques, works of calligraphy, paintings, and beautiful furniture.

Six Eastern Palaces
These can be reached through the right-side gate of the Inner Court. Formerly also used as living quarters for empresses and concubines, they have been turned into museums of bronzes and porcelain.

East Outer Section
This section can also be reached through the right-side gate of the Inner Court but is further along on the right. Built by Emperor Qian Long (1736-1795 A.D.) when he became the Su-

preme Emperor after retirement, the main Hall is similar in architectural style to the Palace of Heavenly Purity. The East Outer Section has a garden (not open to the public) behind two major buildings and three minor halls, each with its own courtyard. Today it is comprised of several museums where various art treasures are on display. They include, among other things, household utensils made of gold, silver, and jade; percussion musical instruments such as the sixteen gold bells and the sixteen jade chimes; several gem-inlaid gold towers, each weighing over 220 lbs. (100 kg.); a dragon robe made of peacock feathers, pearls, and coral beads; and the "jade hill," carved from one solid piece of jade weighing five tons (this work took ten years to complete). It is in the East Outer Section that you will find also the Hall of Paintings and the magnificent Nine Dragon Screen, made from varicolored glazed tiles.

Jing Shan ("Coal Hill")

Going through the Gate of Divine Prowess, the northern end of the Imperial Palace, you will come to Jing Shan (Prospect Hill). It is in the heart of Beijing's inner city and the highest elevated point of old Beijing. Originally there was only a small hill located here (Qing Shan or Green Hill) but at the beginning of the fifteenth century, when the Imperial Palace was being built, unnecessary dirt when constructing the moat was heaped on Qing Shan and five peaks were created. The name Coal Hill (Mei Shan) comes from the fact that coal was once stored here.

When you first enter the grounds you will see Beautiful View Tower. Looking up, you will see five eighteenth-century pavilions, one on each of the five peaks. On the middle peak stands the largest pavilion, the three-story Pavilion of Ten Thousand Springs. This can be reached by a path up the side of the hill and the view from the top is magnificent, coupling not only a view of the Imperial Palace but also modern-day Beijing. At the foot of the hill stands the tree that legend tells us is where the last Ming Emperor, Chong Zhen, hanged himself in 1644 A.D. when his enemies forced the gates of the capital.

Bei Hai Park

Long ago there was a legend that to the east there existed a place that was so deep, one could not see the bottom. To this

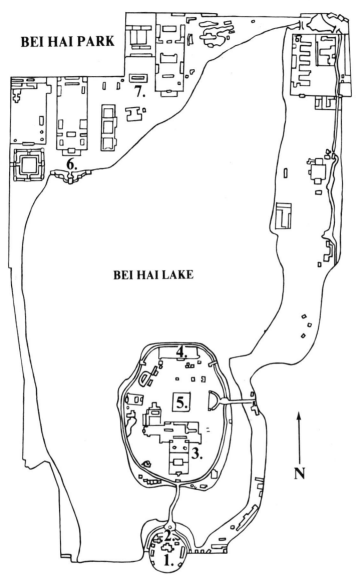

BEI HAI PARK

7.

6.

BEI HAI LAKE

4.

5.

3.

N

2.

1.

1. Round Town
2. Hall of Receiving Light
3. Qiong Hua Island
4. Fang Shan Restaurant
5. White Dagoba
6. Pavilion of Five Dragons
7. Nine Dragon Screen

place all the rivers and oceans ran and disappeared. That area was also said to contain the three islands of Peng-lai (a mythical Taoist paradise) where fairy immortals lived. Emperor Wu of the Han Dynasty, in an attempt to obtain immortality, had a large pond constructed to the rear of his palace. Earth was heaped in the middle of the pond to represent the Isles of Peng-lai. Similar construction was accomplished by emperors of the Sui and Tang Dynasties when their palaces were built. As the years progressed historical legend became the basis for a style of garden construction which is uniquely Chinese and rich in mythology and fantasy. Bei Hai Park's design was based on this legend.

Bei Hai (North Lake) is west of Jing Shan ("Coal Hill"). The area is not only beautiful and scenic but is also closely associated with the development of the city of Beijing. During the Liao (947-1125 A.D.) and the Jin (1115-1234 A.D.) Dy-

White Dagoba crowns Qiong Hua Island, Bei Hai Park

nasties, secondary palaces were built here. Under the Yuan Dynasty (1280-1368 A.D.) Qiong Hua (Precious Jade) Island was renovated three times. It was on this site that Kubla Khan's palace once stood which was the place where Marco Polo stayed when he visited China. With the palace as its center, more buildings were put up further out around the lake so that it became the foundation of the inner city of Beijing.

The lake and surrounding area are enclosed by walls. Before you enter through the main gate you will see Round Town, on the left, enclosed by a wall 14 ft. (5 m.) high. Originally an island, it now houses the Hall of Receiving Light. Within you will find a white jade Buddha (5 ft. or 1.5 m. high) which is ethereal and lustrous, suggesting sublime and tran-scendent repose. In the courtyard is the great Jade Basin. Car-ved in 1265 A.D., this bowl measures approximately 5 ft. (1.5 m.) in diameter, 2 ft. (.6 m.) in height, and over 15 ft. (4.6 m.) in circumference. The Jade Basin was originally used at cer-emonial banquets from which the various ministers and digni-taries drank wine.

Bei Hai Lake surrounds Qiong Hua Island which is 5,166 ft. (1,912 m.) in circumference. On the Island you will find many pavilions and multi-storied buildings with colorful glazed tiles. It is on this Island that the lovely Fang Shan Res-taurant can be found. Occupying the whole center of the Is-land is the White Dagoba built in 1651 A.D. on the ruins of the original palace 119 ft. (35.9 m.) high. If one climbs to the top of the hill on which it stands and gazes out, the scenery near and far spreads itself out and it is a spectacular view.

On the northern shore of Bei Hai is the Pavilion of the Five Dragons. Constructed in 1602 A.D. and jutting out over the water, their reflections resemble five clusters of new flowers blooming on the water's surface. Here you will also find the famous Nine Dragon Screen. This Screen, or wall, is 87 ft. (26.5 m.) long and over 15 ft. (4.6 m.) high. On both sides there are nine dragons chasing a pearl amid the waves. The wall is made entirely of colorful glazed tiles and one gets the feeling that each of the dragons is about to break forth from the wall.

Temple of Heaven Park (Tian Tan Park)

Tian Tan Park is the largest of all parks in Beijing with an area of 667 acres (269.9 ha.). It is covered with ancient pines and green cypresses many of which are over five hundred years old. The main buildings in this park are a group of temples which are noted for their exquisite layout, harmoni-ous color, and unique structure. They comprise one of the most beautiful architectural achievements in the world and are outstanding masterpieces of traditional Chinese architecture.

This group of temples was built at the same time as the Im-perial Palace (1406-1420 A.D.). The feudal emperors who called themselves "the sons of heaven" held ceremonies to worship heaven every year and the Temple of Heaven was built just for this purpose.

The Temple of Heaven, which is the name given to these

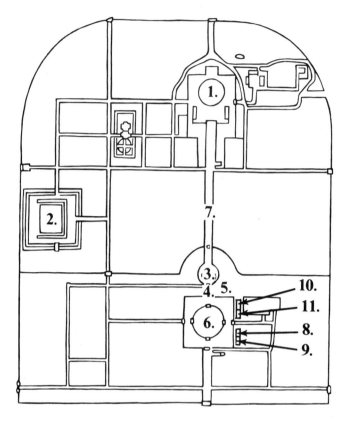

N

TEMPLE OF HEAVEN PARK

1. Hall of Prayer for Good Harvest
2. Hall of Abstinence
3. Imperial Vault of Heaven
4. Triple Sound Stones
5. Echo Wall
6. Circular Mound Altar
7. Red Stairway Bridge
8. **Kuan Fu Chai Seals, Ink Sticks, and Ink Stones Branch**
9. **Ching Yun Tang Stone Rubbings Branch**
10. **Yun Ku Chai Original Pottery and Porcelain Branch**
11. **Bao Ku Chai Original Chinese Calligraphy and Paintings Branch**

ceremonial buildings, has two surrounding walls, both of which are round to the north and square to the south. Such a pattern symbolizes the ancient belief that heaven is round and the earth square.

Entering the western gate of the Temple to the right there is a path which leads through the trees to the Hall of Abstinence. The Hall is a group of buildings surrounded by a square enclosure and a moat. This section of the Temple of Heaven is presently not open to visitors.

Continuing along the entrance path one comes to a raised passage called the Red Stairway Bridge. This broad walk connects the two sets of main buildings in the Temple of Heaven enclosure. On this Red Stairway Bridge there is a platform to the east. It is on this platform that the emperors changed clothing before going to worship.

Turning northward and entering through the Gate of Prayer for Good Harvest, one will see the Hall of Prayer for Good Harvest in its full grandeur. It is a lofty cone-shaped structure with triple eaves and a blue-tiled roof. The entire structure is 123 ft. (37.5 m.) high and is supported by twenty-eight massive wooden pillars each of which symbolizes a different thing. The four central columns, called the "Dragon-Well pillars," represent the four seasons. Surrounding these four there are two rings of twelve columns each, the inner ring symbolizing the twelve months, and the outer ring, the twelve divisions of day and night. The center of the stone-paved floor is a round marble slab which has a natural pattern of a dragon and phoenix. The whole building is a wooden structure joined together by means of wooden bars, laths, and brackets without the use of any iron or bronze.

Hall of Prayer for Good Harvest, Temple of Heaven Park

The Hall of Prayer for Good Harvest served as the place where the emperors prayed for good harvest every year on the fifteenth day of the first moon by the lunar calendar. Behind this Hall is the Hall of Heavenly Emperor, a place to keep the tablet of heaven and other divine symbols during the year. Going back out through the Gate of Prayer for Good Harvest, and proceeding southward, you can visit the Imperial Vault of Heaven and the Circular Mound Altar.

The Circular Mound Altar was the place for making offerings to heaven on the winter solstice. In ancient China the odd numbers (1, 3, 5, 7, 9) were regarded as "sun numbers." So the number of stone slabs in any part of this Altar (terrace floor, staircases, and balustrades) is made in multiples of 9. After the ceremony the tablet of the God of Heaven and the tablets of the Gods of Wind, Rain, Thunder, and Lightning were brought back to be stored in the Imperial Vault of Heaven.

The surrounding wall of the Imperial Vault of Heaven and the center stones of the Circular Mound Altar produce a strange acoustic effect. People can make "telephone calls" through the wall. Two people standing behind the side chambers, one on each side, and speaking softly to the wall, may be heard by each other. This is often referred to as Echo Wall.

On the flight of steps leading down from the Imperial Vault of Heaven there are three rectangular stones. If you stand on the first stone and call out, the sound will be echoed once; on the second, twice; on the third stone, three times. These are called the Triple Sound Stones.

Beijing Zoo

This is the largest zoo in China and has over two thousand animals (four hundred different species). It is located in the northwestern section of Beijing, opposite the bus terminal. The biggest attraction is, of course, the giant panda. There are also yaks from Tibet, tigers from Manchuria, huge sea turtles,

Marble Boat, Summer Palace

elephants, lions, a rust-colored species of panda closely related to the racoon, and much more. Besides those animals native to China, other animals were obtained through exchanges with zoos from all over the world. There is also a beautiful outdoor bird sanctuary and a restaurant with large windows overlooking the zoo.

During the Ming Dynasty (1368-1644 A.D.) the site was a park. It became a private garden under the Qing Dynasty (1644-1911 A.D.) Its development as a zoological park began in 1902 when a Viceroy returned from a foreign tour with a collection of birds and animals from Germany which were presented to the Empress as a gift. The park was renamed Wan Sheng Yuan (Park of Ten Thousand Animals) and a few years later a botanical garden was added and shortly after that they were all opened to the public. But during the civil wars the stock of animals declined to nearly the vanishing point and the gardens were badly neglected. In 1949 the restoration of the zoo was undertaken. Today it is not only a popular tourist attraction but also a favorite place of the Chinese themselves.

Summer Palace

The Summer Palace is a forty-five minute drive northwest from Beijing. The grounds of the palace cover an area of 659 acres (266.7 ha.), over three quarters of which are water (Lake Kun Ming). The fourth quarter is Longevity Hill on which you will find the various buildings.

To escape the heat of the city proper the emperor and his court came here in the summer and the various residences and other edifices became known as the Summer Palace.

In the twelfth century the first palace was built here, called the Garden of Golden Waves. The Yuan Dynasty carried out a large excavation project to increase the lake's size. The Ming Dynasty added the Temple of Perfect Tranquillity and several pavilions and called it the Garden of Wonderful Hills. During the Qing Dynasty the largest construction was accomplished under Emperor Qian Long and he renamed the entire area, Garden of Clear Waves. All his work was done in honor of his mother's birthday and he named the hill, Longevity Hill, in her honor. It is still called that today.

In the mid-nineteenth century the area was burned by the Anglo-French allied forces. In 1888 the Dowager Empress Ci Xi took the money meant for improving the navy and rebuilt the area, giving it its present name, the Garden Where Peace is Cultivated. In 1900 foreign forces again severely damaged the area, but it was repaired in 1903.

The entrance to the Summer Palace is the Eastern Palace Gate. As you pass through this Gate you will see various palaces: on the right, the Palace of Virtue and Harmony, which houses a three-story theater in the center; at the far end, the Hall of Goodwill and Longevity, where the various emperors held audience; on the shore of the lake, the Jade Waves Palace, where Ci Xi held Emperor Guang Xu prisoner; and a little up, also on the lake, the Palace of Joy and Longevity, which was Ci Xi's residence.

A long, covered passageway 7,388 ft. (728 m.) long, follows the side of the lake. This is decorated with historical and mythological scenes. The landscape scenes of Hangzhou date back to the eighteenth century and Emperor Qian Long's birthday present to his mother. As you walk along this covered way you will come to the Hall of Regular Clouds, and, at its end, the famous marble boat built by Ci Xi when she rebuilt the entire area with navy funds.

If you climb the stairs to the top of Longevity Hill there is a beautiful view of the lake and the surrounding countryside including the seventeen-arch bridge of Long Wang Miao Island (located in the center of Lake Kun Ming). The Fo Xiang Ge Pagoda is located on the southern slope of this Hill. Four stories high (150 ft. or 14.7 m.), it contains statues of the Buddha and his followers. North of the Fo Xiang Ge, on the top of

Longevity Hill, is the Zhi Hui Hai (the Sea of Wisdom). This is a rectangular building and the large reclining Buddha inside was cast from fifty thousand pieces of copper, requiring seven thousand men to complete it.

Located near the Marble Boat is a restaurant, Ting Li Guan (Oriole Hall). Housed in a building which was originally a theater, the restaurant specializes in fresh fish. To the north of the restaurant note the gazebo built against the rocks.

If you have the time, the grounds of the Summer Palace contain other pavilions, pagodas, gazebos, and a beautiful garden. It is a delightful area for a relaxing walk.

The Great Wall (Visitors to Beijing are able to enjoy a new view of the Great Wall and Ming Tombs from the air. The helicopter sightseeing services over these famous sites were started from July 1, 1985.)

The Great Wall, first built during the Spring and Autumn Period (770-476 B.C.), was the crystallization of the wisdom of the Chinese working people in ancient times. It was a military project built by various small kingdoms for holding back nomadic tribes coming from the north as well as for protection against each other. After unifying the six states in 221 B.C., the first emperor of the Qin Dynasty issued an order that the walls originally built by the States of Qin, Yan, and Zhao be reinforced and linked together for defense against attack by the slave-owner regime in the northern part of China. This is how the well-known 3,700 mi. (6,000 km.) Great Wall came into being and it has played a significant role in protecting the economic and cultural developments in the central plain area of China.

After the Qin Dynasty, the Great Wall was restored and reinforced by successive dynasties; but the most ambitious efforts were made under the Ming Dynasty. After its founding in 1368 A.D. the Ming Dynasty devoted huge amounts of manpower and resources to the restoration project taking a total of over one hundred years to complete it. When the Wall was being rebuilt it was necessary to use a lot of bricks and stones, and some of the stone slabs were as heavy as one ton. Considering the conditions of the time, one can imagine how extremely difficult the project must have been.

Because of the high quality of its construction, most of the Great Wall built under Ming still stands intact. The section at Badaling, restored in 1957 for visitors, is typical in structure: 26 ft. (7.8 m.) high on the average, 22 ft (6.6 m.) wide at the bottom, and 19 ft. (5.8 m.) wide on the top. On the outer flank of the Wall there were battlements for watching and shooting. The guard towers built at intervals were used as sentry posts and living quarters for soldiers. Beacon towers were built at commanding points on either side of the Wall. These were facilities used in ancient times for communication and signalling (with smoke in the daytime and with fire at night in case of emergency).

The Great Wall at Badaling Pass

In addition to its use as a defensive bulwark and as a communications network, the Great Wall was also a roadway. Wide enough to permit five horsemen to ride side by side or permit passage for soldiers by columns of ten, emperors were able to move men and equipment vast distances quite rapidly through mountainous areas that would ordinarily have been impassible.

The Great Wall begins in the east at Shan Hai Guan Pass (between the provinces of Hebei and Liaoning) and traverses up and down over numerous mountains and valleys through four of China's provinces, two autonomous regions and the municipality of Beijing, ending at Jia Yu Pass in the northwest province of Gansu. The Great Wall skirts many steep passes including the Ju Yong Guan Pass, with its fort, and Badaling.

It is approximately 40 miles (64 km.) from Beijing to Badaling where you can climb a portion of the Great Wall. As you drive towards Badaling you will pass a magnificent white marble gate at Ju Yong Guan. It was originally the base of a tower astride the road and is centuries old. The arch contains bas-relief carvings of Buddhist themes. The walls of this gateway are decorated with inscriptions in Chinese, Mongolian, Sanskrit, Uighur, Tibetan, and Tangut. These inscriptions have been a very valuable reference in the study of ancient languages.

The road will continue upward and approximately 6 mi. (9.7 km.) from Ju Yong Guan you will reach Badaling. It is here that you can climb up either the left or right side of the Wall. Climbing up the left side is more steep than if you go up the right, but many people say the view from the left is more spectacular. Recently a small cafe where travelers can purchase candy, tea, milk, beer, and cigarettes has been opened here.

It is advisable to wear comfortable walking shoes, with good gripping soles. The Wall is steep and can be slippery.

The Ming Tombs

If you go to the Great Wall by bus or automobile you can visit the Ming Tombs on the same day since they form a slight detour from the same road that leads out to the Great Wall. Arrangements can be also made to travel to the Great Wall by train, returning on the train only as far as the vicinity of the Ming Tombs. From there a bus will take the visitor to the

Tombs and return you to Beijing.

The site of the Ming Tombs is in the northwest suburbs of Beijing, 30 mi. (49 km.) from the heart of the city. Tian Shou Hill, which is very high and quite steep, forms the backdrop for a deep, secluded ravine filled with lovely green trees. All around in a shallow basin are the thirteen tombs of the Ming Dynasty emperors. The location of the tombs was chosen with great care and involved the art of divination to assure the most suitable final resting place for the emperors and empresses. The site selected had to have protection from the north, where evil spirits emanate, and also had to have a natural, adequate water supply.

The Ming Dynasty had a total of seventeen emperors but only thirteen are buried here. Emperor Cheng Zu (Yong Le) was the third Ming Emperor but the first of the Ming Dynasty to choose this site. His tomb is considered the "chief tomb" and the others were built, one by one, around it. The original path of the Sacred Way led to his tomb. Each tomb was broken into three parts: a building where sacrifices were offered; a tower for the stele; and the tumulus itself, which covered the underground palace where the body was buried. (A stele was a pillar, usually made of stone, used in ancient times for votive purposes.)

Of the thirteen tombs, Ding Ling, the tomb of the fourteenth emperor of the Ming Dynasty, Shen Zong, and Chang Ling, Emperor Cheng Zu's tomb, are the only ones that have been restored. Ding Ling is completely accessible with the tomb buildings renovated and the tomb itself excavated. At Chang Ling, the tomb buildings have been renovated but the tomb itself has yet to be excavated. The other eleven tombs have survived but are in severely damaged states.

The Sacred Way

The approach to the Ming Tombs is called the Sacred Way. Approximately 4 mi. (6.4 km.) in length, it begins when you pass a white marble gate and ends at the gate of the chief tomb. The first landmark, the white marble gate, was built in 1540 A.D. With five arches it has beautiful bas-relief carvings at its base. Originally the Sacred Way passed through this Gate. Today you will see it to the right of the road. Next comes the Great Red Gate. This is a massive building with three archways, each of which is 120 ft. (36 m.) high and 35 ft. (10.5 m.) wide. Traditionally the center passage was reserved

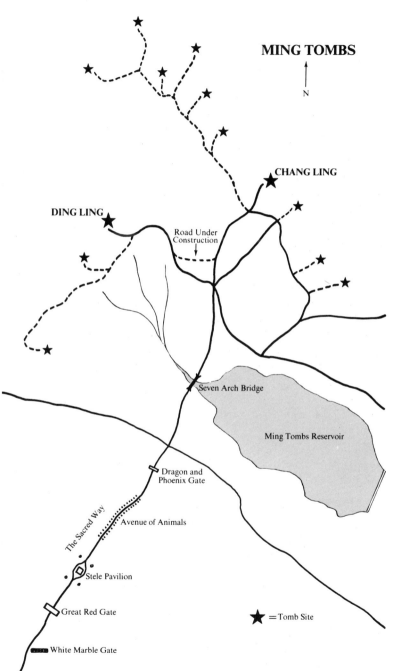

MING TOMBS

N

CHANG LING

DING LING

Road Under
Construction

Seven Arch Bridge

Ming Tombs Reservoir

Dragon and
Phoenix Gate

The Sacred Way

Avenue of Animals

Stele Pavilion

Great Red Gate

White Marble Gate

★ = Tomb Site

for the body of the emperor who was being transported to his final resting place. When visiting the site even the live emperors used the side porticos. This gate gave access to the original grounds which were surrounded by a high wall to keep out all unauthorized visitors. The penalty for intruders was death. A small retinue of officials and workers lived on the grounds permanently and saw to the landscaping and upkeep of the buildings.

Next along the road is the Stele Pavilion, which was erected in 1426 A.D. and is 30 ft. (9 m.) high. The inscribed stele within stands on the back of a tortoise and at each of the four corners are white marble columns decorated with carvings of dragons. Directly beyond this is the world-renowned Avenue of the Animals. The custom of placing animals outside of royal tombs dates from the time of the Han Dynasty (206 B.C.-220 A.D.). There are twenty-four large white marble animals, twelve facing pairs, equidistantly placed on either side of the road in standing and kneeling positions. Six animals are represented: two mythical animals, lions, elephants, camels, and horses. Then the Avenue turns slightly to the right and there is a row of twelve stone mandarin statues dating from the fifteenth century, six on each side. At the end of the Avenue of the Animals is a small portico with three gates. The road runs along on either side leading to the sites of the thirteen tombs.

Ding Ling

The most elaborate of the two restored tombs is that of Emperor Shen Zong (Wan Li) who reigned from 1573-1620 A.D. You will cross a small bridge which is marked with a stele on the back of a tortoise on the far side. Following the road brings the visitor to an entrance gate with three arched doorways. Passing through the wall in which the doors are set, the visitor walks toward a terrace which holds the bases of some stone columns that are all that remain of a building that once stood on the site. On one end three sets of stone steps lead down from the terrace to a tree-lined courtyard. At the other end of the terrace are three stairways, the middle one leading to another small terrace where sacrifices were made. Again only the bases of surviving columns remain of the building that once occupied the spot. Following the path further along brings the visitor to a gateway that opens onto a third court-

Avenue of the Animals, Ming Tombs

yard on either side of which are two small museum buildings.

The first museum, to the right, contains a model and photographs tracing the excavation of the tomb, and possessions of the two empresses buried in Ding Ling (Empress Xiao Duan, the Emperor's first wife who died in 1620 a few months before the Emperor, and his secondary wife, Empress Xiao Jing, who died in 1612 and whose body was moved to Ding Ling only after her son became emperor). The second museum, to the left, contains the possessions of the Emperor. The museum exhibition rooms have some three thousand items including clothing, silver, jade, and porcelain.

At the far end of this third courtyard is the large brick Square Tower and on top of this a Stele Tower. The Square Tower was erected against the Precious Wall which goes around the tumulus. Stairs lead up to the top of the Precious Wall from which it is possible to walk onto the tumulus. Additional stairs lead up to the top of the Square Tower.

Entrance to the tomb proper is near here. The tomb contains three rooms and can be reached by descending three flights of stairs. The first or outer room was of little value as nothing was found here during the excavation. The central chamber contained three altars and funerary lamps. Behind these alters was a very intricately carved throne. The third or final room, which cups the other two like a "T," is where the bodies of the Emperor and Empresses were laid, as well as the considerable treasurers with which they were interred.

The two side chambers on either side of the central chamber are still something of a mystery. Each one had a platform large enough to hold a coffin and from each a corridor led out of the tumulus, but when the excavation was complete, both rooms were found to be empty. It is thought that they were meant for the two empresses but at the last minute the coffins were found to be too large so they had to be interred in the emperor's chamber.

Chang Ling

The second of the two tombs to which some access is possible is that of Emperor Cheng Zu (Yong Le) who reigned from 1403-1424 A.D., and his wife, Empress Ren Xiao Si. At the present time the massive unexcavated mound that covers the tomb is believed to contain an even greater number of precious objects than was found in the tomb of Shen Zong (Wan Li). Opening of this tumulus is planned after further archaeological study has been completed.

To approach the tomb one passes first through one of three doorways in a large gate which forms part of a wall that surrounds the tomb and its grounds. A pavilion housing a Qing stele stands to the right as one enters. At the end of the first courtyard stands the Gate of Eminent Favors which has three passageways and a roof of glazed yellow tiles. This Gate leads into another large courtyard containing carefully pruned trees and the Hall of Eminent Favors can be seen at its far end. The Hall stands on a three-level marble terrace and access is gained by means of three flights of stairs. With a double roof of glazed tiles, it is supported by thirty-two mammoth wooden pillars extending down the 220 foot (67.1 m.) length of the room, which is 105 ft. (31 m.) wide. An additional twenty eight pillars, almost as thick, help to support the lower roof. Exiting from the rear of the Hall, the visitor goes through another gate which leads to the final courtyard. This courtyard is 300 ft. (91.4 m.) long and extends to the foot of the Square Tower which is capped by a Stele Tower. The characters inscribed on it announce "Tomb of Emperor Cheng Zu." There is a 60 ft. (18.3 m.) tunnel which goes through the tower and leads visitors to a terrace from which the unexcavated portion of the tomb can be viewed.

Liu Li Chang Jie (Glazed Tile Works Street)

This is an ancient street in Beijing which deals in antiques,

Passageway leading from the Underground Palace of Ding Ling

books, paintings, calligraphies, rubbings of ancient inscriptions, inkstones, brushes, and ink. Famous throughout the world for its products, it has been called "Beijing's culture street." It is located southwest of Tian An Men Square. One reaches Liu Li Chang from South Xin Hua Street.

Liu Li Chang Jie has a long history. In the Tang Dynasty (618-907 A.D.) it was part of Ji county. Through the years it was a village called Hai Wang on the eastern outskirts of the capital and then the name was changed to Hai Wang Zhuang. During the Yuan Dynasty (1280-1368 A.D.) the glazed pottery works were first established here. The Ming (1368-1644 A.D.) emperors undertook construction of many palaces and the scope of Liu Li Chang was increased. It then became one of the five great pottery ateliers under the Ministry of Works. All the glazed materials required for the construction of the palaces came from Liu Li Chang, which is how it derived its name.

Rong Bao Zhai (Studio of Glorious Treasures)

The Rong Bao Zhai Studio, the largest art shop in China, is on Liu Li Chang and specializes in the sale of traditional Chinese art works. These include watercolor woodblock reproductions, original paintings of modern and contemporary China, as well as artists' supplies such as brushes, inksticks, rice paper, and inkstones. Rong Bao Zhai also has a watercolor woodblock reproduction shop and if you have the time to tour the four processing workshops — tracing, carving, printing, and mounting — you will be amazed at the exquisite workmanship displayed by the artists at work. Modern printing cannot faithfully reproduce these paintings and it is only in the Rong Bao Zhai that reproductions have been successfully made using woodblock printing in which a block of pear wood is made for each color and then individually applied. In the 1960's Rong Bao Zhai reproduced the famous Song painting, "Han Xi Zai's Evening Party" by Gu Hongzhong. Depicting the life of ancient nobles during the Five Dynasties period (907-960 A.D.), the original contained scores of figures all with very complicated colors. The reproduction displayed on the wall of the store is faithful to the original and required three thousand woodblocks for its realization.

SHOPPING

For shopping in Beijing the traveler should begin his exploration with a visit to the Friendship Store which is approximately 2 mi. (3.2 km.) east of the Peking Hotel on Chang An Avenue. A taxi ride is recommended with a return car available from the stand in front. It is therefore unnecessary to have a taxi wait as one must do for most excursions within the City.

Friendship Store

As with the Friendship Stores throughout China, a broad

*Well known artist, Lee Ku Chan, demonstrates art technique
at Rong Bao Zhai, Liu Li Chang, Beijing*

range of products from all areas of the country are available here. Three large shopping floors offer everything from fresh bread and chocolates to jade jewelry, antique porcelain, and army caps. Exchange facilities are available as are packing, customs clearance, and foreign shipping for purchases made both at the store itself and elsewhere.

While there is a great variety of articles at the Beijing Friendship Store, one place cannot contain all the things a visitor may wish to purchase. For this, two different shopping tours are recommended: one concentrating on contemporary items such as clothing and household goods, and the other concentrating on artistic artifacts. Wang Fu Jing Street on the east side of the Peking Hotel is the best area for the former, while Liu Li Chang is the best for the latter.

Wang Fu Jing

Because of its central location and easy access, Wang Fu Jing may be explored at a leisurely pace with the visitor discovering the many shops that follow one another. Time spent enjoying the flavor of the street with its throngs of Chinese shoppers will be a memorable experience. While you will be interested in seeing what the people are purchasing for themselves, they, in turn, will be curious to observe what you are buying as a memento of your visit. Places to be sure to visit are Bai Huo Da Lou (#255), Beijing's No. 1 Department Store; the Chop Store (#261); the Scroll Store (#265); Foreign Language Bookstore (#235); and the Arts and Handicrafts Center (#200).

Liu Li Chang Street

Liu Li Chang, an old street in Beijing, is situated at Hepingmenwai (Peace Gate). It is a famous shopping center dealing in original and contemporary Chinese calligraphy and paintings, original pottery and porcelain, stone rubbings, jade, lacquerware and carvings of bamboo and ivory.

Since the restoration and reconstruction of Liu Li Chang has begun, some shops have been closed. Four shops belonging to Peking Antique Store have been moved to the Temple of Heaven. They are: Bao Ku Chai, Original Chinese Calligraphy and Paintings Branch; Yun Ku Chai, Original Pottery and Porcelain Branch; Ching Yun Tang, Stone Rubbings Branchl and Kuan Fu Chai, Seals, Ink Sticks and Ink Stones Branch. Huaiyin Shanfang, specializing in calligraphy and paintings, has been moved to Beihai Park.

The world-famous Studio of Glorious Treasures (Rong Bao Zhai) at #19 West Liu Li Chang is still there. The other three shops remaining are: Tsui Chen Chai Porcelain & Pottery Branch at #17; Gui Wen Ge, Artistic Seal Carving at #78; and Cho Chin Chai, a workshop for the reproduction of traditional paintings and calligraphy, at #31.

Remaining at 115 East Liu Li Chang are Zhongguo Bookshop, Wen Kui Tang and Sui Ya Zhai which sell ancient Chinese books, Chinese style paintings and calligraphics, and stone rubbings.

HOTELS

There are certain facilities which all hotels in China have. For instance, you will usually find a Post Office and its hours are fixed, 8:00 AM to 6:00 PM on weekdays (Monday-Saturday) and 8:00 AM to Noon on Sundays. All hotels have a foreign exchange desk or a regular bank. Hours differ but the pattern is commonly an early opening (approximately 7:30 AM) with a break for lunch in the middle of the day and then afternoon and early evening hours. They also have morning hours on Sunday. Hours will be posted in each hotel so it is best to check when you first arrive.

All hotels have restaurants of good quality offering both Western-style and Chinese meals serving breakfast, lunch, and dinner. Hours for meals vary slightly from hotel to hotel but in general breakfast is served from 7:00 AM to 8:30 AM, lunch from 12 Noon to 1:30 PM, and dinner, 6:00 PM to 8:30 PM. Most hotels have shops where you can purchase toiletries, souvenirs, and handicrafts and some even have food shops.

There are many hotels in Beijing, and when your tour is initially arranged, your hotel accommodations are also chosen.

Beijing (Peking) Hotel

East Chang An Avenue, Telephone 50 77 66

This is the most famous hotel in China (RMB ¥40-180 per day), and even if visitors are not put up here, they usually visit its restaurants, bar, and shops. The hairdressing salon for men and women, on the second floor, is worth a visit to enjoy the soothing neck massage while your hair is being washed. In the old wing you'll find a "commissary" which sells fresh fruit and delicious cookies. There is a recreation room which houses several billiard tables. Located next to Wang Fu Jing the busiest shopping street in Beijing, the Beijing Hotel, like most hotels, has a bank, a Post Office, a handicraft shop, food and liquor shops, and a bookstore.

Diaoyutai State Guest House

Telephone 86 88 31

Since 1980 the Diaoyutai (Anglers' Resort) State Guest House has set aside some of its villas for foreign visitors so that they might enjoy its traditional Chinese landscape, architecture, tranquil environment and tasteful furnishings.

Located on the western outskirts of Beijing, Diaoyutai is the site of an imperial hostel of the Qing Dynasty (1644-1911) and has one of the best preserved centuries-old gardens in the capital. The guest house itself was built in 1959. Its 15 villas plus a number of other buildings are scattered around three lakes fed by the nearby Yuyuantan Pool and are situated amidst gardens containing thousands of flowering plants, trees and bamboos. The villas have bedrooms, sitting-rooms, reception-rooms, dining-rooms and studies. They are all spacious, bright and well-furnished in the traditional Chinese style.

Fragrant Hill Hotel
In Fragrant Hills Park, Telephone 81 92 42

The Fragrant Hill Hotel, a modern first-rate hotel designed by the world-famous Chinese-American architect Ieoh Ming Pei, is located in Fragrant Hills Park in the scenic Western Hills, 20 kilometres from Beijing. It opened for business in April 1983.

The hotel is a perfect combination of traditional Chinese architectural and gardening styles with up-to-date facilities. The 292 suites consist of 322 rooms with 500 beds, all having magnificent views of the outdoors.

Great Wall Sheraton Hotel
This hotel covers an area of 78,800 square meters and has three rectangular guest room wings radiating from a central service core with 1,007 guest rooms and 12 meeting rooms. One of the finest hotels in the country, it not only provides rooms equipped with color house movie system, radios and message-keeping telephones but also offers various services and entertainments, such as a health club featuring a gymnasium, exercise room, sauna, massages and steam bath, all-weather indoor swimming pool, tour and sightseeing center, house clinic, billiard room, tennis courts, beauty shop, and baby-sitter service.

Heping (Peace) Hotel
Jinyu Hutong, Telephone 55 88 41

The Heping Hotel is near Wangfujing Street and was refurbished in 1980. With the work now complete, it is receiving foreign guests. The hotel is fully carpeted and air conditioned. It has 23 suites and 91 rooms with twin beds.

Huadu Hotel

Xinyuanli Telephone 50 11 66 l

The Huadu Hotel has unique characteristics of traditional Chinese architecture. There are 522 guest rooms with 1,141 beds. All rooms are comfortably furnished with private bath and air-conditioner. The hotel has function rooms, private banquet rooms, a well-stocked gift store, flower house, and winding corridor in Chinese style. The Chinese restaurant serves Sichuan cuisine.

Jianguo Hotel

Jianguomen Wai, Telephone 50 22 33 ´1

The hotel is a joint venture enterprise run by the Chinese and an American-Chinese entrepreneur. It has 455 luxurious rooms and suites furnished in 17-18th century European style. Facilities in the hotel include a coffee shop, a bar, an indoor swimming pool, hair dressing and beauty salon.

The Western restaurant specializes in French and American cuisines with imported main ingredients, and is serviced by chefs from Switzerland. The Chinese restaurant serves Guangdong and Chaozhou cuisines. All the attendants are well trained.

Jinglun Hotel

Jinglun, ideally located in the heart of Beijing at Jianguomenwai, offers world-class facilities and different restaurants to provide international cuisine of your choice. It consists of 659 rooms and suites, and within the Hotel are banking facilities, shopping arcade, indoor pool, massage room and sauna, business center and airlines ticketing offices providing every convenience that the international traveller expects.

Lido Hotel

This hotel is located conveniently on a site northeast of Beijing, between the city proper and the Beijing International Airport, allowing the guests to reach destinations in either direction in only 20 minutes by car. It has 530 rooms arranged in six major hotel blocks — designed in a symmetrical pattern. The central axis is occupied by two public amenities blocks, linking on both sides to five-story guest room wings. Each wing is formed by two E-shaped blocks, enclosing a hexagonal-shaped central core, which contains all service and entertainment rooms. Beijing's first-ever bowling lanes in the hotels were opened in Lido Hotel in December, 1984. The bowling center is capable of accommodating international competition.

Minzu (Nationalities) Hotel

West Chang An Avenue, Telephone 65 85 41

A moderately-priced hotel (RMB ¥ 35-80 per day), it is located not far from Tian An Men Square. Featuring comfortable, no-frills accommodations, there are two restaurants (one serving Chinese food and one serving Western meals). As with Beijing's other hotels, you will find a bank, a Post Office, shops, billiards, and a hairdressing salon.

Qian Men Hotel

Yong'an Road, Telephone 33 87 31

Old, but with excellent service, which is displayed with pleasing charm. Located in a good area for walking, it is quite close to several shopping districts. Qian Men offers a range of necessary tourist facilities although not as extensive as some of the larger hotels.

Xin Qiao Hotel

Dongjiaomin Lane, Telephone 55 77 31

It is moderately priced (RMB ¥ 50-100 per day) and located in the old section of Beijing. The hotel offers a full range of services for the tourist. It has two restaurants, both serving breakfast, lunch, and dinner. One serves basically Chinese food; the other features Western-style meals. Shops, hairdressers, and a billiard room are also available as well as a bank and a Post Office.

Yanjing Hotel

Fuxingmenwai, Telephone 86 87 21

The Yanjing Hotel is the first modern hotel designed and built by the Chinese. It is a twenty-two story building with a total of 515 rooms, 59 of which are suites. All the rooms are fully carpeted and have private baths. The hotel is fully heated and air conditioned. In the hotel there are Chinese and Western-style restaurants and coffee shops, and shopping is available on the main floor.

Yanxiang Hotel

Telephone 50 66 66

Yanxiang Hotel was a small hotel with 144 guest rooms

when it started business in 1981, but the new wing of Yanxiang was completed at the beginning of 1985, 371 rooms equipped with modern facilities, a nine-storied building covering 29,000 square meters. Its restaurant serves both Chinese food in Shandong style and western food in continental and American styles.

Zhaolong Hotel
Telephone 50 22 99

Opened in the autumn of 1985, Zhaolong Hotel is in the eastern part of Beijing, close to embassies, within easy reach of markets. It is an international tourist hotel with modern facilities, jointly funded by the donation of Mr. Pao Yue-Kong and domestic investment, named after Mr. Bao Zhao-Long, the father of Mr. Pao Yue-Kong. The main building is 73 meters high with 22 stories above the ground and 2 below while the attached buildings are of 3 and 6 stories respectively. There are altogether 270 guest rooms including a presidential suite, a 3-room suite, de luxe suites and standard rooms.

Youyi (Friendship) Hotel
Haidian Road, Telephone 89 06 21

This hotel is in the northwestern section of Beijing and inexpensive (RMB ¥ 35-65 per day). It has one restaurant, a foreign exchange office, a Post Office, a guest shop, a hairdresser, and billiard and ping-pong tables. An exclusive to this hotel is an outdoor swimming pool and tennis courts. Youyi is about a twenty-minute ride from the center of Beijing.

RESTAURANTS

There are many restaurants in Beijing offering a full range of cuisines. Unless you plan an extended stay, you will unfortunately not have time to sample them all. Listed below are some of the more popular restaurants your tour is likely to include. For your reference, the Appendix includes a list of sample banquet menus from several of the larger restaurants. These banquets include both moderate and fairly expensive meals. This will permit you to decide in advance what you'd like to eat and also give you an idea of what it will cost.

Beijing Hotel Restaurant
East Chang An Avenue, Telephone 55 65 31

The Beijing Hotel Restaurant consists of two dining rooms,

one Chinese and one Western, as well as additional halls and rooms of varying sizes. The Hotel is convenient for foreign guests and visitors to host cocktail parties and banquets. The Chinese dining room specializes in Sichuan (Szechuan), Guangdong (Cantonese), Jiangsu, and Tan-style cuisines. Chefs with specific expertise are expressly employed for these cuisines. The food in its Western dining room is predominantly English and French. Their pastries are superb and praised by foreign visitors from all over the world.

Beijing Roast Duck Restaurant
13 Wang Fu Jie; Heping Gate Road
Telephone 55 33 10

The Beijing Roast Duck Restaurant was originally opened in 1864. Due to its meticulous ways of roasting, always with the choicest ingredients, the restaurant has kept its unique, traditional flavor for over one hundred years and enjoys a fine reputation around the world. To meet the ever-increasing demand, a new branch has been opened recently at Heping Gate Road. The new Beijing Roast Duck Restaurant has seven stories, with a floor space of 18,000 sq. ft. (1,672 sq. m.) and forty-one dining rooms of varying sizes. It is at present the largest restaurant in the country. Dining rooms for Chinese customers can hold 6,000 people at once. Dining rooms for foreign guests, overseas Chinese, and Chinese from Hong Kong and Macao can hold 2,600 people simultaneously. There is also a banquet hall with a capacity for 600.

The new Beijing Roast Duck Restaurant has kept the original roasting method. It has its own duck farm for raising the large and tender ducks. Two famous preserved vegetable factories, Liu Bi Ju and Tian Yuan, exclusively supply sweet bean paste, which is a necessary dip to accompany the roast duck. Finally, hard fruit tree woods fuel its high-heat ovens because they emit little smoke while at the same time providing the fragrance that guarantees the unique aroma of the roast duck. In addition to the traditional roast duck, there are a variety of other dishes which are also famous.

Bian Yi Fang Roast Duck Restaurant
Chongwenmen Street, Telephone 75 05 05

The Bian Yi Fang Roast Duck Restaurant in Beijing is a time-honored restaurant famous for its culinary art. The old Bian Yi Fang, the earliest roast duck restaurant in Beijing, opened in 1522 during the Ming Dynasty. The Bian Yi Fang now located on Chongwenmen Street started business in 1855. This 120-year-old restaurant is even older than the famous Quan Ju De (Beijing Roast Duck Restaurant).

Feng Ze Yuan Restaurant
Zhushikou Xi Jie, Telephone 33 28 28

Specializing in northern Chinese cuisine, this restaurant is considered by many the best restaurant in Beijing. Although the interior is modest in character, the meals will please even the most demanding gourmet. Often your tour will include either a luncheon or dinner-time banquet at Feng Ze Yuan and you won't be disappointed. Should you go there in a small group, you will find their menu varied, from moderately-priced meals to very expensive, exotic dishes.

Fang Shan Restaurant
Bei Hai Park, Telephone 44 25 73

This restaurant, specializing in Imperial Cuisine from the Qing Court (known to Westerners as Mandarin Cuisine) is located at the edge of the lake in Bei Hai Park on Qiong Hua Island. It is likely your visit to Bei Hai Park will include lunch at Fang Shan.

At the time Bei Hai Park was opened in 1925 a man by the name of Zhao Runhai, a former food supplier to the Qing Court, gathered a few former chefs from the Imperial kitchen and together they opened the Fang Shan Restaurant. The name means that the food and pastries served here are all imitations of the Imperial Cuisine of the Qing Dynasty. Characteristic of the Fang Shan cuisine, and there are well over two hundred famous dishes, is the exquisite preparation of the meals. Each dish is carefully named and wonderfully colorful. Besides its culinary artistry, the restaurant itself is physically beautiful.

Sichuan Restaurant
Rong Xian Lane, Telephone 33 63 56

This popular restaurant serves the spicy food from Sichuan Province, known to Westerners as Szechuan cuisine. It is set in extremely lovely surroundings with several buildings joined together by small courtyards. Your tour may also include a banquet here as this is considered one of Beijing's most beautiful restaurants as well as one of its best.

Ting Li Guan Restaurant
Summer Palace, Telephone 28 19 26

Located within the grounds of the Summer Palace, this restaurant is approximately forty-five minutes by car from Beijing. Your tour of the Summer Palace may include lunch here. The building itself was originally a theater so it is quite spacious. On the expensive side, its specialty is fresh fish.

Cui Hua Lou (Capital Restaurant)
60 Wang Fu Jing, Telephone 55 45 81

The original name has just been returned to this excellent restaurant. Offering a wide range of dishes, it specializes in northern Chinese cooking. Located on the busiest shopping street in Beijing, you may have time for lunch here on one of your shopping tours. One of its many specialities is Grilled Shark's Fin. Since it is rare, it is also expensive.

Donglaishun Restaurant
Dong Feng Market, off Wang Fu Jing, Telephone 55 00 69

Known by foreigners as the Mongolian Restaurant, Donglaishun was opened in 1903. It is located near the Beijing Hotel at the north side of Dongfeng Market, off Wang Fu Jing. Although they have an extremely good menu, their speciality is Chinese-Islamic cuisine and it serves the best sliced mutton hot-pot in China. If you have the time, dinner here will be a memorable experience.

Guangzhou (CANTON)

Guangzhou, capital of Guangdong Sheng (Guangdong Province), is on the bank of the Zhu Jiang (Pearl River). It is 1,443 mi. (2,322 km.) south of Beijing with a population of well over two million people.

As the most important industrial city in southern China, its harbor, Huangpu (Whampoa), has long been one of China's most important ports. As early as the Qin Dynasty (221-206 B.C.), Guangzhou was already developing into a foreign trading center. Originally called Pan Yu, after two nearby hills, it was the capital of an autonomous state until it was joined to the empire during the Han Dynasty (206 B.C.-220 A.D.). The present name of Guangzhou appears as far back as the Three Kingdoms Period (220-265 A.D.).

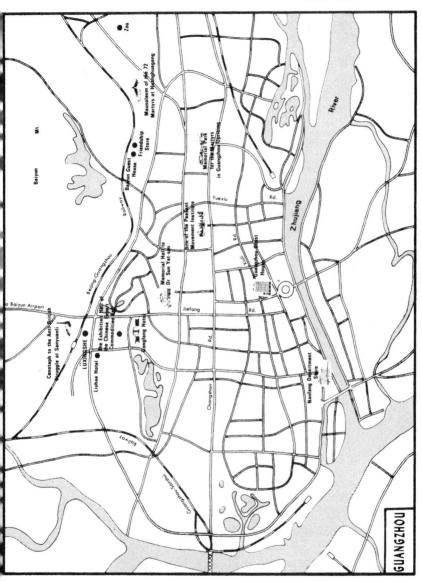

After the first Opium War (1840-1842), Guangzhou was forced to become one of the five large treaty ports by the unequal Nanking Treaty and it was plundered by foreign aggressors. After the Second Opium War (1856-1860) it was again subjected to foreign aggression. The economy of the area was wrecked and the people became more impoverished every day. It is little wonder that from the middle of the nineteenth century Guangzhou became a center of revolutionary and democratic ferment and was active in resisting foreign as well as domestic oppressors. In April 1911 the Chinese Revolutionary League, headed by Dr. Sun Yat-Sen, launched an armed insurrection in Guangzhou against the Manchu which resulted in seventy-two of the rebels being caught and executed.

During the first Revolutionary Civil War (1924-1927), Chairman Mao visited the city many times to lead revolutionary activities. It was here that he founded the National Peasant Institute and directed the National Peasant Movement. The people of Guangzhou waged repeated struggles against hunger, persecution, and civil war. On October 14, 1949, Guangzhou was liberated and Chiang Kai-Shek's troops were routed or fled.

Guangzhou today is a lovely city with broad, tree-lined streets and tropical parks. Even in the city proper one can see acres of farmland. It has a warm climate and abundant rainfall. Its cuisine, known to Westerners as Cantonese, is justifiably world famous.

Located on the Zhu Jiang delta, agriculture plays an important part of life in Guangzhou. Rice, wheat, sweet potatoes, and sugarcane are the main crops. Both heavy and light industry can be found here. There is an iron and steel works as well as factories manufacturing paper, chemicals, textiles, and processed foods.

Your tour may either begin or end in Guangzhou as it is the most frequently used gateway and departure point for foreign visitors. Only 75 mi. (120.7 km.) northwest of Hong Kong, there are several modes of transportation between the two cities. The train takes a little over three hours if you are scheduled on the direct trains which run twice a day. There is additional train service, but it is indirect, requiring passengers to change trains. This indirect train service takes much longer. A new hydrofoil service has been introduced. The trip takes approximately two hours and forty minutes.

PLACES OF INTEREST
National Institute of the Peasant Movement
In 1924 Mao Zedong founded this Institute to train cadres for the peasant movement. He was appointed director. Its teachers included Zhou Enlai and other revolutionary leaders. The Institute closed in September 1926 and its graduates went on to organize the peasant movement in various parts of the country.

The exterior of the building, a former temple of Confucius, is a fine example of sixteenth century architecture. The interior was repaired and restored after 1949. One of the interesting aspects of the Institute is the relative simplicity of both students' and instructors' rooms. You will see Chairman Mao's office and bedroom, the lecture rooms, the dining hall, and the students' dormitories.

Gate at Memorial Park for the Martyrs

Memorial Park for the Martyrs of the Guangzhou Uprising
This park, built to commemorate those who died in the Guangzhou Uprising in December 1927, was opened in 1957 on the thirtieth anniversary of the Uprising. The park contains graceful gardens, pavilions, and exhibition halls.

115

Entering the park through a large gate, one follows a paved stone pathway to a mammoth man-made mound surrounded by a marble wall. This burial mound, or tumulus, contains the remains of the five thousand people who perished during the Uprising.

Sha Mian Isle

This Isle is about a half mile (.8 km.) long and 400 yds. (366 m.) wide. Two bridges (one a footbridge) span the canal that separates it from the City.

After the second Opium War a foreign enclave was established here with permission of the Qing Dynasty. At that time the Isle was little more than a sand bar on the river. The English and the French created it with bulkheads and retaining walls of stone. Four-fifths of the expense was borne by the English and one-fifth by the French. Both established consulates. In addition to the private homes, a number of banks established branches and there were tennis courts and a sailing club for the residents. No Chinese were allowed to enter without permission and the iron gates of the bridges were locked at 10:00 PM every night. Magnificent villas graced the water's edge. There were two churches (now used for office buildings) and administrative buildings.

Today you will find the remains of walled gardens, malls planted with palms, and a line of cannons aimed out over the river. The river bank, lined with banyan trees, is a lovely, cool place to walk. The large mansions, well kept up, are now used by the Government. This little isle, if one has time to explore its grounds, will give the traveler a very tranquil, pleasant feeling.

Huang Hua Gang Mausoleum of 72 Martyrs

Located on Huang Hua Gang (Yellow Flower Hill) this Mausoleum is a little over a mile outside of Guangzhou. Covering approximately 192,000 sq. yds. (160,000 sq. m.), it was built to commemorate the martyrs of the 1911 Revolution. Before Dr. Sun Yat-Sen was victorious in October 1911, many uprisings had failed. In April 1911 an unsuccessful revolt resulted in 88 victims; 72 of these are buried here.

The funds gathered to erect this monument were collected from the Chinese people, both within China and overseas. Built in 1918, its design reflects a diverse number of influences. There are traditional Chinese lions but the Mausoleum also has a small replica of the Statue of Liberty, an Egyptian obelisk, and a pavilion reminiscent of Versailles.

Yue Xiu Park

Inside this 247-acre (100 ha.) park or nearby are located the Dr. Sun Yat-Sen Memorial Hall, the Zhen Hai Tower (Guangzhou Museum), a sports stadium, two olympic-size swimming pools, and an artificial lake. This park is considered the most enjoyable of the many parks to be found in Guangzhou. The flower beds were laid out so that there would be at least one species blooming in all months of the year. There are facilities for the casual stroller as well as the dedicated athlete. If you are so inclined, rowboats are for hire on the lake.

Children at play, Memorial Park of the Martyrs

Dr. Sun Yat-Sen Memorial Hall, Yue Xiu Park

Dr. Sun Yat-Sen Memorial Hall

Located near Yue Xiu Park, this remarkable piece of traditional Chinese architecture has a vast auditorium which can seat up to five thousand people. Through an ingenious design, there is not one supporting pillar to obstruct the view. The building was erected in 1931 and boasts a beautiful blue tile roof. There is a statue of Dr. Sun Yat-Sen in the Garden.

The Zhen Hai Tower

This attractive five-story building dates back to the fourteenth century. Originally used as a watchtower, it is the oldest building in Guangzhou and one of the oldest in China. Today it is a museum with many artifacts tracing the history of Guangzhou.

In front of the museum is a recently constructed veranda containing steles which were discovered locally and also a nineteenth century cannon from the Krupp armaments firm in Germany. Of interest in the Museum is a collection of figurines that were excavated from nearby tombs and examples of coins dating back to the Han Dynasty (206 B.C.-220 A.D.). These are located on the first floor along with bronzes, silk, maps, and other objects dating back to the sixth century.

On the second floor are objects from the Sui and Tang Dynasties (589-907 A.D.), while the third floor is devoted mainly to the Ming and Qing Dynasties (1368-1911 A.D.). The fourth floor is devoted to the independent revolutionary spirit that has long been a part of Guangzhou history. The material records activities against the Qing "Manchu" Dynasty (1644-1911 A.D.) and also anti-imperialist incidents. These include the destruction of the opium that started the Opium Wars, the bombardment of the city by French and English troops in 1867, the Franco-Chinese War of 1881, and events surrounding the successful 1911 Revolution by Dr. Sun Yat-Sen. The history of the revolutionary movement throughout China along with events relating particularly to Guangzhou are the material for the exhibits on the fifth floor.

Temple of the Six Banyan Trees

The temple's most noted feature is its pagoda, which is designated as the "decorated pagoda" to clearly identify it from the undecorated "naked" minaret of a nearby mosque. The temple was established in 479 A.D., and the pagoda built in 537 A.D. The famous poet, Su Dongpo, visited the temple in 1099 A.D., a year after it was rebuilt, and admired the banyan trees growing in its courtyard. He wrote glowingly about them in a poem and the name became attached to the temple.

Inside the main hall are statues of the Buddha and the God of Medicine as well as others dating from the Qing Dynasty. Directly behind the hall stands the octagonal, nine-story pagoda. It is 180 ft. (54.9 m.) tall and each of the nine stories, separated by green-tiled roofs, contains viewing windows. There is a staircase which reaches to the top and the view from there is magnificent. A small garden just outside the pagoda contains a stele with a likeness of Su Dongpo, the poet who gave the temple its name.

Mosque Dedicated to the Saint

Known as the oldest mosque in China, it is reputed to have been established in 627 A.D. by an uncle of Mohammed. The buildings which are to be seen now are quite obviously modern and the iron gates which secure the entrance are normally locked. Entrance can be gained by ringing for the attendant. The courtyard within has several fully-leaved trees to offer protection from the sun and the far side of the courtyard is the prayer room which is identified with arabic script.

The "naked" minaret is 80 ft. (24.4 m.) high. There is an inside staircase which leads to the top and opens onto a small circular balcony, which offers a splendid view of the City.

Guang Xiao Si Temple

This temple is one of the oldest in Guangzhou. Local legend has it that it even existed before the City was established. Whatever the facts are, the temple is very old and has been damaged and repaired many times. Quite extensive restoration was done in 1832 and at the present time, it is again being worked upon.

The building bears the traces of a variety of different architectural influences and the main hall is a place where these various styles seem to have come together quite well. When a school was being moved into the temple several years ago, three statues of the Buddha were accidentally broken by the workmen. These turned out to be hollow and revealed inside over seventy little figurines representing donors and the pious. Most of these unfortunately were lost but those recovered are on display in the history museum.

Behind the central hall is a stone pagoda which is octagonal and 21 ft. (6.4 m.) high. Each of the eight sides has a niche containing a statue of the Buddha. In addition to the stone pagoda, the temple has two iron ones. The pagoda on the east side is in excellent condition. The other, the western one, was severely damaged when the pavilion housing it collapsed and ruined the top four stories. The remaining three stories can still be seen.

Hua Lin Si Temple

The temple was founded in 526 A.D. and a monk from India preached there in the sixth century. The original buildings were destroyed and restored several times and those on the site presently date from no earlier than the seventeenth century. Of the five hundred statues decorating the interior, one of them is said to represent Marco Polo who is identifiable by the large brimmed hat he wears.

Temple of the Chen Family Ancestors

This edifice is distinguished because of its exceptional size, covering an area of 25,000 sq. ft. (2,323 sq. m.) and because of the glazed pottery carvings on its roof. It was constructed in 1890 and it is now utilized as an exhibition space for the art of the City of Guangzhou and the Province of Guangdong.

The Roman Catholic Cathedral

The cathedral was erected between 1860 and 1863 at which time it was consecrated. Designed in traditional gothic style, its pointed towers are 160 ft. (48.6 m.) high. The front elevation is 80 ft. (24.3 m.); the over-all length is 260 ft. (79.2 m.); and the width is 90 ft. (27.4 m.).

Guangzhou Foreign Trade Center

This building, formerly called the Exhibition Center, was opened in 1956 when the Chinese Export Commodities Fair (the Canton Trade Fair) was established. Covering an area of 131,560 sq. yd. (110,000 sq. m.), it is large enough to display export items by the thousands, from art objects to heavy machinery.

Through 1979 twice each year (April 15th to May 15th and October 15th to November 15th) businessmen gathered in Guangzhou for the trade fairs. These grew in importance each succeeding year and accordingly the numbers of businessmen who attended increased. In 1979 over 30,000 representatives of trading firms attended each session of the Fair.

But on November 15, 1979, it was announced that the Exhibition Center would be open all year long and would be renamed the Guangzhou Foreign Trade Center. Although complete plans are not final at this time, it is expected that the Chinese export companies will keep their offices here to enable foreign businessmen to negotiate purchases year-round and that mini-fairs will be scheduled throughout the year. At the time of this writing, several foreign product exhibits, book exhibitions, and a direct-response exhibit were being set up.

The Guangzhou Foreign Trade Center will continue to serve as the facility where foreign buyers are introduced to the full range of Chinese goods available for export. As all these products are exhibited in one building and cover a wide range of goods, Guangzhou is considered China's most important foreign trade city.

Guangzhou Cultural Park

In 1951 a large section of uncultivated land was cleared and turned into this vast park. It has become a busy center of cultural activities and offers a hundred or more different diversions. There are theaters, movie houses, exhibition halls, and much more. In the evening you will be amazed at the large crowds that gather to take advantage of the various entertainments offered.

South China Botanical Garden

This garden was planted in 1956. It covers over 247 acres (100 ha.) and is carefully tended. Walking through the grounds, you will be captivated by the over two thousand species of tropical and subtropical plants to be found here.

Guangzhou Zoo

This is the largest zoo to be found in southern China and one of the largest in the country. It has many varieties of animals including several adorable Giant Pandas.

Zhong Shan Da Xue

Zhong Shan Da Xue (Sun Yat-Sen University) was founded by Dr. Sun Yat-Sen in 1924. Originally called Guangdong

University, it was located near the center of the City. In 1931 the old university moved to larger quarters and after Sun Yat-Sen's death, it was renamed in his honor. On the present university grounds you will find a museum devoted to the career of Dr. Sun Yat-Sen. The building that housed the original university is now occupied by the Lu Xun Museum.

Day Trips from Guangzhou
Bai Yun Shan Park
This beautiful park, also called White Cloud Mountain Park, lies about 9 mi. (14.5 km.) to the northeast of the city. As it is 1,400 ft. (426.7 m.) high, you will have an exceptional panoramic view that includes the City proper, the river, and the entire delta area. It was originally noted for its many temples but more recently has been developed as a resort area. Bai Yun Shan has the reputation of being one of the most luxurious resorts in China.

Foshan
See separate section.

Conghua Hot Springs
This health resort is located 50 mi. (81 km.) from the City. It is one of China's best known spas and water from the natural springs reaches a temperature of 143° Fahrenheit (61.7° Celsius.) It is said to have an especially salutary effect on rheumatism and neuralgia.

Qi Xing Yan (Seven-Star Cliffs)
This very interesting natural wonder is located 68 mi. (108.4 km.) north of Guangzhou and forms a pattern like the Big Dipper constellation. The largest contains the Guang Yin cave which has both a north and south entrance. This cave is filled with stalactites descending from the roof and stalagmites growing up from the floor. It also contains impressive natural stone columns and subterranean streams.

SHOPPING
Prior to the early part of 1980 the time of the year the visitor arrived in Guangzhou determined some of the shopping opportunities. If one stayed during the spring or fall Trade Fairs,

there was a range of stores located on the fair grounds which were not open at other times. Now that the fairs have been established as a year-round event, many will remain open all year long. These stores carry all sorts of traditional handicrafts as well as contemporary leather garments, furs, and textiles.

The Friendship Store

Located at Yuan Jiang Road 1, this store is open year round and offers a broad selection of merchandise including food, clothing, jewelry, crafts, and luggage. One of the most famous items is Guangzhou ivory carving. This ancient craft goes back more than a thousand years and examples of its intricately carved spheres are known throughout the world. The outside ball's surface is covered with designs and pierced through at various points, revealing another equally detailed sphere within, which rotates completely independently of the outside one. These remarkable objects sometimes reach an incredible complexity with one containing over forty carved spheres. See page 38 for customs restrictions which exist on ivory objects.

The Guangzhou Antique Shop

This antique shop (146 Wen De North Street) has a selection of original antiques and authorized reproductions. The selection of items in this shop and those found in Beijing and Shanghai tend to be quite similar since all draw their merchandise from a centralized distribution warehouse.

For those who are curious to investigate small local stores which carry everything from household goods to books and pharmaceuticals, a trip to the intersection of Beijing Road and Zhong Shan Road will be rewarding.

HOTELS

There are five major hotels which accommodate visitors from the United States and Western Europe. Your tour will likely have arranged for you to stay at one of these places. Although there are several smaller hotels in Guangzhou, they are used by Overseas Chinese as well as Chinese visitors from Hong Kong and Macao.

Bai Yun Hotel
Huan Shi Road East, Telephone 6 77 00

This hotel is a new, thirty-three-story building completed in 1977. The entire hotel is totally air conditioned. When it was constructed the builders incorporated some of the natural rock and tree formations of the site into an attractive courtyard within the Hotel.

It is not as centrally located as the Dong Fang but is only a short ride from the main section of town. It does have the advantage of being near the Friendship Store. Prices range from RMB ¥ 30-120 per day depending on accommodations selected.

The bank's hours are from 12:00 Noon to 2:30 PM and 6:00 PM to 8:30 PM on weekdays (Monday through Friday) and 6:00 PM to 8:30 PM on weekends (Saturday and Sunday). The Post office is open seven days a week from 12:00 Noon to 2:30 PM and 6:00 PM to 10:00 PM. Telex facilities are also available. There are two restaurants in the hotel, both a Western and Chinese. When the exclusively Western restaurant is closed, Western food may be ordered in the Chinese restaurant. There are gift shops, a beauty parlor for women, and a men's barber.

China Hotel
The China Hotel is a huge hotel/apartment/shopping/office complex, close to the railway station and just across the street from the China Export Commodities Fair Building. It started business in 1984 and serves some of the best meals in the city. Three lounges and five restaurants as well as a unique "Food Street" featuring a variety of authentic Chinese delights, attract both hotel guests and city residents. In this hotel there is a wide range of facilities, including a complete gynmasium, tennis court and bowling alley.

Dong Fang Hotel
Ren Min Road North, Telephone 6 99 00

This hotel is centrally located and is within walking distance of the railroad station. It is also the more conveniently located of the two for visitors to the Guangzhou Foreign Trade Center since it faces the main entrance of the Center.

The hotel has a new and an old wing and is laid out around a courtyard which contains a pond as well as a pretty garden. Prices for rooms range from RMB ¥40-180 per day depending on the size and location of the accommodation. Individual room air conditioners were added for the 1980 summer tourist season.

There are a variety of services located within the hotel for the convenience of guests. The Post Office has weekday hours (Monday-Saturday) from 12:00 Noon to 2:30 PM and 6:00 PM to 8:30 PM. On Sundays it is open in the evening only, 6:00 PM to 8:30 PM. Cable and telex facilities are also available. The bank maintains the same hours as the Post Office during the week but on Sunday is open from 6:00 PM to 9:00 PM.

There is a dining room located in the old wing serving both Chinese and Western cuisine. You will also find several shops specializing in food and handicrafts, men's and women's hairdressing salons, and rooms for billiards and ping pong.

Garden Hotel

The Garden Hotel was opened in 1984, with 1,170 rooms and suites outfitted with the latest and most comfortable furnishings. Atop the 24-story hotel complex, a revolving restaurant offers a spectacle — from the setting diners can enjoy an unparalleled view of the city. Several lounges, including the Waterfall Terrace Lounge which looks out through atrium windows on a peaceful garden setting, add to the complex's appealing amenities. Shoppers may choose from the arcade's selections or simply walk down the street to the nearby Friendship Store.

White Swan Hotel

Shamian Island, Telephone 8 69 68

The White Swan Hotel is a newly-built first-class tourist hotel. It contains 1,000 rooms, which include first-class 2 or 3-bedroom suites, standard rooms and rooms with gardens. The design of this hotel has taken the exceptional advantages of the quiet and pleasant natural environment, which fully reflects the features of the "Flower City" of south China.

All the service attendants have been trained in a special tourism school. They speak Beijing dialect, Cantonese, English and other foreign languages, and offer cordial and attentive services.

RESTAURANTS

The food of South China is justifiably famous and nowhere can it be sampled in greater variety than in Guangzhou. Known to Westerners as "Cantonese" cuisine, it is perhaps the most widely-known Chinese cooking style. As Guangzhou was the first Chinese port opened to foreign trade, merchants have been helping spread the glories of Guangzhou cooking since the sixteenth century.

Chefs throughout China pay strict attention to the quality of the cuisine, which most people say is the most important aspect of dining out. In Guangzhou almost as much care is taken in preparing the surroundings in which the food will be served. Some of the most attractive restaurants are to be enjoyed not only for their food, but also for their decor.

In Guangzhou there is literally a menu for every taste including snake and wildcat. You can, of course, always order Western-style meals in almost all places. Your stay in Guangzhou should provide sufficient time to sample many of the area's delicacies. Sample menus for two of Guangzhou's more popular restaurants can be found in the Appendix. Some of the dishes found on these menus can also be ordered at other restaurants in the region. Below you will find a listing of some of the better-known restaurants in Guangzhou.

Ban Xi Restaurant

Liwan Road East, Telephone 8 56 55

The speciality of this popular restaurant is Guangzhou cuisine. Situated in a group of palace-like buildings, the focal point is a small lake. On this lake is a houseboat and the various dining halls surround it. The entire interior of the restaurant is beautifully landscaped with little gardens and ornamental pools.

Two of the sample menus located in the Appendix are from Ban Xi. Although the restaurant is well known for its pleasant surroundings and excellent food, an extra-added charm is the attention paid to the appearance of the food. Their "Assorted Cold Hors d'Oeuvres Platter" comes in the form of a bird or a flower. Other dishes will be beautifully garnished and artistically laid out on the serving platters. To eat in this restaurant, whether for lunch or dinner, is a thoroughly enjoyable experience for the traveler.

Bei Yuan Restaurant
318 Dengfeng Road North, Telephone 3 24 71

This lovely restaurant is often called the North Garden Restaurant. It also specializes in the Guangzhou cuisine of the area. Located in what was originally a teahouse, the landscaping is made up of ornamental pools and beautiful gardens with both tropical and subtropical plants.

Your tour will most likely also include lunch or dinner at the Bei Yuan Restaurant. Do try their Chicken Flavored in Shaoxing Wine (see sample menus in Appendix). The flavor of this dish is memorable.

Teahouse of the Guangzhou Restaurant

Guangzhou Restaurant
2 Wenchang Road, Telephone 8 71 36

This excellent restaurant is also housed in a large teahouse and features many specialities of the local cuisine. The building consists of a central courtyard which is surrounded by many terraces and porches.

If you have time to eat in this restaurant it will most probably be upstairs in one of the private dining halls reserved for foreign travelers.

Datong Restaurant
Changti Xihao Road, Telephone 8 86 97

The view from this restaurant is lovely and with the good food, any meal here will be an experience you will long remember. Situated on the top floor of a large building, you can look down on the Zhu Jiang (Pearl River) on one side and the City proper on the other side. Depending on the time of day a pleasant breeze can be felt in parts of the restaurant.

This restaurant specializes in Guangzhou cuisine. As with other establishments in the area, the interior surroundings are a delight to the eye.

Shahe Restaurant

Shahe Road, Telephone 7 76 37

This lovely restaurant on the top floor of a small building has a series of dining rooms surrounding an open court. Foreign visitors eat in various rooms on the third floor which are located by walking up two flights of stairs in the center of the building. The second floor is that portion reserved for the Guangzhou residents.

If you can make time to sample their cuisine, be sure to try at least one of their many variety of noodle dishes. They are superb and unparalleled.

Dong Fang Restaurant

Dong Fang Hotel, Telephone 6 99 00

Located in the Dong Fang Hotel this restaurant is centrally located both to the city proper and the Guangzhou Foreign Trade Center. Besides the main restaurant which offers a variety of Western-style and Chinese cuisines, there are a number of private dining rooms where banquets for small groups of people can be arranged.

Nan Yuan Restaurant

Qianjin Road, Telephone 5 05 32

Also called the South Garden Restaurant, it's speciality is Guangzhou cuisine. Many who have eaten here indicate it is one of the City's best. The food is meticulously prepared and extremely flavorful. The surroundings are exquisite. Beautifully tended gardens and small water pools are an integral part of the setting. Although it is not centrally located, stopping here on one of your excursions through the City should be part of your itinerary.

Vegetarian Restaurant

Zhongshan Road, Telephone 8 68 36

As its name suggests, dishes served in this restaurant are prepared totally with vegetables. No meat or fowl is used in any of the various courses. Imaginatively-prepared, the meals are lovely to look at and extremely delicious. The absence of meat is hardly noticeable.

Snake Restaurant

Jianglan Road, Telephone 2 25 17

The special distinction of this restaurant is its snake dishes. These are an exotic sidelight of southern Chinese cuisine. Although other meat and fowl are served as a part of a meal, the variety of courses made from snake are the rarities and it is to sample these unusual dishes that people come to this restaurant.

Wild Game Restaurant

Beijing Road, Telephone 3 03 37

The chefs at this fine restaurant are experts in the preparation of game dishes. Included among their specialities are courses made from various wildfowl, such as quail, duck, and lark. The wildcat served here is particularly recommended.

Shanghai (SHANGHAI)

Shanghai, one of China's three municipalities (with Beijing and Tianjin), is a flourishing commercial and industrial center. Its population of 10.8 million and its area of 2,355 sq. mi. (6,100 sq. km.) earn for Shanghai the distinction of being China's largest city.

Early records indicate that the City was founded during the Song Dynasty (960-1280 A.D.) at a time when invaders from the north were drawing back to their own borders. It was a small fishing village in the beginning and did not become a town until the middle of the thirteenth century. Compared to other major cities in China it has had a relatively short history.

During the Ming Dynasty (1368-1644 A.D.) many walls were erected to enclose the town and protect it from Japanese pirates. The town prospered from foreign trade in the Qing Dynasty (1644-1911 A.D.) with cotton grown in the area

Bridges over the Wusong Jiang, Shanghai

being a major staple. Prior to the outbreak of the Opium War, Shanghai had grown into a port with 500,000 inhabitants.

After the Opium War Shanghai was forcibly opened as a "treaty port." From that time on aggressors from many countries began to flock in and the city became known as a "paradise for adventurers." Carving out their own spheres of influence, England, France, the United States, and Japan settled here by seizing their respective "concessions" which was characteristic of this colonial period.

The greatest population growth as well as development of the pier and dockside facilities dates from this time. The Bund, Shanghai's fashionable waterfront boulevard along the Huangpu Jiang (Whangpoo River), was lined with many large buildings and residences, but they all belonged to foreigners. The wealth of this era did not extend to the outlying areas where the original inhabitants, the Chinese, lived. In fact unbelievable conditions existed for members of the Chinese community. Lack of sufficient food and shelter was the norm.

The Chinese response to this foreign dominance took several decades to become strong. But on July 1, 1921, the First National Congress of the Chinese Communist Party was held in Shanghai and the local residents as well as all of China began to fight back. During the war with Japan (1937-1945) Shanghai was occupied and the Kuomintang regained it after the surrender of Japan. The city was liberated on May 28, 1949.

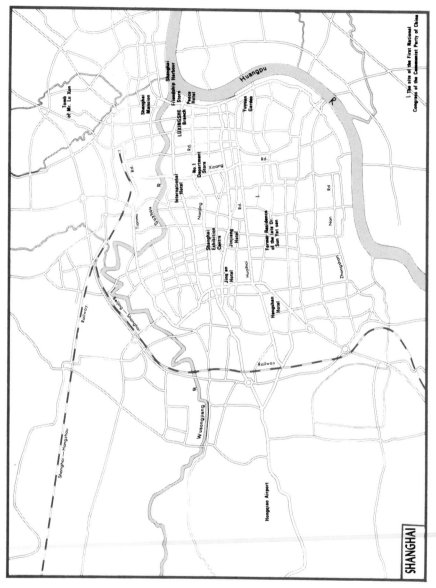

SHANGHAI

Huangpu R

Shanghai Harbour
Friendship Store
Peace Hotel
Shanghai Mansion
LUXINGSHE Branch
Yuyuan Garden
Tomb of Mr. Lu Xun
No.1 Department Store
Xizang Rd.
Rd.
International Hotel
Suzhou R
Tiamu Rd.
Nanjing Rd.
Shanghai Exhibition Centre
Jinjiang Hotel
Former Residence of the late Dr. Sun Yat-sen
Nan Rd.
Jing'an Hotel
Huaihai Rd.
Zhongshan Rd.
Hengshan Hotel
Beijing — Shanghai Railway
Railway
Shanghai — Hangzhou
Wusongjiang R
Hongqiao Airport

1. The site of the First National Congress of the Communist Party of China

Since that time Shanghai has changed from a consumer city of the past into a major industrial city. Today its industrial enterprises total over 10,000. You will find large factories engaged in the production of chemicals, paper, electrical machinery, cars, oil refining, and textiles. With an important harbor for China's foreign trade, Shanghai maintains commercial relations with more than 115 countries all over the world. Ships depart from here destined for more than 300 foreign ports. Shanghai's port facilities extend over 35 mi. (56 km.) and an enormous variety of craft can be seen in its harbor ranging from modest sailing ships to modern ocean-going freighters holding up to 10,000 tons of cargo in their hulls.

Walking through Shanghai you will be aware of its lively and bustling air. It has many sidewalk vendors and endless varieties of small shops with window displays of goods for sale. The streets smell of seafood, cakes baking, and food frying in oil, and everywhere you look you will see crowds of people.

There are over two hundred communes in the surrounding suburbs cultivating cotton, rice, vegetables, and wheat as well as raising livestock, poultry, and fish to supply the city. Education is present in modern-day Shanghai. It has many universities and medical colleges along with primary and secondary schools. Foreign doctors who want to learn acupuncture can be enrolled in a teaching hospital set up expressly for this purpose. Various cultural activities can be found including theater groups, film studios, the symphony, the ballet, opera companies, acrobats, and even a circus.

Because of its years of foreign influence, Shanghai is perhaps China's most cosmopolitan city. The first to open a disco for foreign visitors, Shanghai also offers the tourist art and history museums tracing China's growth through the ages and magnificent examples of Chinese architecture in its temples and buildings. Heavily populated, basically industrial, Shanghai is the home of one of China's most-thriving communities.

PLACES OF INTEREST

Zhong Shan Lu

Zhong Shan Road, most often called the Bund, begins at the Huangpu (Whangpoo River). As you walk along this road you will come to many parks throughout its length on the river's edge. The people of Shanghai come here to read, rest, exercise, or just walk through the beautiful flowered gardens. Sightseers can lean on the wall and watch the river traffic, a blending of modern ships and Chinese junks. Across the avenue from the river wall the skyscrapers that once housed the foreign mansions, clubs, and banks are now occupied by state trading corporations, hotels, and one of the largest Friendship Stores in the country.

Nanjing Lu

Nanjing Lu, translated Nanjing Road, is Shanghai's busiest street. It starts at the Bund, south of the Peace Hotel, and runs westward. It is the city's shopping area with department stores, small shops, restaurants, theaters, and cinemas. To the south of Nanjing Road is the Renmin (People's) Park which was previously known as the Shanghai Race Course. To the west you will see the Municipal Library which was built in 1849.

Shanghai Industrial Exhibition

This large exhibition hall, with its high-spired roof, is filled with more than five thousand exhibits. It is the center where new products of Shanghai are displayed and where residents exchange new techniques. Apart from the main hall there are seven other, smaller halls which display heavy machinery, telecommunications equipment, and handicrafts. You will also find a small store which can be visited.

Lu Xun's Museum and His Tomb

Lu Xun's revolutionary writings are well known and loved throughout China and his museum and tomb have proven very attractive to visitors. He is the most famous modern writer in China and his works have been widely translated. There are exhibitions of his letters, manuscripts, books, and photographs showing his wife, family, and friends.

The tomb is in Hong Kou Park close to the museum. The tombstone has six gold characters in the calligraphy of Chairman Mao which translate to "Mr. Lu Xun's Tomb." On the flowered lawn in front of the tomb is a statue of Lu Xun sitting in a chair. When he died in 1936 he was buried in the Wan Guo Cemetery. In 1956, to commemorate the twentieth anniversary of his death, his ashes were transferred to the present site in Hong Kou Park to bring his tomb closer to the museum. The original museum was located in the house he had lived in the last few years of his life.

Within the museum the displays are divided into twenty-four sections. Each section traces the course of the writer's career in great detail through photographs, writings, rubbings, and copies of his lectures. The exhibits begin with his childhood and continue through his death and include various materials written about him after 1936.

Arts and Crafts Research Institute

This institute was set up in December 1956 to exhibit various types of China's folk art and to help continue the traditions attached to their production. The specialities shown are wood boxes, bamboo, porcelain, ink blocks, ivory and lacquerware carving, clay figurines, paper-cuts, colored lanterns, artificial flowers, mosaics, and embroidery.

Shanghai Museum

Established in 1952 this museum is housed in a former bank building. At present the halls display Chinese bronzes, ceramics, and paintings arranged in chronological order.

The first floor features pottery and bronzes from the Stone Age as well as the Shang and Zhou Dynasties (1766-770 B.C.). Among the special objects are a three-legged cauldron, an ancient bell, and a large axe decorated with stones. Also on this level are displayed weapons and household items from the Warring States Period (476-221 B.C.).

Carvings and tomb figurines from the Qin and Han Dynasties (221 B.C.-220 A.D.) can be found on the second floor. The figurines are extremely detailed and include barnyard animals as well as men and soldiers in characteristic working or warring postures. Also notable is a fine collection of pottery from the Tang Dynasty (618-907 A.D.).

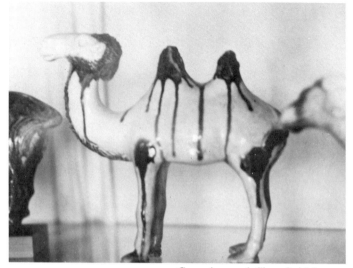

Ceramic camel, Shanghai Museum

The third floor begins with artifacts from the Song Dynasty (960-1280 A.D.) and continues through objects produced in more recent times. There is beautiful cloisonné work, paintings, calligraphy, and porcelain as well as a selection of marionettes and shadow puppets.

Museum of Natural Sciences

Located next to the Shanghai Museum, this museum is also housed in a building which was originally a bank. Smaller than its neighbor, it contains displays showing a wide variety of the natural sciences.

Temple of the Jade Buddha

Built in 1882, the outside walls of this temple are a magnificent yellow. There are two statues of Buddha--one seated and one reclining. Both have been carved from single pieces of white jade.

Renmin Park

Also called People's Park, it is laid out in the heart of the city. Originally built as a race track, it is now a lovely park with lawns and ponds.

Figure at Temple of the Jade Buddha

Children's Palace

There are actually many of these in Shanghai. Once the mansions of millionaires, children between the ages of seven and seventeen receive specialized instruction in these schools. The most popular subjects taught are ballet, music, drama, mechanics, handicrafts, and painting. The children, holding visitor's hands, are the guides for tours of the palace.

137

Yunsun Steamboat

This steamboat started operating in late November 1979. It travels back and forth through the three-gorge area of the Changjiang (Yangtze River). The view of river life and the shore is quite extraordinary.

Yu Yuan

Translated Yu, the Mandarin's Garden, it was originally designed in the sixteenth century by provincial governor, Pan Yunduan, in honor of his father, Pan En, who was himself a government minister. Construction took over twenty years to complete. It is ingeniously laid out to create the feeling of spaciousness within a small area.

Yu Yuan is a garden within a garden. Divided into two parts, the outer garden contains pavilions, rock gardens, and ponds and leads to the inner garden, which is a smaller version of the outer garden. Consisting of many closely-packed pavilions, it suffered extensive damage over the years but was restored in 1956.

Rockery and pavilion, Yu, the Mandarin's Garden

Not only is it distinguished by its beautiful grounds, which are characteristically southern Chinese in style, but Yu Yuan has political significance as well. In the outer garden you will find a small museum, called the Beautiful Spring Hall, which was built to commemorate the Society of Little Swords. One of the loveliest spots in the Garden, it was used as the Society headquarters during the 1853 Uprising. The museum includes a map of the siege of Shanghai and examples of the types of short swords used by the Society members.

At the entrance to the Suitang Hall is a table inscribed with the characters Jian Ru Jia Jing or "Approaching a Scenic Wonderland." One continues along a covered promenade the ceiling of which is covered with ornamental paintings. On a stone wall nearby is the engraving, Xi Shan Qing Shang, which translates to "A Tranquil View of Hills and Streams." Just inside the gate stands a famous artificial mountain made from rocks, a masterpiece created by the outstanding craftsman, Zhang Nanyang, of the Ming Dynasty. Though the rocks are only 39 ft. (12 m.) high they present a scene of peaks and valleys that combine charm and majesty.

As you walk along you will pass pavilions, lodges, ponds, and brooks. A stream of clear water flows by covered promenades, waterside pavilions, and through a moon gate to a pond in front of the Building of Ten Thousand Flowers. In front of this building are magnolia and other stately trees over a hundred years old.

In your meanderings you should not miss seeing Yu Ling Long, a large translucent, jade-like stone. The stone was found during the Song Dynasty. After much moving and many misadventures, it was placed in Yu Yuan by Pan Yunduan.

Site of the First National Congress of the Chinese Communist Party

On July 1, 1921, the first meeting of the Chinese Communist Party was held here and was attended by Chairman Mao. Located near Fuxing Park, the site was restored after liberation to its appearance at the time of the first meeting. The revolutionary relics on display are reproductions.

Temple to the Town Gods

At one time temples like this existed in virtually every town throughout China. Today few are left and this temple is one that has survived. Historically it was customary to erect statues to those persons under whom the town had received protection. The two statues remaining in this Temple are of Lao Zi and Huo Guang.

Garden of the Purple Clouds of Autumn

This park lies directly in back of the Temple to the Town Gods and contains an ornamental pond with landscaped hills surrounding it. Because of the location, it is commonly referred to as the Inner Garden. It was originally laid out during the Ming Dynasty (1368-1644 A.D.) and later acquired by a rich merchant. Finally the town itself took over the park in 1726 A.D. as an addition to the Temple.

Long Hua Temple

The four halls within this temple were constructed during the Qing Dynasty (1644-1911 A.D.) and contain statues of the Buddha, the Celestial Guardians, and the Celestial Defenders. The only pagoda in Shanghai stands here. The precise construction date of the present structure, with its seven stories and numerous balconies, is uncertain. History tells us that there was a pagoda on this site during the Three Kingdoms Period (220-265 A.D.) but it was destroyed and rebuilt several times. The present pagoda represents the latest restoration.

Sanghai Zoo (Xi Jiao Park)

This zoo is situated in a western suburb of Shanghai near the airport and occupies an area of nearly 200 acres (70 ha.). The birds and animals on display here represent over 300 species and number more than 2000. Among them are such rare birds and animals of China as the giant panda, golden monkey, red-crowned crane, Northeastern tiger, Asian elephant, and Chinese alligator. There are also rare birds and unusual animals from other parts of the world.

Jin Jiang Club

The Jin Jiang Club opened at the end of 1979 in a building which prior to 1949 housed the Colonial French Club. Admission is limited to foreign tourists, businessmen, and overseas Chinese. It consists of a French-style restaurant, a bowling alley, pinball machines, and an olympic-sized swimming pool. The club covers several acres of grounds and its gardens are beautiful. The interior is decorated with paintings and furnishings from the turn of the century. Plans are underway for building a tennis court within the grounds. A rarity in China, you may use your MasterCard to pay your bill.

Song Jiang Xian

This town is about 12-½ mi. (20.1 km.) southwest of Shanghai and easily reached by rail. It is famous for a variety of fish called the Song Perch. The pagoda near the Xing Sheng Jiao Si Temple was first erected during the Song Dynasty (960-1280 A.D.). The present square, nine-storied structure was restored in the Qing Dynasty (1644-1911 A.D.).

SHOPPING

The main shopping area is Nanjing Road East, conveniently placed between the Peace Hotel and the People's Park. The road is clogged with pedestrians and traffic and has one of the most varied selections of stores to be found in China.

The Friendship Store, one of the largest in China, is the only major shop not located on Nanjing Road. You will find the Friendship Store on the Bund.

The shops along Nanjing Road East are open to both tourists and Shanghai residents and range in size from the very large to the very small. A walk along the street will bring the visitor to a store that carries almost everything he could possibly imagine. There is a Toy Shop (#98), a Music Store (#118), a Bookstore (#351), and Artificial Flower Store (#522), a Paper-Cuts Store (#751), and a Number 1 Department Store (#800) to name just a few. There are many, many more shops along this bustling street and enough time should be allotted to explore each and every one.

HOTELS

Dahua Guesthouse

914 Yan'an Road (W.), Telephone 52 30 79

Occupying a nine-story building with 90 rooms and suites for travelers, this hotel is well furnished and gives excellent service. Room rates range from RMB ¥ 30-50 per day.

Donghu Guest House

7 Donghu Road, Telephone 37 00 50

The Donghu Guest House, near the busy Huaihai Road, is a separate garden villa providing a quiet serenity in a bustling downtown area. There is an open-air swimming pool and tennis court open to guests. The main building is a three-storied villa of English style, with ten bedrooms. On the ground floor there are two equisitely furnished parlors and one dining hall. The ten rooms, on the first floor, have mahogany furniture, TV sets, central heating, air-conditioning and other facilities. The hotel is also famous for its special dishes of Sichuan and Guangdong cuisines, Western food and snacks. The Donghu Guest House is 13 kilometers from the airport and 7 kilometers from the railway station.

Hengshan Hotel

534 Hengshan Road, Telephone 37 70 50

If your stay in Shanghai is concurrent with a particularly busy time you may be housed in this hotel which is a few miles from the center of town. Single-room rate at the Hengshan is RMB ¥ 30; double rate is RMB ¥ 52; and suites are available at RMB ¥ 150.

Heping (Peace) Hotel

20 Nanjing Road East, Telephone 21 12 44

The Heping Hotel is conveniently located on the Bund and overlooks the Huangpu Jiang (Whangpoo River). Like most of the hotels in Shanghai, it is a large, imposing building with comfortable rooms. The furnishings are especially notable for their solid, vintage flavor. Accommodation costs run from RMB ¥ 30-80 per day.

There is a dining room on the eighth floor which has a splendid view of the waterfront and the river and serves both Chinese and Western meals. There is also a coffee shop located in the lobby. About a block away on Nanjing Road is located the Shanghai Cakes and Pastries Store, which specializes in Western-style baked goods.

The Jing'an Hotel

370 Huashan Road, Telephone 56 30 50

This hotel occupies a nine-story building and features a beautiful and secluded inner garden. The hotel offers 104 rooms and suites for travelers. It is frequented by businessmen and dignitaries and offers outstanding service. Room rates range from RMB ¥ 30-80 per day.

Jinjiang Hotel

59 Maoming Road South, Telephone 53 42 42

Formerly a French Mansion, this hotel consists of four buildings. There are several restaurants in the hotel serving a variety of excellent Chinese and Western foods. There is also a cafe, open until midnight, that serves wine and coffee.

The single-room rate in this eleven-story hotel is RMB ¥ 30; double rate is RMB ¥ 55; and suites are available from RMB ¥ 150-300. Within the hotel compound is an arcade featuring commercial shops, a post office and telex facilities.

Longbai Hotel
2419 Hongqiao Road Telephone 32 92 88

The hotel is surrounded by different kinds of flowers and cypress trees hence the name Longbai. It has 161 suites and rooms. There are indoor gardens, lobbies of different size, meeting rooms, banquet halls and dining halls. Besides a cafe, stores, it also has an outdoor swimming pool and a tennis court.

The hotel specializes in Sichuan dishes and French food.

It is one kilometre from the airport and 20 kilometres from the railway station.

Shanghai Mansions
20 Suzhou Road North, Telephone 24 62 60

Even if you are not scheduled to stay here, visitors are frequently taken to this hotel to enjoy the marvelous view of the city. The period furnishings are similar to those of the Heping Hotel and the room charges run from RMB ¥ 30-75 per day. Some of the more expensive rooms include a balcony overlooking the river. There is a good restaurant which serves breakfast, lunch and dinner. Telex service and stamps are available at the mail counter and you can also mail your letters there. A beauty shop, a barber, and a small gift store are located off the lobby.

Ruijin Guest House
118 Ruijin Road (No. 2), Telephone 37 26 53

The Ruijin Guest House is situated on Ruijin Road (No. 2), hence the name of the hotel. Though near the shopping center, it retains its peacefulness in a busy area and attracts visitors with its ease and comfort. There are five different styles of villas in the hotel and it used to be available only to heads of states. Each villa has a bright and special hall, a banquet hall and dining rooms and has 7 to 14 suites or single rooms. Each room is well furnished, and the bedroom is spacious and tastefully decorated with mahogany furniture. With central heating, air-conditioning and sanitary facility in the rooms, tourists can certainly get a good rest. The hotel provides facilities for telex and telegram. First class chefs specialize in Sichuan, Guangdong and Western dishes. The Ruijin Guest House is 14 kilometers from the airport and 6 kilometers from the railway station.

Sea Gull Hotel

60 Huangpu Road, Telephone 25 15 00

The Sea Gull Hotel, located at the junction of the Huangpu River and Suzhou Creek, was built in 1984. The hotel mostly accommodates international seamen, foreign workers' visiting groups, tourists, businessmen, overseas Chinese and compatriots from Taiwan, Hongkong and Macao.

With a height of 52 meters the hotel has fourteen stories covering an area of 8,600 square meters. It has a good location and commands a panoramic view with the Huangpu River and Souzhou Creek, interweaving with two wide belts, lying just at its foot. The buildings rising up to the heavens stand along the bund and one gets a special view of the port city. There are 108 rooms (including suites) with 216 beds from the fifth floor up to the twelfth floor. The color of the interior walls of rooms on each floor is different and bright. All the rooms are light and sunny, and equipped with color TV sets, fire detectors and private bathrooms, and with exquisite, simple and unsophisticated furniture. The hotel provides various service facilities and there is a movie theatre with a capacity of 1,000 seats. There are 7 dining halls and banquet halls, big and small, accepting 600 people for dining at the same time. The hotel makes the Guangdong cuisine its specialty, but guests can have a wide selection, including Sichuan and Yangzhou dishes. The western dining hall on the third floor serves French food cooked by famous chefs.

Shanghai Hotel

460 Huashan Road, Telephone 31 23 12

Easily accessible; here are 604 suites and rooms with 1,208 beds. In addition, it has 16 dining halls with unique styles. Guangdong cuisine is its speciality. European and Japanese food are also available.

Lighting, acoustics, telecommunication, air conditioning and many other modern facilities are all basic installations in the hotel.

Xijiao Guest House
1921 Hongqiao Raod, Telephone 37 96 43

The Xijiao (Western Suburb) Guest House in Shanghai, reconstructed on the basis of several former private gardens and plant nurseries, is a hotel for state guests. It is close to the city center. Enveloped in an atmosphere of peace and tranquility, the hotel has now seven blocks of building. Inside the elegant villas in the garden, there are a few luxurious suites and magnificent parlors. Bar, cafe, small ballroom, banquet halls and glass-roofed indoor garden are ready for use. Flowers blossom all the year round. The whole garden is clothed in greenery. The service facilities in the Guest House handle telecommunication and postal matters, deal in various kinds of arts and crafts, souvenirs, etc. Its service also includes foreign exchange, booking train, ship and air tickets, taxi, massage, hairdressing.

Xingguo Guest House
72 Xingguo Road, Telephone 37 45 03

The Xingguo Guest House is situated in a beautiful area. Dingxiang Garden, attached to the Xingguo Guest House, is characterized by its Qing Dynasty garden style. Half of the garden is surrounded by a wall some 100 meters long covered with glazed tiles and in the shape of a dragon. The uplifting dragon head is of a man's height and looks true to life. The Garden also provides a rural scenery of idyllic beauty together with a hundred kinds of beautiful flowers and plants. The Xingguo Guest House consists of more than ten villas, each of a different style. The two-storied villas with four to nine suites or rooms each is complete with all modern conveniences. The roomy salons are luxuriously furnished, each having its own features. The guest house provides taxi services, post, telex, etc. Since the hotel has well-known chefs, it serves famous food of Beijing, Guangdong, Sichuan and Yangzhou. The Xingguo Guest House is 11 kilometers from the airport and 9 kilometers from the railway station.

RESTAURANTS
Shanghai is the largest city in China and its citizens come from all over the country. As a result the various restaurants serve cuisine which is the local speciality but often combine it with the uniqueness of cuisines brought from other regions.

There are not many large restaurants in Shanghai with those most frequented by foreign visitors being in the various hotels. There are a great variety of small restaurants and a listing of some of them follows. In the Appendix you will find several sample menus from three of Shanghai's more popular restaurants.

Xin Ya Restaurant

The dishes native to Guangdong, known to Westerners as Cantonese, are served here yet have a style of their own. The various meals served combine Shanghai care in beautiful presentation with the Guangdong cuisine's unique flavor. Some of the traditional dishes which can be ordered are the sweet and sour pork and the fried beef with oyster sauce. If you visit here in the summer, don't fail to order the winter melon pond. The outside surface of the melon is scored with intricate patterns and your enjoyment is doubled by the tasty melon inside and the designs on the outside.

Nanhua Yanyun Restaurant

The speciality of the house is Beijing (Peking) cuisine featuring dishes which are crisp yet tender, appetizing, and aromatic. Dishes which the house is proud of include sauted fish slices in wine sauce, quick fried crisps, and Beijing duck.

Sichuan Restaurant

The dishes of this restaurant preserve the strong local flavors of Sichuan Province. Special seasonings used include chili, sour and hot sauce, cayenne pepper, and black pepper, in varying combinations provide many different tastes. Dishes that show off this style of cooking especially well are pork shreds in hot sauce, pork slices with cabbage in hot sauce, and cabbage with chili.

Yangzhou Restaurant

The saying goes that the distinguishing feature of Yangzhou cuisine is soup so crystal clear you can see the bottom of the bowl and sauce so thick it turns cream white. This restaurant is particular about flavor control so that its dishes suit both southerners and northerners. Its celebrated dishes include boiled fish head and crystal pork seasoned with salt and saltpeter.

People's Restaurant

The specialities offered here are drawn from both the Suzhou and the Wuxi areas. Among the stewed, braised, and simmered dishes that are noteworthy are: Assorted Three Delicacies, Duck in Spicy Sauce, and Mandarin Fish with Pine Nuts.

Lixin Vegetarian Restaurant

The feature of this restaurant is that all of its strictly vegetarian dishes are served in the shapes of chicken, duck, fish, and pigs. The ingredients include bean products, vegetables in season, and dried nuts.

Moslem Restaurant

The food here is prepared carefully according to Islamic customs. Among its best known dishes are fried steak, deep-fried fillet, fried beef shreds, and self-rinsed mutton in hot pot. The desserts here are exceptionally sweet and tasty.

List of Major Restaurants in Shanghai

Name	Style	Telephone
Xinya Restaurant	Guangdong	22 36 36
Mei Xin Restaurant	Guangdong	37 39 91
Xing Hua Lou Restaurant	Guangdong	2 97 40
Yan Yun Lou Restaurant	Beijing	22 32 93
Sichuan Restaurant	Sichuan	22 22 64
Mei Long Zhen Restaurant	Sichuan	53 53 53
Chengdu Restaurant	Sichuan	37 64 12
Lu Yang Cun Restaurant	Sichuan • Yangzhou	53 72 21
Yangzhou Restaurant	Yangzhou	287
The People's Restaurant	Suzhou	53 73 51
Dongfeng Restaurant	Suzhou • Guangdong	21 80 60
Da Hong Yun Restaurant	Souzhou	22 34 75
Lao (Old) Shanghai Restaurant	Shanghai	28 98 50
Yueyanglou Restaurant	Hunan	28 26 72
Moslem Restaurant		22 48 76
Gongdelin Vegetarian Restaurant		53 13 13
Vegetarian Restaurant of The Jade Buddha Temple		53 57 45
Lubolang Restaurant	Snack Pastries	28 06
Red House Restaurant	French • Italian	56 57 4

4. Other Places To Visit

Dragon Gate Grottoes, Luoyang

Anshan (ANSHAN)

The city of Anshan, famous for its iron and steel production, is located in the southeast of Liaoning (Liaoning Province). Prior to 1949 it was a small town of a little over 100,000 people. When the People's Republic of China was founded, emphasis was put on developing the iron and steel works located here. Today the population is well over one million people and its iron and steel manufacturing plants are among China's largest.

For such an industrial city its avenues are broad and tree-lined. One cannot miss the evidence of the factories towering over the city, but the over-all atmosphere does not suggest that the population grew because of the growth in industry. The iron and steel complex at Anshan embraces ore mining, ore dressing, iron smelting, steel making, steel rolling, chemical, power, transport, machine repairing, and other ancillary plants. A tour of a portion of these facilities is sometimes possible but your Lüxingshe guide should be advised of your interest. If feasible, the visit will be arranged.

PLACES OF INTEREST
Tang Gang Zi Spring

At the Tang Gang Zi Spring, which is about 9 mi. (15 km.) south of Anshan, is located a lovely park. More than 1,000 tons of mineral water flow daily from the hot springs here. The water is crystal clear and rises to a temperature of 161° Fahrenheit (72° Celsius). Amidst the trees and historical buildings is a sanatorium and people come from miles to bathe in the water which is said to have great therapeutic properties.

Qian Duo Lian Hua

Also called the Hill of a Thousand Lotus Flowers, it is 12 mi. (20 km.) outside of Anshan. The name is derived from its many mist-enshrouded peaks which suggest budding lotus flowers.

Other Attractions

If your stay in China includes a stop at Anshan, others spots to visit include Fragrant Cliff Monastery, Dragon Spring Monastery, Delicate Pagoda, West Pavilion which dates back to the Tang Dynasty (618-907 A.D.), and the Qian Shan (Chienshan Mountains). In this mountain range the Thousand Hills Sanatorium was erected after 1949. With its springs, brooks, pines, and attractive buildings, this area makes an ideal holiday and health resort.

Baotou (PAOTOW)

Baotou is a developing industrial city of the Inner-Mongolia Autonomous Region. One of China's important steel centers, it is often referred to as "a steel city on the prairie."

The city has a long history of civilization. Stone knives, stone axes and bone needles, dating back to the neolithic period, have been unearthed here. The ruins of over forty cities and tombs of the Han Dynasty have been discovered at Baotou.

PLACES OF INTEREST

Wudangzhao Temple

Located in the Wudang Valley of the Daqing Mountains, this well-known temple was built in 1749 A.D. during the Qian-long reign of the Qing Dynasty. Wudangzhao Temple, standing imposingly and magnificently, covers an area of 50 acres (20 ha.) and consists of approximately 2500 rooms. Its structure is exquisite and, coupled with its decorations, is a good example of the style and architecture of China.

Changchun (CHANGCHUN)

Located in the center of the Northeast Plain, Changchun, the capital of Jilin (Kirin Province), is more than one hundred years old. It contains China's first large auto plant. It produced the initial batch of Liberation Heavy Trucks in 1956; then followed with cross-country vehicles, Red Flag sedans, and other types of motor vehicles. With a population of over 1,200,000 people, it also houses industrial plants that turn out locomotives, tractors, machine tools, optical instruments, electric motors, and electrical appliances. Changchun's burgeoning arts and crafts include embroidery, jade carvings, carpets, and cork pictures. All these industries are new and have developed rapidly since 1949 to make Changchun today a thriving industrial city.

As with most industrial cities in China, Changchun does not look like one. It has many trees along its wide streets and is exceptionally clean. It is the home of the Jilin University, Chang Chun Film Studios, one of China's most famous film studios, and also has a large hotel and a shopping district.

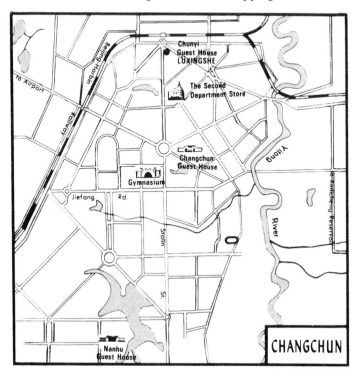

PLACES OF INTEREST

Laodong Park

Laodong Park, often called the Workers Park, was once a fetid, open ditch. Today it is a lovely park planted with pines and willows. There are pleasant lotus ponds with bridges and attractive pavilions to rest in.

Xinlicheng Reservoir

Situated on the upper reaches of the Yitong Jiang (Yitong River), 12 mi. (20 km.) from Changchun, Xinlicheng Reservoir is a major project for harnessing the river. The land surrounding the catchment area is well forested. River clams are raised to produce cultivated pearls and the reservoir is also stocked with fish. There are orchards and a deer farm. It is considered one of Changchun's most scenic spots.

Changjiang (YANGTZE RIVER) Gorges

"Changjiang (Yangtse River) Gorges" is a general term for the Qutang, the Wu, and the Xiling Gorges. Beginning by the Baidi (White King) City, of Fengjie County, Sichuan Province, and ending at the Nanjin Pass of Yichang County, Hubei Province in the east, this stretch of the river which runs about 124 mi. (200 km.) is known as one of the largest gorges in the world. The common features of the three gorges are steep mountain crags on both sides of the river, swift currents, dangerous shoals and incessant bellowing waves. Each of the three gorges has its own characteristics, however, the Qutang Gorge is known for its majestic steep crags which rise abruptly into the clouds; the Wu Gorge is famed for its elegant beauty; and the Xiling Gorge is best known for its rapids and shoals.

Qutang Gorge

The Qutang Gorge, also known as the Kwei Gorge, is only about 5 mi. (8 km.) long. It is the narrowest of the three gorges. With two chains of great cliffs facing each other along both banks, resembling a gateway, this is Kweimen or "Qutang Pass"—the valve controlling the flow of the entire river.

Wu Gorge

The Wu Gorge, taking its name from the Wu Mountains, has

a total length of over 25 mi. (40 km.). The scenery is considered to be the finest of the three gorges—stately cliffs rising on both sides of the river and stretching off into the distance. As all of the peaks are 4,900-6,500 ft. (1,500-2,000 m.) above sea level, the mist-clad "Twelve Peaks" of the Wu Mountains lining the banks of the Wu Gorge are the prettiest. Six on the northern side can be seen at a glance from a boat, but of the six on the southern side only three are visible. The other three can be seen only by going up about 19 mi. (30 km.) along the Qingshi Stream. Of the 12 peaks, the Fairy Princess Peak is the highest and the most beautiful. Standing at the top is a human-like stone column which resembles an elegant young lady gazing down on the river. This is the Fairy Princess Stone of the Fairy Princess Peak. As it stands at the very summit of this cluster of mountains, this peak is the first to be lit up by the light of dawn and the last to darken at dusk. Because of this it has been given the additional name of "Rose-tinted Peak." Legend has it that the 12 peaks are the embodiments of the 12 fairies and the Fairy Princess Peak is that of Yao Ji, the daughter of the Western Queen Mother.

At the eastern end of the Wu Gorge the river becomes wider. This is the wide estuary of the Fragrant Stream, which stretches some 28 mi. (45 km.) between the Wu and the Xiling Gorges. The nearby village here on the northern bank of the Changjiang is supposed to be the place where Qu Yuan — the patriotic poet of the Warring States Period (475-221 B.C.) was actually born and brought up. There is a Qu Yuan Tomb, a Qu Yuan Temple and a Qu Yuan Stream here. Also this region was the home of a famous Han Dynasty Beauty—Wang Zhaojun. Legend has it that one day while washing herself in its waters Wang Zhoajun dropped a string of pearls into the stream, thus the waters acquired their fresh and fragrant aroma.

Xiling Gorge

The Xiling Gorge extends 47 mi. (76 km.) from the mouth of the Fragrant Stream to Nanjin Pass in Hubei Province and is the longest of the three gorges. It is known primarily for its treacherous rapids and dangerous reefs and shoals.

The Nanjin Pass marks the end of the Xiling Gorge. Flanking both sides of the river are precipitous cliffs which control access to the west. Passing through the Nanjin Pass the river widens dramatically and the water flows rather smoothly into the vast expanse of a plain.

The whole stretch of the Changjiang Gorges is not only known to the world for its majestic natural beauty, but also for the rich history and fascinating legends that are such a part of it. It is, therefore, a memorable experience for those who decide to make the trip.

Changsha (CHANGSHA)

Changsha, located on the Xiang Jiang (Hsiangchiang River), is the capital of Hunan (Hunan Province). It was here that Chairman Mao spent part of his school years and carried on early revolutionary activities.

The city has a long history. It was a large town over two thousand years ago during the Spring and Autumn and Warring States Periods (770-221 B.C.) when it was called Qingyang. In 221 B.C., after the first emperor of the Qin Dynasty unified various states and principalities, the Changsha prefecture was set up. Agriculture has always played an important part in its history. The land is very fertile and even a dry spell cannot cause much harm as water from the river can be diverted to irrigate the crops.

In addition to its many acres of farmland on which are grown rice and tea, Changsha also has a paper mill, textile and shoe factories, and other industrial plants. You can cross the river on a ferry boat and have a good view of the busy river traffic or stroll through the lovely gardens in the southern corner of the old town.

PLACES OF INTEREST

Qing Shui Tang (Clear Water Pond)

In the autumn of 1921, after attending the First National Congress of the Chinese Communist Party, Chairman Mao returned to Hunan and set up the Xiang District Committee of the Communist Party of China with himself as its secretary. It was established here at No. 22 Qing Shui Tang and the original house has been restored. The name Qing Shui Tang (Clear Water Pond) dates back to the early 1900's when there was a pond behind the house. The pond has long since dried up.

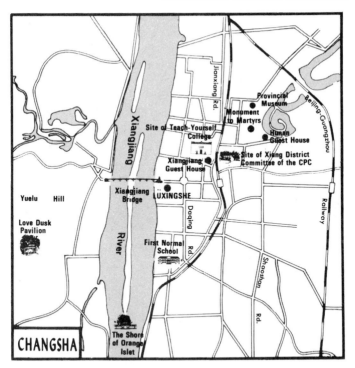

After restoration, the house was turned into a Museum covering both the history of Changsha and the part the Communist Party played in its development.

The First Normal School of Hunan

From the spring of 1913 to the summer of 1918 Chairman Mao studied and worked for the revolution here. Although the original buildings were destroyed, it was rebuilt after the People's Republic of China was founded. Today it houses a museum which contains photographs, books, and other materials relating to Chairman Mao.

Juzi Dao

This island is in the Xiang Jiang west of Changsha. About 3 mi. (5 km.) long, it is sometimes called "Long Island," although most often it is referred to as Orange Island. On it stands the Juzi Zhou Tou Memorial Pavilion. In this Pavilion is a large stone table on which is engraved Chairman Mao's poem, "Changsha."

Yang Kai Hui's Home

Comrade Yang Kai Hui, who died a martyr's death, was Chairman Mao's wife and close comrade in arms. Her home is some 36 mi. (60 km.) from Changsha and her tomb is located on the premises.

Yue Lu Hill

This lovely hill is covered with maples which turn into a mantle of red in late autumn. There are scenic spots like the Love Dusk Pavilion on the hill. In his youth Chairman Mao came here often to climb and sleep in the open in order to build up his strength and willpower.

Hunan Ceramics

Pottery is one of the oldest crafts in Hunan. Perhaps best known of the traditional products is porcelain. Visitors are welcome at the Jian Xiang Porcelain Factory to see how the pottery is made. At this factory there has also been set up a ceramics exhibition for the visitor's perusal featuring the various crafts native to this province.

Mawangdui Tombs

The archaeological finds at the Mawangdui Tombs, which were discovered in 1972, date back 2,100 years to the Western Han Dynasty (206 B.C.-24 A.D.) and contain the remains of the Marquis of Dai, his wife and son together with funerary objects.

Among the more than three thousand relics found was the corpse of a fifty-year-old woman which was in an excellent state of preservation. Her body had been wrapped in more than twenty layers of silk and linen. There was a silk painting draped over the inside of the coffin depicting scenes of life at that time and others from legend.

Also discovered were beautiful lacquerware, wooden figurines, bamboo books, pottery, a musical instrument not known today, bamboo baskets containing clothes and food, flutes, and a bronze mirror among other things. The body and a portion of the relics are now on display.

SHOPPING

There are a variety of shops in Changsha to choose from:

The Friendship Store is located on May First Square and carries a big selection of items.

The Ceramics Store is in the Hunan Exhibition Hall at 13 Dong Feng Road. Here you will find a broad variety of local products.

Hunan Provincial Arts and Crafts Department Store displays a variety of artifacts produced in the Province. It is located at 49 May First Square.

Shaoshan Road Department Store carries a selection of decorative and household items.

RESTAURANTS

There are several restaurants in Changsha in which you may sample the distinctive cuisine of Hunan. In addition to the restaurants in the Hangzhou and Overseas Chinese Hotels, there is the Huo Gongdian Restaurant, the You Yi Cun Restaurant, and the Furong or Hibiscus Restaurant.

Chengde (CHENGTEH)

The city of Chengde is an economic center in northeastern Hebei Sheng (Hopei Province). On the main railway line from Beijing (Peking), it is used as a central point of storing and shipping products from and to neighboring cities. Its location by the Wulie He (Wulie River), on elevated terrain, with numerous surrounding peaks, lends it a rare picturesque quality. At Chengde the Emperors of the Qing Dynasty constructed a group of buildings, similar to the Summer Palace in Beijing, to which they came every summer to escape from the heat.

PLACES OF INTEREST

Bi Shu Shan Zhuang

Also called Cool Mountain Villa, it is in the north of the city. Historically it was called Rehe, Jehol, or Chengde Palace. Emperors of the Qing Dynasty (1644-1911 A.D.) lived and conducted state affairs here in the summer. Construction started in 1703 (during the reign of Emperor Kangxi) and was completed in 1790 (during the reign of Emperor Qianlong). The estate encompasses 1,384 acres (564 ha.) and is surrounded by a 6 mi. (10 km.) long battlement stone wall. The Imperial residence is on a hill overlooking a lake. Taking a stroll through the densely-wooded grounds you will be rewarded with beautiful views of palaces, pavilions, terraces, and scattered islands. Pine and cypress trees line the paths, there are many springs and brooks, all help to keep the area always cool and comfortable. From the Snow-Capped Pavilion on the South Hill one can enjoy a fine view of jagged rocks and the Wai Ba Temples.

Wai Ba Temples

Of the eleven temples built between 1713 and 1780, only seven remain. Five incorporate the Han style of architecture: the Pu Ren Monastery (Temple of Universal Goodness); the Pu Ning Monastery (Temple of General Peace); the An Yuan Temple (Ili Valley Temple); the Shu Xiang Monastery; and the Xu Mi

Fu Shou Temple. The remaining two, the Pu Tuo Zong Cheng and the Xu Mi Fu Shou Temples, are copies of lamaseries in western and eastern Xizang (Tibet) respectively, combining large red terraces with smaller white ones.

The glazed-tile arches of the Pu Tuo Zong Cheng Temple and an octagonal seven-storied pagoda of glazed tile on the hillside display a blending of the architectural features of the Han and Zang (Tibetan) nationalities. All these temples, forming a magnificent harmonious unit, are a monument to the cultural exchange between the various nationalities. They are evidence that the splendid culture of the Chinese nation was created and developed through the common effort of the people of all fraternal nationalities in China.

Chengdu (CHENGTU)

The present provincial capital of Sichuan Sheng (Szechuan Province), Chengdu is also its economic and cultural center and has been since as far back as 400 B.C. It has had several other names in history. Long noted for its brocade, during the Eastern Han Dynasty (25-220 A.D.) an official was appointed

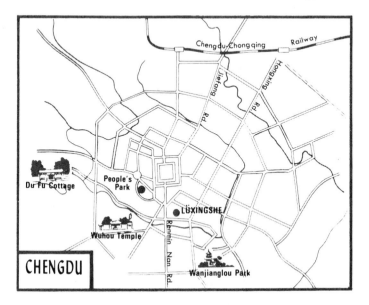

to control and devlop the fast-growing brocade industry. Thus the city became known as Jincheng (Brocade Town). When it was discovered that the brocade turned brighter and fresher after being washed in river water, the nearby stream was given the name Jin Jiang or Brocade River.

During the Five Dynasties era it was for a time the capital of China and hibiscus was planted all along the city wall. Because of this it then became known as Furong or Hibiscus. Today flowers and trees grace the wide streets and the many parks. Agriculture and light industry are the dominant mainstays of the region. Brocade is still manufactured along with other textiles and handicrafts. If you stay in Chengdu perhaps you will be able to see an operatic production. The Sichuan Opera has been in existence for many years and is slowly gaining world-wide fame.

There are many universities located in Chengdu. Perhaps the most famous is the Sichuan University, founded in the late 1920's. Also you will find several medical colleges, as well as scientific and technical institutes.

PLACES OF INTEREST
Du Fu Caotang

The Tang poet, Du Fu, came to Chengdu in the winter of 759 A.D. Du Fu Caotang or Du Fu's Hut is a small thatched hut he erected the year following his arrival. Du Fu lived in this hut off and on for nearly four years and it is here he wrote many of his more than 240 poems. The hut is located in the western part of the City by Huanhuaxi Jiang (Flower Washing River). By this river a temple was erected during the Song Dynasty (960-1280 A.D.) in Du Fu's honor. Over the years it has frequently been renovated and enlarged to its present scale. Within this group of buildings is the Temple Gongbuci, which has a stone statue of the poet, and also a museum which houses copies of Du Fu's work and various paintings reputed to have been done to glorify his poems.

Wang Jiang Park (River View Park)

This park is located in the southeastern suburbs. Overlooking the river are three buildings: Pavilion for Admiring Beauty, Chamber for Washing Brocade, and Chamber for Reciting Poetry. All three date back to the early part of the Qing Dynasty (1644-1911 A.D.) The park also has a good collection of bamboo including two rare types: the "mottled" and the "human face."

Qingcheng Shan (Green Town Mountain)

Qingcheng Shan is southwest from Chengdu approximately 42 mi. (67.6 km.). With undulating hills and a total of 108 monasteries, temples, and pavilions nestled among lofty ancient trees, this excursion center and summer resort is worthy of its name, "the quietest spot under heaven."

Baoguangsi

Baoguangsi (Precious Light Monastery), founded during the Tang Dynasty (618-907 A.D.), is located to the west of Chengdu. Lohan Hall, part of the monastery, houses a collection of over five hundred Qing statues. These are not only considered the best in the province but have been used over the years for the study of traditional Chinese sculpture.

SHOPPING

There are several stores in Chengdu for the tourist to browse in. Among the larger ones are the Chengdu Friendship Store, the Chengdu Arts and Crafts Department Store, the Chengdu Municipal Fine Arts Company, and the Sichuan Antique Store. All carry a variety of items including silks and brocades made in nearby plants and beautiful handicrafts from the province.

RESTAURANTS

Cuisine of Chengdu is typical of food served in Sichuan Sheng (Szechuan Province). It is hot and spicy and very flavorful. While visiting here you have many fine restaurants to choose from. Some of the larger are: Jinjiang Guest House; Rong Cheng Restaurant; Chengdu Restaurant; Furong Retaurant; Yaohua Restaurant; and Dong Feng Restaurant.

Chongqing (CHUNGKING)

Chongqing is also located in Sichuan Sheng (Szechuan Province) where the Changjiang (Yangtze River) and Jialing Jiang (Chialing River) meet. Although it is an old city with a history of over three thousand years, there are very few ancient buildings or temples.

In the early part of the twentieth century it was a backward consumer city. During World War II it became the Kuomintang seat of the government. (During that period Zhou Enlai and others served there as Communist Party representatives.) As a direct result of the importance it held during those years, many industries developed. After the People's Republic of China was founded the city grew even more. Today it has more than 2,300 factories producing steel, iron, and machinery. It is a large coal-mining district. With its population of over six million people this mountain city has taken over an entirely new look — clean, with a transportation system that covers the region.

PLACES OF INTEREST

Beiwenquan Park (North Hot Springs Park)

This park is situated 31 mi. (52 km.) from the center of the city on the side of the Hot Spring Temple. The Temple dates back to 423 A.D. but the park was only opened to the public in 1927. The scenery is magnificent. With the Red Silk Mountain behind it, looking out over the Jialing River, the view combines mountain ranges, ravines, and rushing water. The carbonated mineral spring water is used in the swimming pools. There are also temples dating back to the Ming and Qing Dynasties (1368-1911 A.D.), fish ponds, caves, and fountains.

Nanwenquan Park (South Hot Springs Park)

Noted for its hot springs and places of historical interest, this park is in the southern suburbs about 14 mi. (24 km.) from the center of the city. Its scenic spots are known as the "Twelve Landscapes of Nanchuan" and if you have the time to explore them you will find each with a charm all of its own. Indoor and outdoor baths are fed by sulphurous springs with a temperature of approximately 100° Fahrenheit (38° Celsius).

Jinyun Shan (Red Silk Mountain)

This mountain has an elevation of 3,399 ft. (1,030 m.). Located 5 mi. (8 km.) from Beiwenquan Park it makes an ideal summer resort as the temperature during the heat of the summer is some 14° Fahrenheit (6° Celsius) lower than in the city. The mountain has nine peaks. Shizifeng (Lion Peak) is the highest and overlooks the Jialing River commanding a view of the beautiful outlying districts. More than 1,700 species of subtropical plants are found on the mountain. The famous local tea, Jinyun, is also grown here. The Jinyun Temple, over 1,500 years old, contains many artifacts of high artistic and historical value.

Hongyancun

Hongyancun or Red Crag Village is where the Delegation of the Communist Party of China, the South China Bureau of the CPC Central Committee, and the 18th Group Army had their headquarters during the War of Resistance against Japan. In August of 1945 Chairman Mao lived here for a short time while he negotiated with the Kuomintang. In 1958 it was turned into the Hongyan Revolutionary Memorial Hall containing furnishings and papers tracing its political and historical significance.

No. 40, Zengjiayan

This was the residence of the South China Bureau of the CPC Central Committee. It was often used as an office by Zhou Enlai when he was the CPC representative. It has also been called the "Zhou Mansion." When Chairman Mao came to Chongqing for various negotiations in 1945 he used this house to meet Chinese and foreign correspondents. After liberation it was turned into a branch of the Hongyan Revolutionary Memorial Hall.

Crime Exhibition Halls

These exhibitions are in Zhazidong (Dregs Cavern) and Baigongguan (Bai Mansion). They are at the foot of Gele Hill in the northwestern suburbs. These were two of the secret prisons run by an international secret service set up in 1942 based on an undercover agreement to suppress the Chinese Revolution. Now the two prisons have been turned into a museum showing how the Communists stood up to torture and other execution.

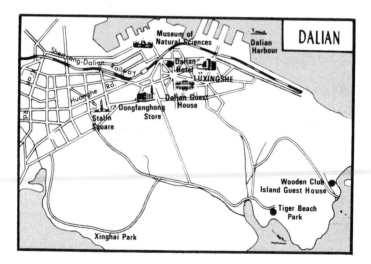

Dalian (TALIEN)

Dalian is located on the southern tip of Liaoning Sheng (Liaoning Province). Surrounded by the sea on three sides, it is one of China's major foreign trade seaports. Dalian's harbor is wide, deep, and ice free and can accommodate ocean-going vessels carrying 40,000 tons of cargo all year round. Agriculture and industrial factories also play a large part in modern-day Dalian. Fields of grain dot the countryside. Large plants produce ships, electrical motors, textiles, and chemicals.

Dalian has long been known as a tourist and health resort. People come from all over the country to enjoy the many beaches along its coast. It is also a cultural center housing a university and several specialized colleges. Screened by mountains and looking out to the sea, Dalian, despite its industrial nature, is an attractive scenic spot.

PLACES OF INTEREST
Dalian Harbor
Construction of the harbor was started in 1899 and completed in the 1930's. It was renovated and expanded after 1949. Today it has modern harbor facilities with deep berths for freighters of the 40,000-ton classification.

Glass Works
This factory was greatly enlarged in 1958. It produces glass utensils, glass containers, and artware. Among the many artistic pieces created by the workers are glass fish, flowers, and birds. The designs are lovely and the objects look free and natural. A tour of this facility will include not only how various pieces are made but also an opportunity to purchase some of the products made here.

Shell Mosaics Workshop
Shells and conches found in rivers, lakes, and on the seaside are used to make shell mosaics in this factory which was built in 1959. The various articles are shaped as flowers, birds, landscapes, and figurines. Skilled craftsmen take the many colored shells of different shapes and sizes and arrange them into extremely attractive ornaments. A tour of this workshop can also be arranged if you so desire.

Museum of Natural Science
This Museum, built in 1950, has a total floor space of 26,676 sq. ft. (2,470 sq. m.). The displays are arranged into four different sections: marine life, minerals, plants, and animals. The exhibit is extremely large and totals over 2,700 objects.

Datong (TATUNG)

Situated in the northern part of Shanxi Sheng (Shansi Province), Datong has often been called "a sea of coal." Large deposits of coal can be found southwest of the town and with these as the center, Datong has become basically an industrial center. 3,900 ft. (1,216 m.) above sea level, the terrain does not lend itself to agriculture. Coal mining and the nearby railroad have turned Datong into a thriving community.

Through the ages it was an important garrison town on China's northern frontier and a center of cultural exchange between many nationalities. More than 1,500 years ago, during the fifth century, it was the capital of China. During that time, one of the great art treasures of China became part of this area, the magnificent carvings in the famous Yungang Grottoes.

PLACES OF INTEREST
Yungang Grottoes
The carving of these rock temples began in the fifth century. The Yungang Grottoes are one of several massive groups of ancient rock temples in China today. Fifty-three caves contain more than 51,000 bas-relief carvings and statues. Twenty-one of them are quite massive with the others ranging from medium to small in size. The largest statue towers 56 ft. (17 m.) and the smallest is just a few centimeters high. In between the various caves can be found several buildings one of which is named the Old Monastery of the Stone Buddhas which dates back to the Qing Dynasty (1644-1911 A.D.) Construction of this monastery and surrounding temples protects several of the caves and it is thought that the buildings were erected to protect the caves and the carvings within. If one were to go through all twenty-one caves, it would be found that all the figures are different both in posture and expression.

Nine Dragon Screen
In the center of the town stands the magnificent Nine Dragon Screen. Over five hundred years old, it was built using five different colored glazed tiles. The nine dragons are caught in varyying life-like movements rising out of the sea and chasing what some believe to be suns, which are symbols of immortality. Moved several decades ago to make room for industrial expansion, it is still in perfect condition today.

Huayan Monastery

This Monastery dates back to the early part of the fifth century. Only one building, the Hall for Keeping Buddhist Scriptures, is part of the original construction. It still contains thirty-one well preserved clay sculptures. As these clay statues date back to the fifth century, they are among China's most highly treasured examples of ancient sculpture. During the twelfth century the Great Temple of Treasure was rebuilt on its original site. Inside this temple, facing the entrance, are five Buddha statues flanked by twenty statues of Celestial Guardians. Murals are painted on all four walls. It is one of the largest Buddhist temples of wood still in existence in China today. During the Qing Dynasty restoration of the remaining buildings of the original monastery was undertaken and it is these temples and halls that comprise the balance of the site today.

Dazu County (TATZU COUNTY)

Dazu County is located in Sichuan Sheng (Szechuan Province) 103 mi. (165 km.) northwest of Chongqing. In Dazu County you will find stone carvings representing the best of China's late-period grotto art. The stone carvings, a type of religious art, mainly depict Buddhist figures. Started in 892 A.D., the carving reached its climax around 960-1279 A.D. Scattered at some forty sites, there stood more than fifty thousand stone figures which are often called the "Dazu Carvings." The two largest groups are located on North Hill and Baodin Hill. These are the finest carvings and they are protected by the national government as key historical relics. There are main roads leading from the county town of Dazu to North Hill (1.2 mi./2 km.) to its north and Baodin Hill (9.3 mi./15 km.) to the northeast.

Emei Shan (MOUNT OMEI)

Emei Shan rises straight out of the ground on the left bank of the Dadu He (Tatu River) in the southwestern part of Sichuan Sheng (Szechuan Province). At an elevation of 10,227 ft. (3,099 m.), "Emei towers over the western horizon," as the noted Tang poet, Li Bai (Li Po), sang in his verses.

A rugged path of green stone steps leads 36 mi. (60 km.) up the mountain to a host of temples of blue bricks and green tiles spread out neatly near the top. Construction began as early as the third century. By the sixteenth century the mountain had come to be known as a great Buddhist sanctuary.

There are a total of more than seventy-five temples and buildings to be found on Emei Shan. The majority are of great religious significance as in ancient times monks lived and studied on the mountainside.

PLACES OF INTEREST

Tiger Taming Temple

This temple was built in the sixth century. It is 2,640 ft. (800 m.) above sea level on a hill which resembles a crouching tiger. Screened off by thickly-forested hillocks, it is a bit of antiquity hidden in the remote mountains.

Thunderclap Temple

Legend tells us that this temple is situated where a rivulet can be heard rumbling like thunder. It stands at a height of over 2,970 ft. (900 m.) before the pagoda-shaped hill. At night the moon might be mistaken for a lantern hanging on a pagoda.

Grand Level Land Temple

This temple is perched on a long peak halfway up the mountain. From it one commands a magnificent view, particularly after a snowfall.

Temple Dedicated to Service to the Country

Perhaps Emei's most imposing edifices, with the best collection of ancient relics and historical sites, are at the foot of the mountain. This temple was built in the sixteenth century. It has four halls, each higher than the one before. They are grand structures built in a simple, unaffected style, adorned with elaborate carvings on the doors and windows. Set off by pines and cypresses, one feels the atmosphere of solemnity within this temple. Chambers, terraces, and pavilions are spaced out in perfect proportion. The front hall contains the Huayan Pagoda, cast of red copper in the Ming Dynasty (1368-1644 A.D.). The pagoda is 22 ft. (6.7 m.) high with fourteen eaves representing the same number of stories. Carved on it are 4,700 Buddhist images and the text of the Huayan scripture.

Ten Thousand Years Temple

This temple was built in the fourth century and is one of the oldest still in existence on Emei Shan. It has a beamless square hall with a dome entirely arched out of brick, a building technique commonly used during the Ming Dynasty. Within the hall is a 30 ft. (9.1 m.) high sculpture of Bodhisattva Samantabhadre, the first disciple of Sakyamuni, the founder of Buddhism. This sculpture pictures the disciple sitting on a giant elephant which is standing on four lotus blossoms. The proportions are majestic. It is a rare bronze relic cast in 980 A.D.

Golden Top Temple

Also called Huazan Temple, this is the most brilliant edifice on the Emei summit. The first building, constructed in the sixteenth century, was burned down to be replaced by a bronze temple cast in Hubei Province, transported to Sichuan Province and hauled all the way up to the summit. This Golden Top gleams in the sun. It was partially destroyed by fire in 1890. After that it was repaired and another structure, Terrace for Watching Lights, added to it. In front of the temple stands the magnificent Grand Buddha Hall with huge golden characters inscribed horizontally over the entrance: "Unmatched Beauty."

From Golden Top Temple one commands a view of three rivers to the east glinting like ribbons, snowclad mountains to the west, the Chengdu Plain to the north, and mountain ridges to the south. The sight is magnificent and cannot be duplicated anywhere else in China.

Foshan (FOSHAN)

Foshan is 10 mi. (16.1 km.) southwest of Guangzhou (Canton). It is located in Guangdong Sheng (Guangdong Province) and has a population of over 300,000. Its name translates to Buddha Hill and is derived from the three statues of the Buddha which stood on a small hill within the town.

In times past Foshan achieved considerable renown as a religious pilgrimage site and attracted the pious from as far away as India. In addition to its spiritual reputation, the town was also noted for its extensive pottery works. Ceramic, textile, and foundry industries were comparatively well developed since the time of the Song Dynasty (960-1279 A.D.). Later, under the Ming Dynasty, a large volume of ironware was produced for the export trade. During these years it was larger in population than Guangzhou itself.

Today it is still a major manufacturer of pottery. Recent archaeological excavations have uncovered ancient kilns and pottery-making equipment. One should try to visit both this historical site as well as a modern pottery factory. The comparison is one striking example of how far China has progressed over the centuries.

PLACES OF INTEREST
Silk Dyeing and Printing Mill
This mill was established in 1956 to bleach, dye, and print the silk fabrics produced by the Hongmian and Nanhai Textile Mills. Three semi-automatic dyeing machines were designed and made by the mill's own workers. They have greatly reduced the number of printers required and increased productivity tenfold over hand printing.

Shiwan Ceramics Factory
This was built in 1952 and produces mainly ceramic artwork. In addition a small amount of everyday pottery and porcelain articles are still manufactured. Shiwan ceramic artworks have a history of seven hundred years. The pottery and porcelain articles produced today include the four major varieties: human figures, animal figures, utensils, and flower pots. Innovation and improvements have been made in the fields of glaze and colors making the modern pieces more brilliant than the traditional. The once-discontinued red glaze has been restored.

Folk Arts Research Society

This Society was organized in 1955 and has a staff of more than 300 people. The handicrafts produced today include:

Autumn Colors: Dating back to the Yongle period of the Ming Dynasty, which features the utilization of waste paper frag-

Pagoda at Ren Shou Si Temple, now an exhibition center of Foshan handicrafts

ments, wood blocks, clay and adhesives to model, carve, and sculpt clay figurines.

Lanterns: Left-over materials from many sources are glazed together to make colorful lanterns. "Wood shaving lanterns," for example, are made of wood shavings. The traditional palatial lanterns and the "revolving lanterns" are made of iron wire and colored silk fabrics.

Paper-Cuts: Foshan paper-cuts date back to the tenth century. Copper leaf and colored paper are used to make the cutouts. It is a folk art of unique skill with brilliant and magnificent colors and bold and serene lines.

Brick carving: The artisans, with simple tools, used building bricks to carve animated designs of human figures, animals, birds, flowers, and landscapes. Finished bricks are used for architectural decoration.

Cuttlefish Bone Sculpture: A new art of sculpture was invented after 1949. Handicraft works are carved out of cuttlefish bone and made into flowers, plants, birds, animals, and landscapes. The finished product, delicate to the eye, has a glossy white color.

Ancestral Temple

The Ancestral Temple of Foshan is a famous historical building of Guangdong Province built in the northern Song Dynasty. The entire roof stands on a framework of wooden arches. These arches are in various shapes: lotus flowers, swallows, "chun zi" (the Chinese character for spring), and human heads. They are made from the hardwood of the Province and put together into a framework without using a single nail. On the eaves of this building are the famous Shiwan glazed tiles of Foshan while on the roof are sculptured animal figures symbolizing auspicious prospects. The entire building is of carved beams and painted pillars that are brilliant, glistening, and magnificent.

The Ancestral Temple has now been extended and made into a park. Towers, pavilions, and corridors have been built. Trees and shrubs have been planted. It is a lovely place to take a leisurely walk.

Ren Shou Si Temple

This temple has now been converted into an exhibition hall. Here one will find a complete display of the wide variety of pottery and folk arts Foshan is famous for. Lanterns, figurines, paper-cuts, and porcelain are among the many items to be found.

Zu Ci Miao Taoist Temple
Originally this was used as a theater. You will see the original stage located in the courtyard. Constructed in the Ming Dynasty (1368-1644 A.D.), it now houses a museum. Among the objects on display are artifacts excavated locally that date back as far as the Han Dynasty (206 B.C.-220 A.D.).

Fushun (FUSHUN)
Located in Liaoning Sheng (Liaoning Province), this city is widely known as "coal city." Coal deposits are known to have existed here over two thousand years ago. Since 1949 there has been rapid development in the coal, petroleum, and related-power industries. Today the city has become one of heavy industry, mainly fuel. Its population is over one million. Some of the people do engage in farming with cotton, wheat, and tobacco being some of the main crops. But the majority of the inhabitants are engaged in coal mining or one of the related industries.

If your tour includes a visit to Fushun you will find it hard to believe that the town has grown around the coal-mining industry. Characteristic of China, it is a clean city. There are public parks with beautiful gardens. Flower beds can be found on every other street. Industry exists and the town is dependent on it. But outwardly one finds it difficult to relate the landscape to the dust and dirt considered an integral part of coal.

PLACES OF INTEREST
Da Huo Fang Reservoir
Construction of this reservoir, located on the upper and middle reaches of the Hun He (Hunho River), started in 1954 and took four years to complete. It is one of the key projects in harnessing the Hun He. Although it is utilitarian in nature, it is also one of the most scenic spots along the river.

Fushun Exhibition Hall
In addition to a small shop selling handicrafts, you will also find on display in this Exhibition Hall ancient artifacts from the surrounding region. Two native products, used to make modern arts and crafts, are also on display. The first, plumbago (graphite) is carved into gleaming cigarette holders, ashtrays, figurines, birds, and animals. The second, amber, is either transparent or translucent. Colors range from white to yellow to red. Amber is used in making beads, brooches, rings, necklaces, cigarette holders, and other ornaments.

Fuzhou (FOOCHOW)
Fuzhou is the capital of Fujian Sheng (Fukien Province). Situated on the longest river in the Province, the Min Jiang (Minchiang River), it has a population of well over half a million people.

Civilization existed at Fuzhou as far back as the sixth century. In the early tenth century it was the capital of an autonomous state. Sugar, tea, and other crops, coupled with the fishing industry, have helped Fuzhou remain one of China's more prosperous towns. Today agriculture still plays an important part in the town's economy. Since 1949 factories have also been added for such products as paper, chemicals, and umbrellas.

PLACES OF INTEREST
Hua Lin Temple
Built on the slope of the nearby mountain, this temple dates back to the Tang Dynasty (618-907 A.D.). It was destroyed on many occasions through the centuries and restored several times. The present temple dates back to the Qing Dynasty.

Gushan (Drum Hill)
This hill is located on the northern bank of Minjiang River east of Fuzhou and is approximately 3,250 ft. (1004 m.) high. On top of the hill there is a huge, flat rock that resembles a drum, hence the name "Drum Hill." The Yongquan Temple, first built in 908 A.D. still maintains the structure of the Jiajing period of the Ming Dynasty (1522-1566 A.D.). The One-Thousand-Buddha Ceramic-Pagoda in front of the temple built during the Song Dynasty (960-1279 A.D.), the white jade Sleeping Buddha in the temple, and the scriptures of various dynasties kept there, are all of great value. At Ling Yuan Cave and Drinking Water Rock, located to the east of the temple in beautiful and tranquil surroundings, one will find clear spring water running. On the rocks, there are several hundred carvings, rarely seen in southeast China. West of the temple, there are 18 caves in a pine tree forest. From Drum Hill one has a magnificent view of the city of Fuzhou with the Minjiang River flowing eastward.

Fuzhou West Lake
First developed during the Jin Dynasty, this man-made lake remains picturesque after many changes. Flower shows are often held in the West Lake Park. In the museum here, "boat coffins" from Wuyi Mountain, and canoes of the Han Dynasty, all priceless treasures of Chinese culture, are on display.

Mawei Port
Mawei shipyard is located at this important foreign trade port in Fuzhou. The International Seamen's Club offers service to foreign friends from around the world.

Arts and Crafts Factory

The well-known Fuzhou laquerware is produced here as well as reproductions of various antiquities made in gold or silver. Other products of Chinese arts and crafts are also made here.

Camel Hill, Guilin

Guilin (KWEILIN)

Guilin is a charming city with magnificent peaks and rivers, beautiful rocks, and fantastic caves. It has some of the most beautiful scenery in all of China. Today Guilin has a population of 320,000 and an area of 300 sq. mi. (780 sq. km.). It is in the northeast section of Guangxi (Kwangsi Chuang Autonomous Region) on the western bank of Lijiang River.

Since 1949 Guilin has become an industrial center producing pharmaceutical products, tires, machinery, fertilizers, silk, cotton material, and many others. Secondary industries include wine, candy, and bamboo chopsticks. The city is noted for its profusion of flowering cassia trees which have a strong, sweet scent. There are many by-products of the cassia: perfume, wine, tea, cinnamon, and herbal medicine.

Guilin is perhaps most famous for its karst landscape which has been the subject of many paintings and poems. This phenomenon is created by the erosion of limestone which forms steep hills, underground channels, and caverns. The Lijiang, Guilin's main waterway, winds among clusters of steep hills which seem to rise abruptly out of the ground. The smooth meandering river, flanked by occasional green meadows and sheer cliffs, is a lovely sight.

Guilin's hills rise perpendicularly from level ground into groups of exotic-shaped pinnacles, each one different. Nearly all have caves and every cave is unique. The stalactites and stalagmites in myriad shapes, sizes, and combinations fascinate old and young alike. Along the Lijiang, between Guilin and Yangshuo, the green hills on both banks, merging with their reflections in the placid blue waters, have always inspired artists, poets, and photographers.

Enough cannot be said about the beauty of Guilin and its surrounding countryside. It must be seen to be believed.

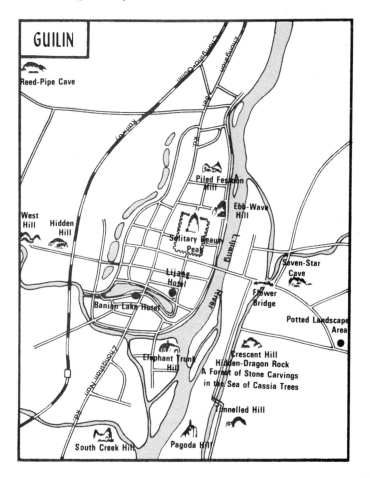

PLACES OF INTEREST
Du Xiu Feng (Solitary Beauty Peak)
Du Xiu Feng is a 500 ft. (152 m.) hill in the center of Guilin. It stands in splendid isolation and the view of the surrounding landscape from the top is excellent.

Xiangbishan (Elephant Trunk Hill)
Xiangbishan has become well known as Elephant Trunk Hill. Amidst the hills is a rock formation. Viewed from Guilin it looks like an elephant's trunk dipping into the water.

Yueyashen (Crescent Hill)
This interesting hill was named after the shape of a rock on its western side which looks like a crescent moon. At the foot of the hill is the Seven-Star Park where sweet cassia trees grow in profusion and the scenery is superb. In this park you will find Seven-Star Cave. Originally the bed of an underground stream, the cavern is about a half mile in length and full of stalactites and stalagmites of various shapes.

Ludiyan (Reed Pipe Cave)
This unusual cave is certainly one of Guilin's major scenic attractions. Inside this vast cavern are fantastic stalagmites and stalactites, earning it the name of "Nature's Art Palace."

SHOPPING
There are two major stores in Guilin, the Guilin Friendship Store and the Yang Qiao Department Store. Between them

Guilin

Primitive ferry station, Guilin

the visitor can find a variety of items including many products from the local region.

RESTAURANTS
Cuisine of this area is basically that of Guangdong (Cantonese). Among the many restaurants one can visit to sample this exquisite food are Rong Hu Restaurant, Li Jiang Restaurant, Guilin Restaurant, and Tong Lai Restaurant.

Handan (HANTAN)
Situated in the southern part of Hebei province, Handan is a city with an ancient civilization dating back to 546 B.C. During the Han Dynasty it became one of the five thriving cities (namely Handan, Xi'an, Luoyang, Zibo and Chengdu) in China. Many relics and places of historic interest are located in and around the city.

PLACES OF INTEREST
The Cong (Clustered) Terrace
Built in 325 B.C. this Terrace was the place where Duke Wuling of the State of Zhao used to review military parades and

watch various entertainments. From the Terrace, one gets a splendid view: to the west are the Taihang mountains rising in the distance; below are weeping willows reflecting in the clear gentle water; and to the south is the city of Handan shrouded in mist.

Xiangtangshan (Mt. Xiangtang) Grottoes

These grottoes are actually located in a mine. The work in them started in the Northern Qi Dynasty (550-577 A.D.) and continued in the later dynasties of Sui (581-618), Tang, Yuan and Ming (1368-1644). There are 16 grottoes altogether with over 3,000 Buddhist statues. It is a facinating place to study the cultural heritage of China.

Hangzhou (HANGCHOW)

Hangzhou, famous for the scenic beauty of Xi Hu (West Lake), is the capital of Zhejiang Province (Chekiang Province). It is situated on the Qiantang Jiang (Chientang River) and is at the southern end of the Grand Canal. With an area of 165.6 sq. mi. (429 sq. km.) Hangzhou has a population of 980,000.

Hangzhou's silk weaving, which dates back to the seventh century, is as beautiful as its brocades. It is well known for many handicrafts including sandlewood fans, silk parasols, scissors, and bamboo ware. It is the home of the high quality green Longjing tea called Dragon Well tea. Mandarin oranges, bamboo, timber, and sugar cane are among its other agricultural industries.

Once a consumer city, it is now not only an agricultural city but also a prosperous industrial one. Its industries include iron and steel, machine making, oil refineries, electronics, power generators, light trucks, and small tractors. The city has many writers and artists, twenty-four hospitals, and a dozen schools.

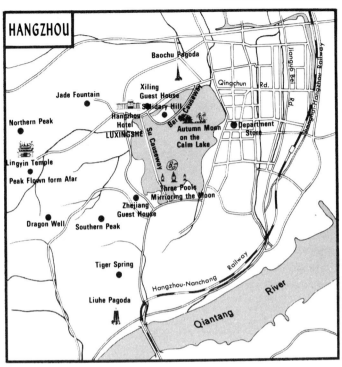

PLACES OF INTEREST
Xi Hu (West Lake)

Enclosed by hills on three sides, Xi Hu (West Lake) mirrors the surrounding landscape to form a panorama of great beauty. It covers 1,235 acres (500 ha.) with a shoreline of 9 mi. (15 km.). Luxurious trees and flowers grow around the lake. It has been a scenic resort since the Tang Dynasty (618-907 A.D.). The Su and Bai Causeways divide the lake into three parts.

Xiao Ying Zhou Island

This looks like an island but is actually an area of the lake surrounded by circular embankments which were built with earth dredged from the lake bottom. Constructed in the early part of the seventeenth century, this island is sometimes called "Three Pools Mirroring the Moon" because of the three stone pagodas on the southern part which stand in the water. From the south to north the island is linked by the Nine-Bend Bridge. Xiao Ying Zhou is adorned with attractive buildings and tiered halls. The scenery shifts rapidly as one strolls along, first appearing as "an island in the lake," and then "a lake on the island."

Bai Causeway and Su Causeway

At the northern part of the lake the Bai Causeway begins from the Duanqiao Bridge near Lakeside Park. Spring here is beautiful with peach blossoms and budding willows mingled together. This causeway is low lying and runs a short distance in a south-westerly direction to Solitary Hill. At the foot of this hill one crosses Xiling Bridge to reach the Su Causeway, which runs north and south across the western end of the lake. The Su Causeway is named after Su Dongpo, a poet of the northern Song Dynasty, who undertook the dredging of Xi Hu when he was prefect of Hangzhou. At the southern end is a park called Huagang Guan Yu (Viewing the Fish in Huagang Pond) where one can enjoy the flowers and view the fish.

Huagang Guan Yu

This pond is situated between the Yingpo Bridge and the Suo-lan Bridge. Here a small creek once flowed from nearby Hua-jia Hill and emptied into the lake. According to historical records gardens were built and ponds dug as far back as the Song Dynasty. Different kinds of rare fish were raised for people to view and admire. A special pavilion for watching the fish was built on the south side of the pond during the Qing Dynasty. This spot came to be known as "Viewing the Fish in Huagang Pond."

Crooked Bridge, Xi Hu, Hangzhou

Xi Hu Scenery, Hangzhou

Gu Shan (Solitary Hill)

Gu Shan is the largest island in Xi Hu. It has an area of 47 acres (19 ha.) and it is here one finds Zhongshan Park and other scenic spots. There is also a museum and a library which house the largest collection of cultural artifacts in Zhejiang. From the top of the hill one can get a bird's eye view of the whole lake. Wandering on the hill one comes upon springs and streams among the rocks and caves. There are also pagodas, temples, and cliffs with stone carvings.

Ling Yin Monastery

This magnificent edifice was originally built in 326 A.D. and is one of the great attractions of Hangzhou. Used as a place for spiritual retreat, it was restored in the early part of the twentieth century. Its main temple contains many bas-relief carvings of Buddhas.

Huang Long Dong (Yellow Dragon Cave)

This unusual tourist attraction includes a large rock jutting from the slope of a hill. The rock has been hewn into a dragon's head. From its mouth, spring water spills out and forms a limpid pool. A favorite summer resort is located nearby.

Liuhe Pagoda (Pagoda of Six Harmonies)

This pagoda was built in 970 A.D. and rises high over forested

hills to a height of 198 ft. (58.8 m.). It is constructed with thirteen stories on the outside and seven on the inside. From here
one will have a good view of the river meandering far into the
distance. The grounds are carefully tended and have been
planted with flowers which bloom all year round.

Other Attractions

Hangzhou is a sightseers paradise. Among its other tourist attractions:

Yu Quan or Jade Spring: This natural spring bubbles up near
Clear Ripples Monastery where various kinds of carp are
raised.

Hu Pao or Tiger Spring: This spring has been called "China's
Third-Best Spring." Its crystal-clear water is said to contain
beneficial minerals.

Yun Qi: This is a quiet, restful foot-path stretching through
lovely thick groves of bamboo. It extends for a distance of
1,093 yds. (1,000 m.) and is a very relaxing place to walk and
talk.

Yu Huang Shan or Jade Emperor's Mountain: From its 989 ft.
(300 m.) elevation, one gets a superb view of the town of
Hangzhou and Xi Hu.

*Liu Lang Wen Ying or Listening to Orioles Among the Willows
Park:* What was once a desolate plot overgrown with brambles
has, since 1949, been turned into a spacious and beautiful
park.

Hangzhou Silk and Brocade Mill: Brocades, woven silk pictures, tapestries, cushions, and other goods are produced here.
If you are interested in a tour, please be sure to ask your Lüxingshe guide to make arrangements.

Mei Jia Wu Tea Production Brigade: Longjing (Dragon Well)
tea, one of China's most celebrated green teas, is grown here.
It is famous for its fine color, aroma, flavor, and the beautiful
shape of its leaves.

SHOPPING

There are a myriad of shopping places for the tourist to visit.
Among them are: Hangzhou Friendship Store; Hangzhou An-
tique Store; Xiling Seal Shop; Hangzhou Embroidery Fac-
tory; Zhejiang Arts and Crafts Department Store; Hangzhou
Municipal Arts and Crafts Department Store; Longjing Tea
Store; Shi Feng Tea Store; and the Jiefang Road Department
Store.

HOTELS

There are many small hotels in Hangzhou. They dot the lake shore surrounded by some of the best scenery in Hangzhou.

RESTAURANTS

The chefs are excellent at this resort area and are particularly known for using fresh ingredients. The Lou Wai Lou, near the Hangzhou Hotel, is specially recommended. Most of the Hangzhou specialities are served here including fried shrimp cooked with Longjing tea. Or you may choose from among the many fresh fish offered and it will be cooked to your liking. At the many tea houses you may enjoy fried noodles with mushrooms and noodles with fried shrimp and eel.

A partial listing of the restaurants in Hangzhou follows: Lou Wai Lou; Shan Wai Shan; Hangzhou Restaurant; Zi Wei Guan; Yanan Restaurant; Tian Xiang Lou; Gui Yuan Guan Restaurant; Sucan Zhai (Vegetarian); Tian Wai Tian; Ru Yi Zhai (Vegetarian); and the Zhejiang Restaurant.

Harbin (HARBIN)

Harbin is the capital of the Heilongjiang Province (Heilungkiang Province). Situated in the middle reaches of the Songhua

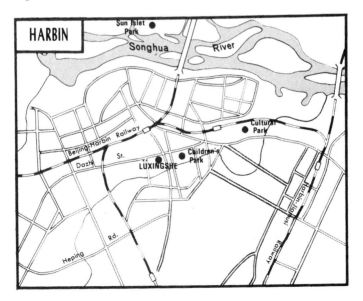

Jiang (Sunghua River), it is a busy river port. As railways and highways converge at Harbin, it is also an important hub of communication.

Harbin used to be a fishing village and its name, in Manchu dialect, means drying fishnets. Unlike most of China, it has a very short history. Harbin was incorporated as a town in 1898. Since 1949 it has become an industrial city. Today you will find factories engaged in the production of automobiles and related products as well as its food processing centers of tobacco and grain.

Scenery here is picturesque. The Songhua Jiang flows through from west to east. In summer the swimming is excellent. Taiyang Dao (Sun Islet) in the northern part of the river is a rest and recuperation area. In winter the scenery is outstanding.

PLACES OF INTEREST

Arts and Crafts Factory

If your tour includes a visit here you will see the various handicrafts of the region including flowers and miniature pavilions made from wheat stalks, feather pictures, and jade carvings.

Heilongjiang Provincial Museum

Built in 1923, this Museum has a collection of some 130,000 historical artifacts and over 100,000 animal specimens. Its

Harbin Monument, Heilongjiang

halls, now open to the public, show the evolution from ape to man as well as displays of prehistoric animals and animals of today.

Taiyang Dao (Sun Islet)

Taiyang Dao is one of northern China's most scenic spots and famous throughout the country as a resort area. This island is in the Songhua Jiang which flows through Harbin. There are many large sanatoriums, lovely villas, fine pavilions, and kiosks surrounded by trees and flower beds.

Children's Railway

Located in Children's Park, this railway was built in 1956. It is managed by children and has two stations, Harbin and Beijing, along its 1.2 mi. (2 km.) length. The toy train has a diesel engine and seven carriages seating 190 passengers. Round trip takes 20 minutes.

Harbin Zoo

Located on the western outskirts of the city, the Harbin Zoo covers 103.8 acres (42 ha.). On display are 149 species of animals and birds, including lions, tigers, leopards, monkeys, bears, and deer. The more notable attractions are the northeast tiger, the red-crown crane, and a fierce bear native to Heilongjiang.

Stalin Park

High above this Park, on the south bank of the Songhua Jiang, is a majestic monument with sculptures on top dedicated to flood fighters. The park itself is landscaped with flowers and trees. It contains various statues, a youth palace, a cultural club, and other public recreational facilities. There is also a good restaurant, a refreshment booth, and a boat house.

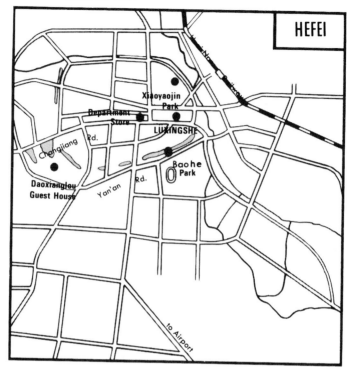

Hefei (HOFEI)

The city of Hefei is located in central Anhui Sheng (Anhwei Province). Today it is not only the provincial capital but also a major industrial city. With a history of over 2,000 years, before 1949 it was a very small consumer city without the ability to produce even a thumbtack. After liberation, emphasis was placed by China on building up the city's resources and now one will find more than four hundred factories. Major industries include iron and steel, machine building, chemicals, electronics, and various light industries. In Hefei there is the capacity for turning out nearly 10,000 different products. The city has now taken on a new look and its population has reached half a million.

PLACES OF INTEREST
Xiao Yao Jin

Legend has it that long ago there was a ford on the Feishui River, in what is now the northeast corner of the city. It is said that at the end of the Eastern Han Dynasty (25-220 A.D.) Sun

Quan was defeated here by Zhang Liao, one of Cao Cao's generals. Today this ancient battlefield is a beautiful park with shady trees and flowering plants. Within the grounds there is a lake for boating in summer or ice skating in winter, tea houses, and restaurants.

Bao Gong Temple

This temple, dedicated to Lord Bao, is located on Xiang Hua Dun (Fragrant Flower Mound) on the Bao He River outside the south gate of Hefei. Lord Bao's reputation as an honest and fearless official and an impartial judge has come down through the ages. As the legend goes this is where Lord Bao, also called Bao Zheng or Bao Xi Ben, once studied in his childhood. He was born in Hefei during the Northern Song Dynasty (970-1127 A.D.) and rose to high office. After 1949 the temple and the river were landscaped into a park called Baohe Park, later renamed People's Park.

Ming Jiao Si Temple

Inside the east gate of Hefei you will find this temple. During the eighth century local officials petitioned the Emperor for a temple to house an 18 ft. (5.5 m.) iron statue of the Buddha. Their request was granted and Ming Jiao Si Temple dates back to that time. Connected to it is the "Terrace for Appointing Generals" which was constructed during the twelfth century.

Hohhot (HUHEHOT)

Hohhot is the capital of the Inner Mongolia Autonomous Region, which was established in May 1947 as the first national minority region in China. The area, bordering with the Soviet Union on the northeast now occupies 424,710 sq. mi. (1,100,000 sq.km.). Its population of 19 million consists of ten percent Mongolians. The remainder are Han and other minorities including Manchu, Hui, and Tahur. Hohhot is known for its grasslands and the major economy is animal husbandry — horses, camels, sheep, and cattle.

Hohhot is north of the Dahei He (Dahei River), a tributary of the Huang He (Yellow River) and is on the Beijing-Baotou Railway line. It is the political, economic, cultural, and communications center of the Inner Mongolia Autonomous Region.

Today Hohhot is one of China's major centers for woolen

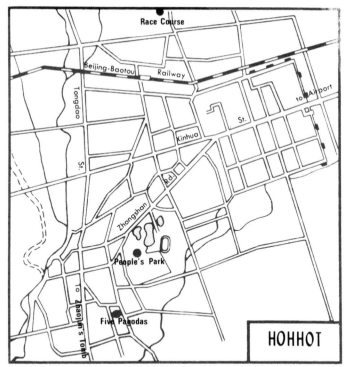

textiles. The city's industrial development has included many factories for woolen textiles, leather, sugar, machinery, iron and steel, construction material, and animal products.

PLACES OF INTEREST

Wu Dang Zhao Monastery

This monastery is in Bastou city, 150 kilometres from Hohhot. It was erected in the middle of the eighteenth century. The grounds cover over 50 acres (20.2 ha.) with a circumference of over 23,100 ft. (7000 m.) Modeled in the Tibetan style after the Budala Palace in Lhasa, Tibet, the building has simple but massive lines and a flat square roof with ridges topped by gilded brick parapets. Many of the rooms are filled with bronze vessels and ornaments. There are seven different halls for Buddhas, halls of the sutras, and a repository for the ashes of "Living Buddhas."

People's Park

This park is 116 acres (46.5 ha.) in area and has a lake covering 25 acres (10.4 ha.). It contains a Martyrs Tower, a zoo, a beautiful flower garden, a water sports area, and a recreation area. More than six hundred animals are housed in the zoo. At the "water sports" area, boating is popular in spring, summer, and autumn; and in the winter, it is a wonderful place to go ice skating.

Zhao Jun Tomb

This is also known as Qing Zhong (Green Grave). The tomb is that of Wang Zhaojun, a concubine of Emperor Yuan Di of the Han Dynasty (206 B.C.-220 A.D.), who was married off to Chan Yu, King of the Xiongnu Tribe in 33 B.C.

Wu Ta Pavilion

This site has several names, "Five Pagodas," and "Diamond Pagoda for Buddhist Relics." Built in 1732 A.D., it is 29 ft. (7.8 m.) high. The upper part of Wu Ta consists of five square-topped pagodas on a pedstal, the highest one, in the center, is 21 ft. (6.3 m.) tall. The pagodas are of masonry faced by beautifully carved glazed brick on which appears writings in Mongolian, Tibetan, and Sanskrit.

Carpet Works

This factory specializes in reproducing carpets following ancient designs. Lovely to look at as well as extremely practical, the rugs are all faithful reproductions of excellent workmanship.

Ranchers weaving wooden frame of their round houses,
Xinjiang Uygur Zizhiqu

SHOPPING

The department store in Hohhot is a two-story building worth a visit to see the people both from the city and from the grasslands. They sell Mongolian costumes, skull caps, blankets, and other local handicraft products.

HOTELS

There is one major hotel here, the Hohhot Hotel. The rooms are comfortable and the dining room is excellent. Mongolian mutton is their speciality and is superb.

Wu Ta Pavilion, Hohhot

Fog Pines of Huang Shan

Huang Shan (YELLOW MOUNTAIN)

Huang Shan is south of the Changjiang (Yangtze River) in Anhui Sheng (Anhwei Province). The mountain is truly magnificent with its many peaks. Its natural landscape has remained largely untouched except for the construction of roads and houses.

Huang Shan is memorable for its clouds and changes in weather. Sometimes seas of clouds enshroud the peaks, leaving only the tops peeping out like islands. Its pine trees grow in rock crevices in unusual forms, some hanging upside down and some spreading out horizontally. The steep peaks are comprised of piles of strangely shaped rocks, split by deep secluded ravines. The static pines and rocks against the restless, moving clouds create changing scenes of great natural beauty.

193

PLACES OF INTEREST
Hot Springs
Water from the springs is odorless and good to drink. It contains minerals beneficial in the treatment of gastric ailments, skin afflictions, and rheumatism. Hot Springs is one of the many attractions of Huang Shan. Gushing forth from the foot of Purple Cloud Peak, the springs never run dry even during the most severe droughts, nor overflow their channels during excessive rains. All the year the temperature of the water remains at 104° Fahrenheit (40° Celsius). Pools have been built for drinking, swimming, and medicinal baths.

Lian Hua Feng (Lotus Flower Peak)
The mountain peak called Lian Hua Feng towers above all others. It is the highest peak with an elevation of 6,138 ft. (1,860 m.). Famous pines such as the "Flying Dragon" and the "Twin Dragons" are found here. From the summit the neighboring peaks look dwarfed and in the distance the whole scene gradually merges into one shade of color.

Meng Bi Sheng Hua (Tip of a Magic Writing Brush)
Meng Bi Sheng Hua, rising out of the profusion of trees and flowers, is a pillar of stone tapering into a sharp point on which stands a twisted old pine. People metaphorically describe it as the "Tip of a Magic Writing Brush," that is, a brush painting all the lovely scenes of Huang Shan.

Shi Xin Feng (Beginning to Believe Peak)
Unlike some of the others, this peak is small and dainty but it has a charm of its own. It is noted for its gorgeous greenery and quaint rock shapes. The beauty of the Huang Shan is so captivating one can't help feeling as if one has stepped into a Chinese landscape painting and exclaiming, "Now I believe it." Hence the name, "Beginning to Believe."

Pai Yun Ting (Cloud Dispelling Pavilion)
This pavilion is particularly interesting because it has in its vicinity an abundance of fantastic rocks. Each rock has its own name denoting what it resembles. You can make out "An Immortal Sunning His Boots," "A Celestial Maid Embroidering," "A Fairy Maiden Playing the Lute," "Wu Song Fighting the Tiger," and "An Immortal on Stilts."

Hua Shan (HUASHAN MOUNTAIN)

The Hua Shan is in Shaanxi Sheng (Shensi Province) approximately 72 mi. (120 km.) east of Xi'an (Sian). The mountain is 7,986 ft. (2,433.8 m.) above sea level and is magnificent with

Sacred Mountain on Hua Shan

its three peaks. The Tomb of Qinshihuang, the first emperor of the Qin Dynasty (221-206 B.C.), was recently excavated here.

In ancient times, some mountains were considered sacred in China. Hua Shan was one of the most famous, considered the most revered mountain in western China. The three peaks are called Lotus Peak, Immortal's Peak, and Peak Where the Wild Geese Land. At the foot of the mountain is where sacrifices were made as part of the many religious pilgrimages that journeyed to Hua Shan.

Walking you will come across pine trees, springs, and waterfalls. There are inns, restaurants, and small shops in the area.

Jiayuguan Pass (CHIAYUKUAN PASS)

Jiayuguan Pass is situated at the southeastern foot of Jiayu Hill in Gansu Sheng (Kansu Province). Built in 1372 A.D. it is the terminal point (or the western extremity) of the Great Wall. From the gate tower of Jiayuguan Pass one sees the snow-covered Qilian Shan (Chilien Mountains) in the distance and the rugged and imposing Jiayu Hill. One also sees the Great Wall winding its way up and down the mountain ridges.

Jiayuguan Pass of the Great Wall

The view from the gate tower is inspiring. Here one naturally calls to mind the famous lines of a Tang poet:

"Bright the moon as in Qin times,
Under the Han, this same pass,
10,000 li away in distant climes,
Loved ones have still not come back."

Jilin (KIRIN)

Surrounded by mountains and hills, Jilin is a beautiful city in northeast China in Jilin Sheng (Kirin Province). After 1949, to take advantage of the province's rich supply of chemical raw materials, three big chemical plants were built: Jilin Chemical Fertilizer Plant, Jilin Fuel Plant, and the Jilin Carbide Factory. The Jilin Thermal Power Plant was built to provide power for these enterprises.

Jilin also has an abundant supply of ginseng, sable, and antlers. Spring, summer, and autumn are ideal times to visit. If your trip coincides with the winter season, skiing and ice skating are very popular here.

PLACES OF INTEREST
Songhua Lake

This man-made lake flows through Jilin. Fed by water from the Changbai Shan (Changpai Mountains), it covers 185 sq. mi. (480 sq. km.) and has a storage capacity of 353 billion cubic feet (10 million cubic meters). It is a multi-purpose project for power generation, flood prevention, irrigation, raising fish, and navigation. The lake is as smooth as a mirror and is surrounded by forested hills. It is a good place for year-round fishing.

197

Songhua River

The waters of Songhua Lake, after running through the turbines of the Fengman Power Station, enter the Songhua River. Cool in summer and warm in winter, the river does not freeze over even in the coldest weather. It acts as a natural temperature regulator for the city of Jilin. It is a lovely stroll along the willow-lined embankments in summer. In the winter the clouds of water vapor rising off the river turn the willows and pines into a frosted scene from fairyland. It is one of the most picturesque sights in North China.

Beishan Park (North Hill Park)

This lovely park occupies a hilly area of about 320 acres (128 ha.) in the northwestern part of the city. On the main peak which stands 891 ft. (270 m.) above sea level is a collection of old buildings. Two beautiful pavilions face each other from the top of two hills. Below, the two hills are connected by Phoenix Harness Bridge across an artificial lake. In summer, when the lotus is in full bloom and the trees provide shade, people come here to picnic or to row on the lake.

Jinggang Shan

Jinggang Shan (CHINGKANG MOUNTAIN)

Jinggang Shan lies in the middle section of the Luoxiao Shan (Lohsiao Mountains) on the borders of Hunan and Jiangxi. In

October 1927 Chairman Mao led the forces of the Autumn Harvest Uprising to the Jinggang and established the first armed independent regime of workers and peasants.

Ci Ping, a village in the Jinggang Shan, was the military center of the revolutionary base area and was also the seat of the leading offices of the government and army in the Hunan-Jiangxi Border Region. Some of the original buildings are still there and have been turned into museums.

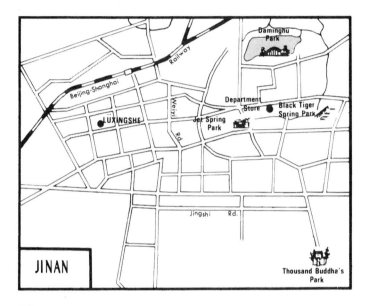

Jinan (TSINAN)

Jinan, capital of Shandong Sheng (Shantung Province) is on the southern bank of Huang He (Yellow River), north of Tai Shan (Mt. Taishan). The Beijing-Shanghai and Qingdao-Jinan Railways meet here. It is one of China's most prosperous cities with a population of 1,200,000.

Industries situated in Jinan produce machine tools, fertilizers and other chemicals, and textiles. It is also known for its peanuts, tobacco, fruits, and vegetables. As the provincial cultural center it houses several universities, theaters, and cinemas. Perhaps its most famous tourist attraction is its bubbling springs.

The town walls were built over 2,600 years ago when the city was called Lu although recent excavations have uncovered evidence of civilization dating back to the Shang Dynasty (1766-1122 B.C.). The name was changed to Jinan 2,100 years ago because it was located to the south of the ancient Jishui River (whose course corresponds roughly to the lower reaches of the present Huang He). In 1116 A.D. Jinan was established as a prefecture and in 1368 A.D. it became the provincial capital. Jinan was incorporated as a city in 1929.

PLACES OF INTEREST
Bao Tu Springs
This park, also called Jet Spring Park, is located in downtown Jinan. It has sixteen jet springs of varying sizes, the largest having three fountains bubbling day and night. Its water is so pure and sweet that people call it "The First Spring Under Heaven."

Da Ming Lake
The natural beauty of this park is enhanced by a lake surrounded by hills dotted with pavilions, kiosks, halls, and towers. The lakeside is lined with weeping willows swaying over beds of lotus. The park holds flower shows and ceramics exhibitions.

Hei Hu Springs
Hei Hu (Black Tiger) Springs is one of the four major groups of springs in Jinan. From a deep cave, water gushes forcefully and noisily through the stone, tiger-head gargoyles.

Liu Bu (Willow Grove Monuments)
Liu Bu, with its collection of interesting artifacts, is located 21 mi. (34 km.) southeast of Jinan. Of historic interest are the ancient buildings and stone statues dating from the sixth through the eighth centuries. Among the sights you will see are the Four-Portal Pagoda, the Dragon and Tiger Pagoda, and Thousand Buddha Cliff.

Qian Fo Shan (Thousand Buddha Hill)
The well-known Qian Fo Shan towers over all like a green jade screen 1.5 mi. (2.5 km.) south of Jinan. Its scenic spots include Xing Guo (Revive the Country) Monastery, Long Quan (Dragon Spring) Cave, and Yi Lan (Panoramic View) Pavilion.

Shandong Provincial Museum

The museum was built in 1954 for the protection and display of valuable cultural relics unearthed and collected from various parts of the province. The exhibits include production tools, articles of daily use, and objects of cultural and artistic value from primitive, slave, and feudal societies.

SHOPPING

There are a variety of shopping opportunities in Jinan. A favorite purchase of visitors would be the lovely feathered pictures which are made here by cutting and pasting together the feathers of pheasants, peacocks, and swans. Stores which should be visited are: Jinan Municipal Friendship Store, Shandong Provincial Antique Store, and the Jinan Municipal Arts and Crafts Department Store.

RESTAURANTS

If your itinerary includes Jinan, there are many restaurants to choose from, among which are Ju Feng De Restaurant, Jiang Quan Restaurant, Yan Xi Tang Restaurant, and Da Ming Hu Restaurant.

Jingdezhen (CHINGTEHCHEN)

The town was called Xinpin in ancient times. Pottery was produced here as early as the Han Dynasty (206 B.C.-220 A.D.). The town became the center for porcelain-making during the Jingde Reign (1004-1007 A.D.) of the Northern Song Dynasty. Porcelain produced in that period carried these words, "Made in the Jingde Region," hence the present name Jingdezhen. Over the centuries Jingdezhen porcelain has developed a unique style which has made it world famous. It is white as jade, clear as a mirror, thin as paper, and resounds like a musical instrument. Jingdezhen porcelain can be found in wide variety and with very fine decorations.

Soon after 1949 small, privately-owned workshops were turned into large, state-owned ones and art galleries were set up. Various part-time schools, with lectures and demonstrations on ceramics, have been organized by the large ceramics factories. To improve the quality and artistic style, scientific

Porcelain plate from Jingdezhen

experiments have been carried out on a large scale. Bowls, plates, cups, and pots are produced in complete sets. Some sets consist of a dozen pieces, others as many as one hundred pieces. There is a greater variety in the design and color of vases, porcelain lamps, and writing accessories today than there was in 1949. The use of pottery and porcelain for industrial purposes is also increasing.

The basic change in Jingdezhen has been the increase in the amount of factory buildings. Otherwise the town is much as it was decades ago. Located in Jiangxi Sheng (Kiangsi Province), its current population is over 250,000 people all connected with the manufacture of porcelain and related industries.

PLACES OF INTEREST
Jingdezhen Museum
This small museum was recently opened. It houses many examples of porcelain which trace the history of the town and the history of the porcelain industry and how they are interrelated.

Fu Liang Cheng Pagoda
This pagoda dates back to the Song Dynasty (960-1280 A.D.). It is on a small hill several miles from the center of town.

Jinghong (CHINGHUNG)
Jinghong, formerly known as Cheli, is a county in the center of Xishuangbanna (Hsishuang Panna Autonomous Prefecture of Tai Nationality) in Yunnan Sheng (Yunnan Province). It was the seat of the Cheli Civil and Military Governor General's Office successively through three dynasties (1271-1911 A.D.). In 1927 it was renamed Cheli County and in 1954 made into four bannas (meaning "counties" in the Dai language) — Jinghong, Menglong, Mengyang, and Mengwang. It was again merged into Banna Jinghong County in 1960. The Lancang Jiang (Lancang River) runs obliquely across the territory which is inhabited by the Dai, Han, Hani, and other nationalities.

Jinghong abounds in rice, sugar cane, tea, cotton, teak, and a large variety of fruit. It also produces camphor, sisal hemp, shellac, and rubber. Industrial development in the fields of electric power, metallurgy, machine tools, tea processing, sugar refining, and timber processing has been notable since 1949.

China has fifty-five minority nationalities living in border and mountain regions. The Dais, exceeding 500,000 in all, live in compact communities in Xishuangbanna and elsewhere in Yunnan. Records in the Han language about this nationality date back to the first century A.D. Envoys with entourages of musicians and magicians were sent to Luoyang, the capital of the Eastern Han Dynasty by the Dai chieftain, on whom the court conferred the title of Grand Governor General of the Han. Ties between the Dai and other nationalities were developed and consolidated.

Before 1949 all mountains and forests here belonged to the feudal lords who controlled the army, the courts, and the prisons. Savage tortures were often employed. The people had no personal freedom. Methods of agricultural production were extremely backward. With the manorial system abolished and land distribution after 1949, the Dai people and other minority nationalities enjoy full freedom and equal political rights. Great efforts have been made by the government to help develop local industries, agriculture, culture, education, and health service.

The Dais have a written language and a calendar of their own. Their New Year falls in the first half of April. This is their biggest annual traditional celebration, also known as the Water-Splashing Festival. Tradition has it that people splashed each other with water in memory of some legendary Dai girls who had fought to rid the people of a fire demon. During the festival other activities to ward off diseases and disaster, to invoke good grain harvests, and to enlarge the herds during the coming year include boating and displays of bamboo firecrackers. When Han cadres working in this area and local inhabitants of other nationalities pay their New Year visits to Dai villages, they are also greeted with water splashing by way of welcome.

The Dai people have a rich and colorful culture; they are especially good singers and dancers. Traditional folk singers have always been popular. The peacock dance, the fish dance, the elephant-foot drum, and the mang gong are unique creations of this nationality. The Dais are also fine sculptors and painters.

Peacock Dance of the Dai Nationality, Yunnan

PLACES OF INTEREST

Menghan Temple

This temple is 6 mi. (9.7 km.) outside of Jinghong. Built in ancient times to revere Buddha, the special Hall in this temple is unique as the statue is in the center of the building. The temple also has a tall pagoda.

Menghai Temple

In the opposite direction, approximately 18 mi. (29 km.) outside the city one will find this temple. It is much larger than the Menghan consisting of a covered passageway, monks' living quarters, libraries, and many other small halls. It also has two pagodas, both square, with intricately carved statues of animals around the outside.

Jiuhua Shan (NINE FLOWERS MOUNTAIN)

Mt. Jiuhua, an ideal summer resort, is in Qingyang County, Anhui Province. On this scenic mountain of ninety-nine peaks one finds caves, springs, waterfalls, and ancient trees. In the Han Dynasty it was also known as Mount Ling Yang or Mount Jiu Zi. Traveling down the Changjiang, the famous Tang poet Li Bai (Li Po) likened the mountain to nine lotus flowers:

> *"Looking far ahead from Jiujiang;*
> *I saw the peaks of Mount Jiuhua*
> *Emerging from the Heavenly River*
> *Like nine beautiful lotus flowers."*

Hence Mount Jiu Zi was renamed Jiuhua (nine flowers).

Between the foot of the mountain and the summit of Tian Tai (Heavenly Terrace Peak), there are a large number of ancient temples, monasteries, and other monuments. The earliest temple was built in the Eastern Jin Dynasty (317-420 A.D.), but the place reached its prime only in the Ming and Qing Dynasties (1368-1911 A.D.) when the number of ancient temples had grown to about three hundred. Only fifty-six, mostly of that period, remain today. Among them the more notable are Rou Shen Bao Dian (The Hall of Monk Wuxia's Figure in Sitting Posture), Qi Yuan Si (Temple of Earth God Garden), Bai Sui Gong (Longevity Palace), and Tian Tai Zheng Ding (The Pinnacle of the Heavenly Terrace). They have in their keeping more than 1,300 ancient documents, seals, fine pieces of calligraphy, paintings, and Buddhist scriptures.

Jiuhua is one of the four famous Buddhist mountains. The others are Pu Tuo of Zhejiang, Emei of Sichuan, and Wutai of Shansi. Poets of many dynasties have described Mount Jiuhua in glowing colors. For example, Liu Mengde of the Tang Dynasty wrote: *"Nine peaks vying to show their beauty — a fantastic view one cannot but admire."* He showed his admiration of the strange rock formations in these lines:

> *"Nine Dragons flew up majestically to prop the sky,*
> *A sudden clap of thunder and they became rocks towering high."*

Su Zimei and Wang Anshi of the Song Dynasty compared the peaks to Celestial Beings: *"Nine immortals treading on air are dimly discernible among the clouds."* They and other poets have made the mountain popular throughout the country.

Jiujiang (CHIUCHIANG)

The city of Jiujiang, in Jiangxi Sheng (Jiangxi Province), lies on the south bank of Changjiang (Yangtze River) in its middle reaches. To the north of Lushan, it is near the Boyang Lake and faces Hubei Province across the river. It is, therefore, generally known as the gateway to Jiangxi.

Jiujiang is famous for its traditional arts and crafts, leather goods, bamboo, and wood products. Crunchy candies, tea cakes, and sealed-vat wine, all of which have a long history, are delicacies at home and abroad.

The city is an important port on the Changjiang the terminus of the railway to Nanchang (capital of the province), and the center of a network of highways leading to Nanchang, Xiushui County, Jingdezhen, and Lushan.

Through history Jiujiang has always been an important port for China and for the province. This is still true today with tea and porcelain being two of its major export products.

PLACES OF INTEREST
Gantang Lake

The lake, originally named the Jingxing Lake, covers an area of about 45 acres (18.2 ha.) and is in the center of the city. It is a natural lake fed by clear water flowing down from the Lushan Mountain. A gentle breeze springing up on the lake stirs the blue ripples, ruffles the reflection of the mountain, and sways the soft willows on the banks. On one end there is a dyke 165 ft. (50 m.) long, built by Governor Li Bo in 821 A.D. (Tang Dynasty). After 1949, it was raised, widened, and covered with asphalt. The Si Xian Bridge, built in the Sung Dynasty (960-1280 A.D.) has been repaired and painted. The dyke, now lined with trees and landscape gardening, is a very attractive sight.

The Yanshui Pavilion

The pavilion on the lake covers an area of 19,872 sq. ft. (1,840 sq. m). According to the "Annals of Jiujiang," Governor Li Bo, when building the dyke, constructed a moon-shaped sluice gate in the middle of the lake. Zhou Dunyi, of the Sung Dynasty, added the pavilion which was first named Qin Yue (Moon on the Lake) and then renamed Yanshui (Vapor on Water), derived from the poetic line, "Hill and water shrouded in vapor." In 1573 A.D., the Ming General, Huang Tengchun, rebuilt the pavilion. Most of the existing structures in it were built towards the end of the Qing Dynasty (1644-1911 A.D.) by the monk, Gu Huai, with money received from donations. The main structures are: the Wharf, Chung Yang Hall, Cui Zhao Veranda, Wu Xian Studio, Zhong Miao Chamber, and the Yi Pavilion. Besides the sluice gate there are two stone scabbards, meant symbolically to house the Shuang Jian (Double Sword) Peak of Lushan Mountain.

In 1972 the pavilion underwent large-scale repairs and was turned into an exhibition hall for historical relics. On display are four hundred objects of historical value collected by the people of the prefecture and the province. A winding bridge has been added so that the visitors can walk from the bank to the pavilion. The splendor of the architecture, the fragrance of the flowers, the freshness of the willows, the attractiveness of the fish — all these are there, inspiring one to write a poem or paint a picture.

Jiuquan (CHIUCHUAN)

Jiuquan, in the western part of Gansu (Kansu) Province, used to be an important town on the road to Central Asia, Western Asia, and Europe in Han, Tang and later dynaties. It was also where the famous "Silk Road" passed.

PLACES OF INTEREST
Jiuquan Spring

It was said that a general of the Han Dynasty named Huo Qubin poured a jar of wine bestowed by Emperor Wudi into a spring pool to share with all his soldiers. Hence the name, Jiuquan, meaning Wine Spring.

Drum Tower of Jiuquan

Jiuquan was famous in Central Asia and Europe by the name "Suzhou." In the thirteenth century, the Venetian merchant Marco Polo praised Jiuquan in his writings. Now all the beautiful ancient buildings of his age have gone except the fourth-century Drum Tower standing at the center of the town.

Jiayuguan Pass

This magnificent castle dating back more than 600 years, is

surrounded by a square-shaped wall more than 765 yds. (700 m.) long and covers an area of more than 7½ acres (30,000 sq. m.) One has a fantastic view of the desert at the top of the castle.

Mural Paintings of the East Jin Dynasty (317-420 B.C.)

Found in a tomb chamber at Dingjiazha, Jiuquan, the attractive paintings are rich both in color and content. They vividly illustrate ancient myths and legends as well as the life and labor of human beings of the period. These paintings have a longer history than the Dunhuang Murals, but there is a similarity in style between the two.

Kaifeng (KAIFENG)

Kaifeng is in Henan (Honan Province) on the banks of the Huang He (Yellow River). Kaifeng has five districts and one county under its jurisdiction covering a total area of 96 sq. mi. (491 sq. km.).

With a history of three thousand years, Kaifeng is known throughout the world as one of the six major centers of ancient Chinese civilization. As early as the Yin-Shang period (c. 1324-1066 B.C.), when Chinese society turned away from nomadic life to an agricultural existence, a city was built here. It then became the capital of seven different dynasties. The magnificent buildings,preserved until this day, display the great talent and creative power of the people in ancient China.

Before 1949 there was limited industry in Kaifeng. After liberation several large, up-to-date factories were built to include chemical processing and the manufacture of agricultural machinery. As the Longhai Railway passes through Kaifeng, it has grown as a distribution center for nearby communities. Today it has a population of 530,000 and agriculture is still an important part of life here.

PLACES OF INTEREST
Tieta (Iron Pagoda)

This is a thirteen-story octagonal pagoda of glazed brick, 180 ft. (54.7 m.) high, erected in the first year of Emperor Huangyou of the Northern Song Dynasty (1049 A.D.). From a distance the pagoda appears to be made of cast iron because of its color, hence its name, Tieta or Iron Pagoda.

Longting (Dragon Pavilion)

This interesting pavilion is a legacy of the Qing Dynasty (1644-1911 A.D.). A pair of large, imposing stone lions guard the front of the pavilion. Inside you will see an immense stone pedestal with beautiful carvings of dragons and clouds.

Iron Tower of Kaifeng

Yuwangtai (King Yu Terrace)

This was originally called Chuitai (Music Terrace). According to legend more than 2,500 years ago Shi Kuang, a noted musician of the state of Jin, once performed here. Under the Ming Dynasty a temple was built on the terrace in honor of the legendary King Yu who tamed the floods. It was renamed then Yuwangtai or King Yu Terrace.

Xiangguosi (Prime Minister Monastery)

This monastery was first established in 555 A.D. It has several large and interesting halls including Great Treasure Hall and Octagonal Hall. In the latter there is a statue of Guanyin (Goddess of Mercy) of a Thousand Arms and a Thousand Eyes carved out of ginkgo wood. The posture is expressive and the workmanship superb.

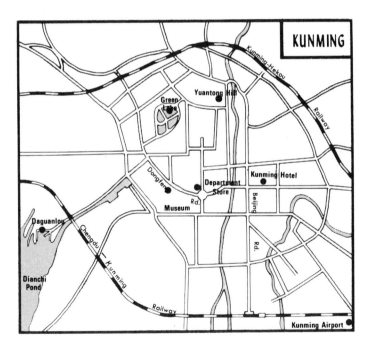

Kunming (KUNMING)

Terminus of "The Burma Road" of World War II, Kunming, the capital of Yunnan Sheng (Yunnan Province) is a city on

China's southwestern frontier. It is inhabited by many Chinese minorities and has a history of more than two thousand years.

Before 1949 the city had only fifty or so small factories and workshops. Today the number of enterprises exceeds four hundred including metallurgy, machine tools, electric power, textiles, optical instruments, printing and dyeing, and chemical and plastics industries. There is also a medium-sized iron and steel complex. Kunming machine tools and optical instruments are held in high repute throughout the country.

The rapid growth in industry coupled with Kunming's location (it is a center for rail and air services), has turned the city into one of China's more prosperous industrial centers with a population of well over one million people.

PLACES OF INTEREST
Dian Chi Lake

Dian Chi, or Tienchih Lake, is to the south of the City and is also known as Kunming Lake. It covers an area of some 120 sq. mi. (300 sq. km.) and was formed by a fault on the Central Yunnan Plateau. A cruise on the lake, which reflects the surrounding hills, is a memorable experience.

Xishan (Western Hills)

As you see Xishan from a distance, this thickly forested area on the western shores of Dian Chi coupled with the undulating ranges of the mountains, presents a grand spectacle. Xishan or Western Hills is really four hills: Huating, Taihua, Taiping, and Lohan. They lie in a line to form a contour which resembles a sleeping beauty with her hair flowing down to the sea. Therefore Xishan is also called "Sleeping Beauty Mountain." Forests stretch for several miles with ancient buildings such as Huating Temple, Taihua Temple, and Sanqing Pavilion nestling, almost invisible, among the thick foliage. The mountain commands a complete view of the city and of Dian Chi.

Daguanlou

Daguanlou or Grand View Mansion was first built in 1690 A.D. on the shores of Dian Chi. It is now a beautiful park covering a total of 150 acres (60 ha.) of land and water. In front of the ancient mansion are a pair of scrolls containing a poetic

Exercise class on shore of Dian Chi, Kunming

couplet of some 180 characters written in clear, bold strokes by the Qing poet, Sun Ranweng. The right side of the famous couplet praises the beauty of Kunming, the left reflects on great vicissitudes in Chinese history. It is the longest couplet that is known to have been composed in China.

Qiongzhusi Temple

The temple known as Qiongzhusi was built in the early years of the Yuan Dynasty (1280-1368 A.D.) on the Yuan (Jade Table) Hill in the western suburbs. It contains five hundred Luohans (clay figures) which took Li Guangxiu, a Sichuan folk artist under the Qing, seven years to complete. Simple in style yet extremely life-like, this collection of clay figures is nationally recognized as a remarkable example of ancient Chinese sculpture.

Yuantong Park

This mountain park contains a zoo with some four hundred animals. One unique feature: flowers are cultivated in four different gardens according to their blooming seasons. Oriental cherry trees are in the Spring Garden, camellias and magnolias in the Summer Garden, sweet cassia in the Autumn Garden, and plum trees in the Winter Garden. The Spring Garden is perhaps the most magnificent. It has a collection of several thousand Yunnan and Japanese cherry trees which, in full bloom, look like crimson clouds floating in the distance.

Anningwenquan (Tranquil Hot Springs)

One of the most famous hot springs in China, Anningwenquan or Tranquil Hot Springs, is located 24 mi. (40 km.) from Kunming. The water, pure enough to drink and warm enough to bathe in, gushes out at a rate of 1,700 tons every twenty-four hours. An ideal vacation and health resort, Anningwenquan is known as the "First Hot Spring Under Heaven."

SHOPPING

There are a variety of shopping opportunities to be found in the following stores: Yunnan Provincial Antique Store, Yunnan Provincial Arts and Crafts Department Store, Kunming Municipal Arts and Crafts Department Store, Kunming Department Store, and the Yunnan Nationalities Trade Store.

RESTAURANTS

Two of the larger restaurants located in Kunming are Kunming Restaurant and Beijing Restaurant. Both will provide superb examples of various styles of Chinese cuisine.

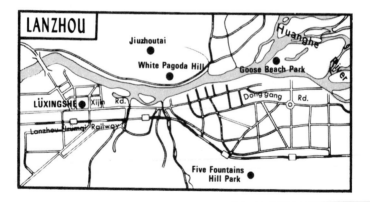

Lanzhou (LANCHOW)

Lanzhou, a city in the central part of Gansu Sheng (Kansu Province) is the provincial capital. Located in the northern foothills of the Gaolan Shan (Kaolan Mountains), the Huang He (Yellow River) flows through the city. Since ancient times it has been an important communications hub between southwest and northwest China and the Central Plains. Since 1949 railway lines have been built linking Lanzhou to Tianshui,

Wu Quan Park, Lanzhou

Ürümqi, Baotou, and Xining. As a result, the city's position has been greatly enhanced.

Lanzhou is definitely the economic, cultural, and communications center of the Province. Several universities and colleges are located there. It has also become an important industrial city engaged mainly in oil refining, machine tool manufacture, the weaving of woolen textiles, and the production of chemicals. Today the population is close to one million and still growing.

PLACES OF INTEREST
Wu Quan Hill
Wu Quan or Five-Spring Hill is located to the south of Lanzhou and as its name implies, has five springs: Hui Spring, Juyue Spring, Mozi Spring, Ganlu Spring, and Meng Spring. Of particular interest is the Chong Qing Temple, later dates back to 1374 A.D. Artifacts in the shrine include the Tai He (Great Harmony) Bell, and statues, cast in bronze, of Buddhist attendants.

Bai Ta (White Pagoda)
On a hill north of the city of Lanzhou is Bai Ta, a seven-storied white brick pagoda built during the reign of Emperor

Jingtai (1450-1456 A.D.) of the Ming Dynasty. Below the pagoda there are Ming bronze bells, elephant skin drums, and other relics. After 1949 the pagoda was renovated and new pavilions, promenades, and towers were constructed in the environs. Water can now be pumped to the top of the hill so trees have been planted which adds to the beauty of Bai Ta.

Workers' Cultural Palace
Of particular interest are cypresses from the Han Dynasty (206 B.C.-220 A.D.) and locust trees from the Tang Dynasty (618-907 A.D.) as well as famous frescos considered to be of high artistic value.

Yan Tan Park
In the northeastern part of Lanzhou is Yan Tan Park with an artificial lake and swimming pool. The surrounding area abounds in vegetables, melons, and other fruit. More than twenty-five varieties of apples are grown here.

Leshan (LESHAN)
Leshan, once known as Jiading or Jiazhou, is a thirteen-hundred-year-old city in southwestern Sichuan Sheng (Szechuan Province) where the Min Jiang (Minchiang River) and the Dadu He (Tatu River) converge. It is a junction for land and water traffic along the way to southern Sichuan.

PLACES OF INTEREST
Lingyun and Wulong Hills
The main scenic spots of Leshan are found on Lingyun (Cloud High Hill) and Wulong (Black Dragon Hill) which tower over the city separated by a stream.

On Lingyun Hill an enormous Buddha, 231 ft. (70 m.) tall sits erect with an armed guard standing on either side. It is carved into a cliff overlooking three rivers. To the left a path with nine turnings winds down the cliff from the top of the Buddha's head, at the crest of the hill, to the statue's feet. Legend has it that Monk Hai Tong of Lingyun Monastery, disturbed to see so many boats capsizing in the turbulent river, initiated the carving of this Buddha to subdue the waters and ensure the safety of the boatmen. It was completed in the

19th year (803 A.D.) of the reign of Zhenyuan in the Tang Dynasty after ninety years of work. The figure, not only a great work of art, incorporates the unique technical features of hidden drains which have been skillfully cut through the body to prevent the surface from weathering.

Wulong Hill, southeast of Lingyun, stands along surrounded by water and covered with bamboo and other trees. Wulong Monastery, built in the middle of the Tang Dynasty, is on the hill. Here a small museum has been set up with calligraphy, painting, Buddhist canonical books, and other artifacts of various dynasties. Also included are stone inscriptions by Su Dongpo, a noted man of letters of the Song Dynasty.

For the convenience of visitors a regular motorboat service to Lingyun and Wulong is now available. A road has been built up the hills and they are also linked by a suspension bridge.

Lhasa (LHASA)

Lhasa is the capital of the Tibet Autonomous Region. In the Tibetan language, Lhasa means "the sacred place." Buddhism is prevalent here. Therefore, there are many old temples and monasteries. Besides the well known and ancient Potala Palace, the Drepung Monastery (1416 A.D.) and Sera Monastery (1419 A.D.) enjoy great fame for their marvelous architecture and splendid decoration.

Before the liberation, there were no highways in Tibet and transportation was most inconvenient. Now, Lhasa is the junction for the Sichuan-Tibet and the Qinghai-Tibet Highways. There is direct air service connecting Lhasa with Chengdu and Xian.

PLACES OF INTEREST
The Potala Palace

The Potala Palace was built on the Red Hill of Lhasa in the seventh century. The Tibetan King, Songtsen Gampo, built it for his wife, Princess Wen Cheng of the Tang Dynasty, who came from Xian to Lhasa to marry him. The Potala Palace, a thirteen-story building containing 1,000 rooms, can be seen from many miles away.

The Jokhang Temple

The magnificent Jokhang Temple is situated in the center of Lhasa. In front of the gate stands a stone tablet from the Tang Dynasty, on which both Chinese characters and Tibetan script were inscribed. Nearby is the Tang willow tree planted by Princess Wen Cheng. They indicate the traditional friendship between the Han and Tibetan peoples.

The Norbulingka

Situated in a western suburb of Lhasa, the Norbulingka is a large, walled park thickly shaded by lush trees and aglow with flowers. Bridges span the clear brooks which flow past graceful pavilions. The park used to be the summer palace of the Dalai Lama. Now people come here on holiday.

Lianyun Gang (LIENYUN HARBOR)

With hills behind it the Lianyun Gang of Jiangsu Sheng (Kiangsu Province) faces the Dong Hai (East China Sea). Its many scenic spots, especially Yun Tai Hill, attract visitors throughout the year.

PLACES OF INTEREST
Yun Tai

Also referred to as Terrace of Clouds Hill, this may very well be the Flowers and Fruit Mountain described in the famous Ming Dynasty novel "Pilgrimage to the West," where Sun Wu Kong, the celebrated Monkey King, found his favorite haunt, the Water Curtain Cave. Three other places in China, Jiu Qu (Nine Bends) Stream of Wu Yi Mountain in Fujian Province; Mt. Heng Shan in Hunan Province; and Binxian County of Shaanxi Province make the same claim, but Yun Tai Hill bears the closest resemblance. The author of the novel, Wu Cheng'en, was also a native of Huai'an Prefecture, a town not far from Lianyun Gang.

In the ancient past it might indeed have been an isolated hill in the sea for, as the story goes, "The country of Aolai is close to the sea in which there is a famous hill." Today's Yun Tai Hill in springtime, when the bright flowers are in full bloom, still looks like a place in fairyland. Though the cataract is no more, gazing at the cliff one can still conjure up the sight of a magnificent waterfall cascading down over it. The hilltop commands a beautiful view of the sea.

Along the shore is a vast expanse of salt fields which look like a plain covered with snow. An ancient pagoda rises from amidst golden ripples of blossoms. It was built by the Tang Dynasty general, Yuchi Gong. At the top of the hill stands San Yuan Gong, a Taoist monastery.

Liuzhou (LIUCHOU)

Liuzhou is a rising industrial city situated by the Liu Jiang (Liu River) in the center of the Guangxi Zhuang (Kwangsi Chuang) Autonomous Region. It is the junction of the Hunan-Guangxi and Guizhou-Guangxi railways which link central-south China with southwest China. Liuzhou has a mild climate, abundant resources, and beautiful scenery.

To the south by the Liu Jiang there is the Ma'anshan Hill rising straight out of the ground. From the top, the view of the city is lovely. The Liu Jiang flows from north to south, and is spanned by a railway bridge close to Eshan Hill. It then turns gradually eastward. A highway bridge crosses it as it runs through the city, then it turns slowly northward again along the foot of Dengtai Hill. The meandering river looks like a green jade belt, turning half of Liuzhou into a beautiful peninsula.

Liuzhou, with a history of over 2,100 years, was called Kunzhou in ancient times. It was given its present name in 634 A.D. Considered to be barren and barbaric in those days, Liuzhou was a place to which court officials who had fallen into disfavor were exiled. Liu Zongyuan, a noted statesman and poet of the Tang Dynasty, was banished from the court to Liuzhou in 815 A.D. During his four years as governor of the city, he had plenty of opportunity to associate himself with the local poor and instituted some measures to benefit the people. Many of his literary works reflect the sufferings of the poor.

In one of his poems we find the lines, "A thicket of trees on the peak shuts out the view. The winding river flows languidly, adding to my pent-up sadness." These two lines describe the scenery of Liuzhou at that time and reveal the poet's political

frustration. Later generations, in honor of this poet and statesman, erected the Liuzhou Temple and the Tomb of Liu Zongyuan in Liuzhou Park.

Li Yu Feng (Upright Fish Peak) and Xiao Long Tan (Little Dragon Pond) are near Ma'anshan Hill. With their old
trees towering all around and the pond water looking clear
and green, they are great attractions to tourists visiting
Liushou.

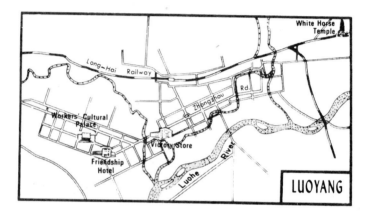

Luoyang (LOYANG)

The city of Luoyang is a newly industrialized city in western
Henan Sheng (Honan Province). However, civilization in this
area dates back to ancient times. The name of Luoyang in
varying forms can be found throughout history. It even served
as China's capital several times over the centuries. Recorded
history tells us many Chinese officials lived here as well as
many writers and poets.

Today it has more than four hundred factories, including
the Dongfanghong Tractor Plant, a ball bearing plant, and a
mining machinery factory. Its 190,000 workers turn out four
thousand kinds of manufactured goods. In addition to its new
industries, agriculture still plays a major role at Luoyang. Altogether its population has risen to over one million people.

PLACES OF INTEREST
Longmen Grottoes

The Longmen caves date back to the fourth century and are
one of the three greatest examples of grotto art in China. Ex-

tending over a stretch of 3,300 ft. (1,000 m.) Longmen or Dragon Gate Grottoes are comprised of 1,352 caves and 750 niches, with more than 100,000 Buddhist sculptures and 3,600 inscriptions and carved stone tablets.

Baimasi (White Horse Temple)

This temple is 6 mi. (10 km.) east of Luoyang. Built in the eleventh year of the reign of Yongping (66 A.D.) of the Eastern Han Dynasty, it was the first temple to be established in

Celestial Guardian at Fenghian Temple, Dragon Gate Grottoes

China following the introduction of Buddhism into the country. Tradition holds that the Buddhist scriptures were brought here from India on a white horse and the name of the temple seems to lend credence to it.

Working People's Park

This was formerly known as the Wangcheng (Royal Town) Park and was first laid out in 770 B.C. when King Ping of Zhou moved his capital here. The grounds, enlarged to protect the site of the ancient town pending further excavation, now extended to both sides of the Jianhe River which is spanned by a long suspension bridge.

Han Tombs

There are two Han Tombs in the Working People's Park, both of which have been unearthed and restored. One of them dates back to the Western Han (206 B.C.-25 A.D.) and contains the earliest mural paintings ever discovered by Chinese archeologists. Lively and graceful, these 2,000-year old frescos are priceless art treasures. The other is a brick and stone tomb built during the Eastern Han (25-220 A.D.). It is a prototype of many later methods of building arches and provides an invaluable source for the study of architecture in China.

Luoyang Museum

This Museum was established in 1958. It contains more than eight hundred priceless artifacts which are representative of those unearthed in Luoyang.

Peony Gardens

These Gardens include over one hundred varieties of peonies with "Twin Sisters," "Smokey Velvet," and "Violet Kerchief" among the most rare. The "Twin Sisters" peony has flowers of two different colors on the same stem and even petals of two colors on the same flower. The Peony Gardens are at their best in the spring.

Lu Shan (LUSHAN MOUNTAIN)

Lu Shan, 4,860 ft. (1,473 m.) above sea level, is on the southern bank of the Changjiang (Yangtze River). With over ninety peaks, it covers an area of 96 sq. mi. (250 sq. km.). Lu Shan is

Lu Shan

known for its beautiful scenery and bracing climate and has become one of China's most celebrated summer resorts.

PLACES OF INTEREST
Xian Ren Dong (Cave of the Immortals)

Xian Ren Dong is located on the Gu Ling Ridge on the western side of Lu Shan where the precipitous gorges are. The cave is below a sheer cliff and is more than 330 ft. (10 m.) deep, capable of holding several hundred people at one time. Legend has it that this cave was once used by Lu Dongbin, a Taoist monk, for his meditations, hence the name "Cave of the Immortals," which is carved in stone in Chinese characters on top of the moon gate. On one side of the cave is a fabled stone toad which carries the words "Wonderful View of Flying Clouds." Nearby there are pines said to have been planted during the Song Dynasty. The scenery is exceptional.

Xiao Tian Chi (Little Heavenly Pool)
This lovely little pool can be found on the top of a peak in the northeast of the Gu Ling Ridge. It never dries out even during a long drought, and never overflows no matter how heavy the rain. The limpid pool presents a fascinating reflection of a thousand and one patterns of ever-changing cloud formations.

Long Shou Yan (Dragon Head Cliff)
This majestic vantage point is 1,000 ft. (304.8 m.) high. The crag looks very much like a flying dragon with its head uplifted. From the cliff one can look down into deep abysses and hear the water thundering through the ravine.

Fei Lai Shi (The Stone Which Flew Here)
This is a gigantic toad-like rock in the west valley of Mount Lu Shan. Acording to China's renowned geologist Li Siguang, it was formed by glacial action centuries ago.

Wu Lao Feng (Five Venerable Peaks)
In the southeast of Lu Shan there are huge masses of stone rising to 4,739 ft. (1,436 m.) above sea level on top of the peaks. Five of them, standing side-by-side and silhouetted against the sky, resemble venerable elders from whence they derived their name, "Five Venerable Peaks."

Lu Shan Botanical Garden
This garden was established over forty years ago and is the only sub-alpine botanical garden in China. It occupies an area of 728 acres (294.8 ha.) and combines research in agriculture,

forestry, and cultivation of medicinal herbs and horticulture. It has over three thousand species of herbs and the part devoted to medicinal herbs is particularly noteworthy. The agricultural station also works on the domestication of wild plants.

Mogan Shan (MOGAN MOUNTAIN)

Mogan Shan is located in Zhejiang Sheng (Chekiang Province) over 37 mi. (60 km.) from Hangzhou. Legend has it that in the Spring and Autumn Period (770-476 B.C.), the King of the State of Wu (He Lu) sent a husband and wife, Moxie and Gan Jiang, here to forge two huge swords, and Mogan Mountain derived its name from this story.

The mountain is over 2,574 ft. (780 m.) high. Near the top the blue-green bamboo grows thick and dense. Amid the waving green bamboo groves are country villas and pavilions, screened from the sun's glare. The mountain in summer is cool and pleasant, and the spot is called the "pure and cool world." The annals for the locale record, "The mountain owes its scenic beauty to the fact that there are bamboo and springs, and nothing else." The bamboo still grows almost everywhere on the mountain, and the music of the springs is a pleasure to hear.

There are cascades and spring-fed streams all over Mogan Shan. Its springs are located at Yin Shan (Shaded Mountain) Cave, Lu Hua (Reed) Pond, and Tian Chi (Heavenly Pond) Hill. Jian (Sword) Pool's waterfall is an especially magnificent sight. It is said that Jian Pool is where the husband and wife forged their famous pair of swords. The waterfall spills down from an imposingly high cliff. Even from a great distance one can hear the roar of the cascade and the closer one approaches it, the more powerful the sound becomes.

Mogao Grottoes (MOKAO GROTTOES)

The Mogao Grottoes are situated in a valley 16 mi. (25 km.) southeast of the town of Dunhuang (Tunhuang), Gansu. Construction of the grottoes began in 366 A.D. and continued through the fourteenth century. Perhaps the most artistic are those dating from the Tang Dynasty (618-907 A.D.). Today a total of 492 caves are still in good condition with 54,000 sq. yd. (45,000 sq. m.) of murals, over two thousand painted statues, and five wooden buildings constructed in the Tang and Song Dynasties. The Mogao Grottoes are among the most ancient in China.

Mogao Grottoes

Nanchang (NANCHANG)

Nanchang is on a plain in the lower reaches of the Gan Jiang (Kanchiang River) and the Fu He (Fu River) and has a population of 500,000. It is the capital of Jiangxi Province (Kiangsi Province.) It was founded under the Han who called it Yuzhang. Its present name dates back to the Five Dynasties period.

Nanchang is famous for an uprising led here by Zhou Enlai on August 1, 1927, and that date has since been observed as the founding day of the Chinese People's Liberation Army.

Since 1949 great progress has been made in Nanchang's industry. The city has taken on a completely new look with a beauitiful People's Park, the wide August 1 Boulevard, and the spacious People's Square. There are twenty-five new bus

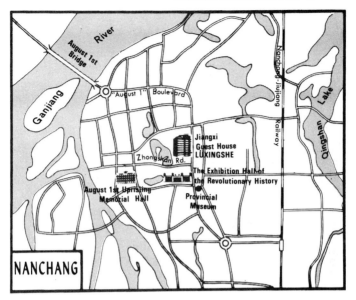

lines and two new bridges over the Gan Jiang, the 4,950 ft. (1,500 m.) August 1 Bridge and a railroad bridge.

PLACES OF INTEREST
Jiangxi Provincial Museum
Built in 1952 there are more than 50,000 valuable cultural artifacts on display here including a large collection of ancient ceramic pieces. There are also sections on geography and history, with descriptions of large scale work projects.

Arts and Crafts Gallery of Jiangxi Province
The pottery and ceramics section of the Arts and Crafts Gallery contains specimens of the world-renowned Jingdezhen china. On display are life-like porcelain carvings, sculptured figurines, elegant celadons, colored glaze ware, and eggshell china. There are also exquisite woven bamboo objects, finely-crafted wood carvings, and porcelain picture plates.

Bai Hua Zhou Island
Bai Hua Zhou, referred to as Island of a Hundred Flowers, is a picturesque island in the East Lake of Nanchang. On it one can visit the Guang Ao Pavilion. From here you can see the

Jiu Qu (Nine Bend) Bridge. The Island was enlarged soon after 1949 and renamed the August 1 Park.

Qing Yun Pu (Genealogical Table of Clear Clouds)

In the southern suburbs of Nanchang, this building was put up over one thousand years ago and was known in the Western Han Dynasty as the Mei Xian Temple. Later, in the Jin Dynasty, it was called the Tai Yi Guan or Tian Ling Guan. When Zhu Da, one of the famous artists of the late Ming and early Qing Dynasties lived here, it was given its present name, meaning literally, "Genealogical Table of Clear Clouds." Outside the grounds there are many streams and inside are tall ancient trees. In September the air in this area is heavy with the odor of flowering osmanthus. Here you will find many precious hand-written scrolls of calligraphy and paintings of Zhu Da, considered by many to be of great artistic value.

Nanjing (NANKING)

Nanjing, meaning southern capital, is situated in one of China's most beautiful natural areas. It is on the lower reaches of the Changjiang (Yangtze River) and is surrounded by the Zijin Shan (Purple Mountain). It is an attractive city with wide tree-lined streets. Nanjing is the capital of Jiangsu Sheng (Kiangsu Province) and has a population of over three million. The city covers an area of 301 sq. mi. (780 sq. km.).

Famous as one of China's ancient cities, Nanjing was built more than 2,400 years ago. From the third century to the beginning of the fifteenth, it was the capital of eight different dynasties.

There are 1,500 industrial and mining enterprises in the city including coal mining, metallurgy, petroleum, machine tool manufacturing, auto and ship building, and telecommunications instruments. It also has a large iron and steel industry.

The sixty-three agricultural communes in the suburban districts produce rice, grain, cotton, tea, apples, watermelons, cherries, and many vegetables. Over twenty-eight million trees have been planted since 1949. The city has fourteen institutions of higher learning, more than 340 middle schools, and over 1,500 primary schools. There are also 107 hospitals in the area.

PLACES OF INTEREST
Yu Hua Terrace
According to legend, a sixth-century Buddhist Priest named Yun Guang recited sutras here. Heaven was moved by his devotion and showered him with flowers. From this arose the name "Terrace of the Rain of Flowers." The vari-colored pebbles found in abundance here are also called rain of flowers stones. The park is known for its many springs. Packages of the colorful pebbles are sold to tourists as souvenirs.

Sun Yat-Sen Mausoleum
This is the mausoleum of Dr. Sun Yat-Sen who was born on November 12, 1866, in Cuiheng Village, Guangdong, and died

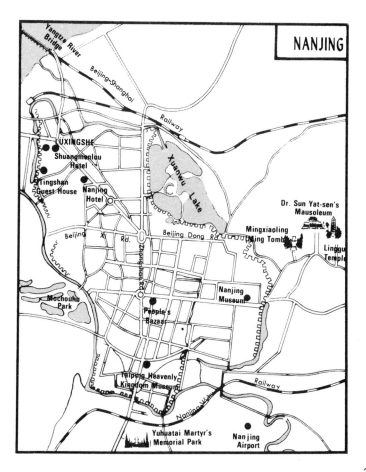

Dr. Sun Yat-Sen Memorial in Nanjing

in Beijing on March 12, 1925. In accordance with his wishes he was buried here in 1929. Dr. Sun Yat-Sen devoted forty years of his life to revolutionary activities. During the 1911 Revolution he led the Chinese people to establish the Republic.

The mausoleum is on the southern slope of the Zijin Shan in the eastern suburbs of Nanjing and covers an area of 321 acres (130 ha.). From the entrance to the Memorial Hall there are 392 steps. At the center of the hall is a white marble statue of Dr. Sun Yat-Sen in a sitting position. In the vault where he is buried there is a marble statue of Dr. Sun Yat-Sen in recumbent posture. The grounds are covered with pines, cypresses, and fruit trees as well as trees sent in his honor from abroad.

Ming Xiao Tomb

This is the tomb of Tai Zu founding Emperor of the Ming Dynasty (1368-1644 A.D.). Today only a stone gate and courtyard remain from the original construction. The sacred way leading to the tomb is flanked by stone statues of ministers, generals, and animals.

Xuan Wu Lake

One of Nanjing's scenic spots and a center for recreational and cultural actitivies, the lake is an extensive body of water with a circumference of 9.3 mi. (15 km.). It has five islands linked by causeways and bridges. Before it was made into a park in 1911 it had been the exclusive resort of the feudal aristocracy. Renovated and expanded after 1949, it is now six times its former size. There is a zoo, swimming pool, and theater.

Nanjing Museum

Established in 1950 as a museum for Jiangsu Province, it collects, preserves, and displays important historical objects discovered in the province. The display areas have distinctive features of Chinese architecture modeled on the wooden structure from the eleventh century.

The museum has exhibits from prehistoric times to the Qing period. There are bronzes from the Shang Dynasty, Han pottery, coins, weapons, tools, rare photographs of the area, paintings, clocks, exquisite furniture, textiles, and handicrafts from various dynasties.

Chang Jiang (Yangtze River) Bridge

This bridge, a great engineering feat, was designed and constructed by Chinese people. It is a modern, double-decker, double-track rail and highway bridge. Construction started in 1960 and was completed in 1968. Before the bridge was constructed there had been no direct rail traffic to Shanghai and Beijing, only the slower ferry service. The railway section to-

Chang Jiang Bridge

tals 22,348 ft. (6,772 m.), and the four-lane highway section is 15,144 ft. (4,589 m.). One of the towers contains an observation platform as well as a scale model of the bridge.

Zijin Shan Observatory

One of China's major astronomical research institutes, the Zijin Shan Observatory of the Chinese Academy of Sciences is on the third peak of Zijin Shan (Purple Mountain), to the east of the city. Building began in 1929 and was completed in 1934. There is a collection of ancient astronomical instruments on display including a celestial sphere and a sun dial designed over three thousand years ago.

Zijin Shan Observatory

Memorial Hall of the C.P.C. Delegation at Plum Tree Village

This was the site of the Office of the Chinese Communist Party Delegation headed by Zhou Enlai and Dong Biwu (Tung Pi Wu), which met with representatives of the Kuomintang. The offices and living quarters of the delegation at Plum Tree Village are kept as they were when in use at that time.

Gu Lou

One receives a fine view of the town from this observation point. This massive tower, called Drum Tower, was built during the Qing Dynasty (1644-1911 A.D.); close by is the equally impressive Bell Tower.

Ling Gu Pagoda

The original sixth-century pagoda that bore this name was located about five miles away and was destroyed by fire as were several of its replacements. During the Ming Dynasty it was taken down and reconstructed on this site.

SHOPPING

During your tour of Nanjing, there are several stores you may wish to browse in: People's Market, Nanjing Department Store, Nanjing Friendship Store, and the Nanjing Antique Store.

Jinling Hotel

2, Hanzhong Road, Telephone 4 11 21

Jinling Hotel, 37-story with the height of 110.4 metres, is a modern first-rate tourist hotel. The hotel has 804 guest rooms and suites with 1,288 beds. Xuangong, the revolving lounge on the 36th floor, is divided into three parts: bar, ballroom and teahouse with 160 seats. It takes 63 minutes to come full circle. Sitting in Xuangong one can taste delicacies, enjoy sweet music while having a magnificent panoramic view of Nanjing. The hotel is installed with safety alarm, air conditioner, closed circuit TV, sound equipment, gymnasium, sauna, etc.

RESTAURANTS

There are several restaurants in Nanjing that offer more than one of the various Chinese cuisines: Old Guangdong Restaurant, Da San Yuan Restaurant, Sichuan Restaurant, and Jiangsu Restaurant.

Nanning (NANNING)

Nanning is the capital of the Guangxi Zhuang (Kwangsi Chuang) Autonomous Region. It has been an important political and military center in southern China for over 1,600 years and is now the economic and cultural center of the region.

Nanning has gradually developed into an industrial center for light industry. There are three hundred light and heavy industrial enterprises with three thousand varieties of product. Xiang Shan (Elephant Hill) brand canned food, Liu Hua

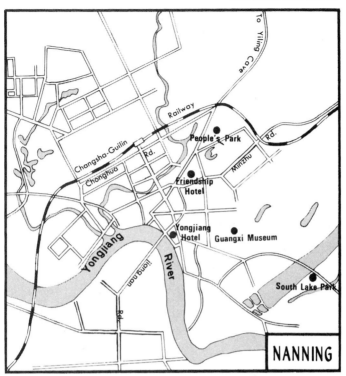

NANNING

(Pomegranate) brand granulated sugar, and Caterpillar tractors are among its exports.

The area of Nanning is now twelve times as great as it was in 1949 and the population has grown to over 500,000. Newly built houses and factories are equivalent to ten times the total built-up area of old Nanning. Large numbers of trees such as Kapok palm, jack-fruit trees, and mango trees have been planted along the streets and in the suburbs. The city is green all the year round.

PLACES OF INTEREST
Yiling Cave

This cave, close to Yiling Village, is more than 12 mi. (20 km.) northwest of Nanning. It is located in the midst of the Nanning Hills which rise abruptly from the flat plains. It is 148 ft. (45 m.) deep and covers an area of 5.5 acres (2.4 ha.). A path 3,000 ft. (916 m.) long has been laid out inside the cave for "would-be" explorers. According to a geological survey, the formation of this cave took almost one million years. Originally this section was an underground stream; later on, the earth's crust rose and it became a cave. Carbon-dioxide-bearing rain water seeping into the cave through the rocks and along the cracks gradually disolved the calcium carbonate limestone. The drops built up into stalactites, stalagmites, stone columns, and "stone flowers" of different shapes. Illuminated by colored lights, they form marvelous figures, landscapes, and scenes.

Inside the cave there is a zigzag undulating "overhead corridor" totaling 990 ft. (300 m.). There are beautiful scenes in the caves with names such as "In Joyous Land of the Zhuangs" and "Remote Thickly-Forested Mountains." "Spectacle

Yiling Stalactite Cave

at Sea" is the most fascinating. One seems to see the ocean with sea gulls flying in the endless azure sky.

Before 1949 Yiling Cave was a haven for people fleeing from the turmoil of war. After 1959 the Government managed to have it repaired and turned into a holiday resort. A paved road was built inside the cave in 1974, lights installed, bridges built, and halls and pavilions put up. An asphalt road leading to the cave has been landscaped on both sides with red camphor, jack-fruit, and other trees. For the convenience of visitors a small shop, a restaurant, parking areas, and other facilities have been added. On the hill one can rest at pavilions built in traditional style and enjoy the chrysanthemums, jasmines, osmanthus, magnolias, and other flowers growing in profusion.

SHOPPING

For your shopping convenience there are several stores to choose from during your stay in Nanning: Nanning Municipal Friendship Store, Nanning Municipal Zhaoyang Department Store, Nanning Municipal Arts and Crafts Department Store, Nanning Antique Store, and Nanning Municipal Bamboo Ware Store.

RESTAURANTS

You will find a wide variety of restaurants in Nanning all offering delicious meals: Nanning Friendship Restaurant, Nanning Ming Yuan Restaurant, Nanning Xi Yuan Restaurant, Nanning Yi Jiang Restaurant, Nanning Nan Hu Park Seafood Restaurant, Nanning Restaurant, and the White Dragon Tea House.

Ningbo (NINGPO)

The city of Ningbo stands at the confluence of the two major tributaries of the Yong Jiang (Yungchiang River) in the eastern part of Zhejiang (Chekiang Province). Because of its history and importance as a trading port, it is known as "Lesser Shanghai." It is the provincial center for foreign trade.

PLACES OF INTEREST
Bao Guo Temple

This temple is the oldest known wooden building south of the

Chang Jiang. The original one built in the Tang Dynasty was destroyed. The present hall of the temple was rebuilt in 1013 A.D. during the Northern Song Dynasty and renovated on a large scale during the Qing Dynasty. Except for the addition of exterior eaves, the main structure has remained unchanged.

As few ancient wooden buildings have survived, Bao Guo Temple is precious because it provides a model for the study of China's ancient wooden structures. By using an ingeniously dovetailed bracketing system called "Dougong" to help support the roof, the architects showed a considerable achievement in the field of applied mechanics. The ceiling of the hall is composed of three parallel pieces of hollowed-out ciasson which is a rarity in Northern Song architecture. The columns are also special. They were constructed of wood and their bases are shaped like a drum or an upturned pot. They are not only practical but artistic.

Tianyige Library

This is one of the oldest libraries in China having been established in 1561. In 1949 only 13,000 out of the original 70,000 volumes remained in its collection. These consisted of Confucian classics, history, philosophy, and belles-lettres. They were printed and hand copied in the Ming Dynasty and before. Among them the most valuable are the Ming Dynasty local histories and lists of successful candidates of the Imperial examinations (some being the only copies left in the whole country). They are part of China's national cultural heritage and provide valuable material for historical research, especially the study of Ming history. The library and its beautiful gardens have been refurbished and its books checked, indexed, and kept in order. A number of lost books have been recovered and a new supply added to its store through contributions of book collectors. Now its stacks have been greatly enlarged to include all sorts of books, transcripts, and manuscripts from the Song through the Qing Dynasties (960-1911 A.D.).

Qingdao (TSINGTAO)

Qingdao (Green Island) is a beautiful seaside city and a fine trading port. On the southern coast of the Shandong Peninsula, it looks out over the Huang Hai (Yellow Sea) at Jiaozhou Bay. The city has a history of only seventy years. It was named after the small island of Qingdao off the coast.

During the half-century when imperialists and KMT reactionaries ruled over the city, the people of Qingdao carried out many strikes, demonstrations, and heroic struggles against them. Since 1949 Qingdao has made great progress in its socialist construction. Now its total industrial output is more than ten times what it was in 1949 and its population totals 1.5 million.

Qingdao is surrounded by water on three sides. The lofty Mt. Lao Shan stands sentinel by the sea. With its blue water, its red-tiled houses, and green trees, Qingdao is a well-known scenic area with many attractions such as The Pier, Luxun Park, and an aquarium, and a bathing beach. Cooled by the sea, it is well known as a health and summer resort. Its local beer "Qingdao" is enjoyed both at home and abroad. The shell mosaics created here are known for their ingenious composition, brilliant colors and simplicity of design which makes them reminiscent of traditional Chinese painting.

PLACES OF INTEREST

Qingdao Harbor

This spacious harbor is formed by two promontories, the Tuando Zui to the northeast of the city and the Jiaozishi Zui to the southwest. These peaks stand 2 mi. (3 km.) apart and enclose the Bay of Jiaozhou. One of China's finest harbors, it covers 180 square nautical miles. Averaging 89 ft. (27 m.) deep at flood tide, it is completely free from silt, ice-free in winter and navigable to 10,000 ton class vessels the year round.

The Pier

Built in 1891, at the mid-point of the shore of Qingdao Bay, the pier stretches 7,320 ft. (400 m.) into the sea. It is an ideal place to enjoy the seascape.

Qingdao Aquarium

Built in 1932, it has a wonderful collection of sea animals and sea plants displayed in their natural environment.

Zhongshan (Dr. Sun Yat-Sen) Park

This heavily wooded park covers 198 acres (80 ha.). In spring there is a profusion of flowering shrubs and plants.

Mt. Lao Shan

One of China's famous hills, it rises out of the sea east of the town. There are various strangely-shaped stones and cliffs. Waves dashing against the rocks below are an awe-inspiring sight.

Shanhaiguan Pass of the Great Wall

Qinghuangdao (CHINHUANGTAO)

Qinhuangdao, facing the sea and screened by mountains, is an important ice-free port in North China. It is in Tangshan Prefecture, in the northeast of Hebei Province, on the Shenyang-Beijing Railway. The city is divided into Shanhaiguan, Beidaihe, and Haigang (Harbor) Districts. The population is 320,000. The area's seafood is abundant, with mackerel and flatfish in spring, jellyfish in summer, and prawns and crabs in autumn.

PLACES OF INTEREST

Shanhaiguan

This pass, called the "First Pass Under Heaven," marks the beginning of the Great Wall. It has been a strategic point since ancient times. Here the towering peaks of the Yanshan Mountains in the north slope down to meet the rushing waves of the Bo Hai Sea in the south. In the Tang Dynasty (618-907 A.D.), it was called Lingyuguan. At the beginning of the Ming Dynasty (1368-1644 A.D.), it was rebuilt by General Xu Da and designated as one of the key cities on the frontier. From the gate tower you can see the Great Walll, like a dragon, winding its way along the mountain ridges, and disappearing beyond the horizon. As the verse goes,

> *"I heard about the ancient pass long ago,*
> *Seeing is believing it is indeed so.*
> *Mile upon mile of silver waves feast the eye,*
> *Across the steep cliffs not even birds can fly."*

Beidaihe

This is a famous scenic spot and summer resort in northeastern Hebei Province on the coast of the Bohai Sea. It is over 60 mi. (90.6 km.) from east to west. The hillside, shaded by pine and cypress trees, is dotted with houses and pavilions commanding a magnificent view of the sea. From here one views the sea sending its waves towards the shore and merging with the sky in the distance. Another attraction for vacationers is its mild climate.

Bathing beach, Beidaihe

Quanzhou (CHUANCHOW)

Quanzhou, a 2000-year-old city, used to be a famous seaport in the middle ages and is now one of the major places inhabited by returning Overseas Chinese and their relatives. Situated on the hillside near mountains and rivers and facing the sea, Quanzhou is surrounded by splendid scenery. No wonder

241

it has been highly praised for having "the most beautiful land-scape in southeast China." There used to be many magnificent religious structures and works of art around this ancient city, hence the name "Buddhist Kingdom of Quannan."

PLACES OF INTEREST

Kaiyuan Temple

This Buddhist temple was built in 686 A.D. in the Chuigong reign of the Tang Dynasty. Among the main structures still in existence are: Tianwangdian (Heavenly King Hall), Daxiong Baodian (Mahavira Hall), Buddhist Study, and stone towers.

Qingjing Temple

This temple, also called Qilin Temple, was built in 1009 A.D. during the Song Dynasty. It is the oldest Islamic church still in existence in China. It is built totally of blue and white gran-ite, similar to the Islamic Church of Damascus in Syria.

Luoyang Bridge and Wuli Bridge

In ancient times, these bridges were considered to be "the best ones on earth." During the Song Dynasty, about 50 stone bridges were built in Quanzhou, of which 12 extended over 290 yd. (266 m.) in length with Luoyang and Wuli bridges ranking as the best and the longest.

Luoyang Bridge, also known as Wanan Bridge, was built in 1059 A.D. in the Jiayou reign, Northern Song Dynasty. It is 912 yd. (834 m.) long and 7½ yd. (7 m.) wide with 48 piers. Wuli Bridge, or Anping Bridge, was built in 1151 A.D. in the Shaoxing reign of the Song Dynasty. It extends about 1.25 mi. (2 km.) in length and is approximately 9-11 ft. (3-3.6 m.) wide with 363 piers. It was once the world's longest bridge.

Qufu (CHÜFU)

Qufu in southwestern Shandong Province was the capital of the State of Lu in the Spring and Autumn Period (770-476 B.C.) and the birth place of Confucius, philosopher and founder of Confucianism.

In 478 B.C., the year following Confucius's death, a hall, Dachengdian, was erected in his memory by Duke Aigong of

Lu. The site chosen was Xingtan, or Apricot Terrace, where Confucius used to talk with his students. This hall was expanded in subsequent dynasties until it became what is now Kongmiao, Temple of Confucius.

Kongmiao, covering one-fifth of Qufu's total area, is set off by a stretch of ancient pines and cypresses and is visible from a distance of several miles. Like the Imperial palaces, it was laid out as a walled-in town. Nine interior gates open to individual courtyards, each having its own special design and forming an impressive separate enclosure.

Dachengdian, the main building, has a dignified grandeur, and is richly ornamented with carved beams and rafters. A terrace with a marble parapet stretches along the front, where the roof is supported by imposing stone columns with bas-relief dragons coiling around them, a style not to be found either in the Imperial Palace in Beijing or at Daimiao Temple on Mt. Tai Shan. Amid pines, cypresses, and an apricot grove opposite the hall, stands an octagonal pavilion with vermilion balustrades and double eaves under a yellow tile roof. This is Xingtan where Confucius taught in the shade of an apricot tree.

The temple houses many relics, including a portrait of the sage, which is said to be one of the rare works left behind by Wu Daozi, a great Tang painter. Confucius' former residence is not far from the temple and his tomb lies in a forest named after him. Kongmiao is one of the three existing ancient Chinese palaces of monumental splendor in the history of world architecture; the other two are the Imperial Palace and Daimiao Temple.

Shaoshan (SHAOSHAN)

Shaoshan, in northwest Xiangtan County, Hunan Province, is the childhood home of Chairman Mao Zedong. He was born here on December 26, 1893, in a village surrounded by hills that are green with pines and cypresses. His former residence and an exhibition hall nearby are open to visitors.

PLACES OF INTEREST
Yinzhi Aqueduct
This aqueduct is one of the projects in the Shaoshan irrigation

system. It was built in Hunan Province during the 1970's. It has been called "Shaoshan Yinhe," meaning Milky Way of Shaoshan."

Shaoxing (SHAOHSING)

Shaoxing, in Zhejiang Province, is situated on the north side of Kuaiji Mountain, in the western part of the Ningbo Shaoxing Plain. Navigable waterways crisscross the urban area where industry and commerce are flourishing. This picturesque city is the birthplace of Lu Xun, a revolutionary cultural giant of modern China. Many of his novels are on display here.

Among the local products from this region is Shaoxing wine, which has been produced here for two thousand years. It is one of China's eighteen most famous beverages. The lakes yield an abundance of fish and shrimp, while tea plants cover most of the hills. Paper fans, lace jewelry, ornaments, and porcelainware are traditional products of Shaoxing.

There are many places of interest in Shaoxing. East Lake which lies to the east of the city was originally a rocky hill covered with bamboo and other trees. Rock found on this hill is green and hard. Since the Sui Dynasty (589-618 A.D.) the rock was quarried to build houses, roads, and bridges, gradually cutting up the hill into cliffs. At the foot, a pond was formed by water pouring down from mountain streams and springs. By the end of the Qing Dynasty (1644-1911 A.D.), a dyke was built here, cutting the pond in two. The inner part became a lake and the outer a river. Dotted with pavilions and stone bridges, East Lake has long been a major scenic spot.

PLACES OF INTEREST

The Lu Xun Memorial Hall

It consists of three parts: Lu Xun's former residence, the San-wei Study, and an exhibition room. Every possible effort has been made to restore the residence and study to exactly the condition they were in during Lu Xun's lifetime. In the exhibition room, more than six hundred items are on display, including manuscripts, letters, photographs, books, periodicals, and various personal possessions.

Temple of Yu

To the southeast of the city is Yu's Temple, built some one thousand years ago. Yu, a legendary hero of the Xia Dynasty (2205-1766 B.C.), is supposed to have performed prodigious feats in controlling rivers. It is said that during an eight-year absence from home he passed his door three times without stepping in. He died while on a tour of inspection four thousand years ago and was buried here.

Northern Yan Dang Shan
(Wild Goose Marsh Mountains)

"Of all the famous mountains I've been to, it is this one whose scenes most beggar description," said Xu Xiake, the great traveler of the Ming Dynasty, in praise of Northern Yan Dang Shan. This picturesque mountain range occupies an area of 116 sq. mi. (300 km.). Its many remarkable features include: over one hundred peaks, sixty-one cliffs, forty-six caves, twenty-six rock formations, thirteen falls, seventeen pools, fourteen barrier ridges, thirteen streams, ten ridges and eight ravines, eight bridges and seven gates, six pits and springs, four ponds and two lakes. From a distance it presents an imposing picture of mountains rising higher and higher, their pinnacles piercing the sky.

Ling Yan Monastery

A quiet and serene atmosphere surrounds the monastery, which is half hidden behind a row of tall ginkgo trees, with only its upturned eaves visible. All around are dense woods and rolling hills. The air is filled with a pleasant aroma of orange blossoms. It is said that during the Yong-he reign of the Jin Dynasty (265-420 A.D.), Nuocuna, a Buddhist Monk, came here from Sichuan with three hundred disciples. He died as he sat contemplating a waterfall. Later he was looked up to as the founder of a Buddhist sect and people erected a pagoda and a temple dedicated to him. From the Song Dynasty on more temples, monasteries, and pavilions were built, one of which is Ling Yan Monastery of the Southern Song Dynasty.

Da Long Qiu Cataract

At the end of Da Long Qiu Ravine, mountain torrents pour down the cliff with a deafening roar. As the cataract plunges into the pool below, the spraying water forms rainbows under the golden sunlight. During long spells of drought when the volume of water diminishes, the falls look like a sheet of thin silk gauze fluttering in the breeze.

Yan Hu (Yan Lake)

On the crest of the mountain there is a lake 3,432 ft. (1,040 m.) above the sea. It is the favorite haunt of wild geese passing by on their long seasonal migrations. From this the lake and mountain derive their names, Yan Hu or Wild Goose Lake. The lake is as placid as a mirror, its shores thickly overgrown with reeds. There are really three lakes: north, middle, and east. The middle lake is the best and reputed by Xu Xiake to be the actual "Home of the Wild Geese." Looking eastward from the rim of the lake one sees peaks rising higher and higher and the East China Sea far in the distance. Yan Ming Tea, fresh fish, fern leaf, hedge bamboo, and a kind of bird called Shanleguan are treasures of this ridge.

Ling Feng Peak

This area, with its many peaks, caves, rocks, and waterfalls, combines a number of scenic spots. Ling Feng Monastery dates back to the year 1023 A.D. On its left is Beidou (The Big

Dipper) Cave, on its right is Guanyin (Goddess of Mercy) Cave, to the north Zhenji (True Tranquility) Temple, and to the west Changchun (Eternal Spring) Cave. In front is a pool called Ningbitan (Congealed Jade) which is fed by converging streams which circle the monastery. All around are rocks of various shapes, one of the most spectacular being Hezhang Feng (Put-Palms-Together Peak), whose shape suggests an eagle flapping its wings. Opposite is another peak called Daoling Feng (Fallen Peak) Park. An earthquake during the Yuan Dynasty (1280-1368 A.D.) shook off its crest and destroyed the ancient monastery, but the site is still discernible. Four huge camphor timbers buried six hundred and sixty years ago were excavated from a stone cavern.

Guanyin Cave

Halfway up the peak one reaches a nine-story tower with a statue of Nanhai Guanyin (Goddess of Mercy of the South Sea) in it. Inside the cave one feels as if in a stone house floating in mid-air. Through a narrow crevice overhead one can see the sky like a long thread. Water falls from the top of the cave like a curtain of pearls and gathers into a cool, clear pond.

Shenyang (SHENYANG)

Shenyang is the capital of Liaoning Province in northeast China. Formerly called Mukden, it has a population of three million. Shenyang is one of China's industrial centers. Its industries include machinery, electric power, chemicals, textiles, food processing, and metallurgy.

An old city with a history of more than two thousand years, Shenyang was the capital of the Qing Dynasty between 1625 and 1644 A.D. Today it has a modern look with wide streets and tall buildings. The Shenyang acrobatic troupe has its own school and dormitories. They are famous in the West as a result of their tour there in 1973.

PLACES OF INTEREST

Imperial Palace Museum of Shenyang

The museum, covering an area of 15 acres (6 ha.) displays historical artifacts of the Qing Dynasty. At one time it served as the Imperial Palace of Nu Er Ha Chi and Huang Tai Ji,

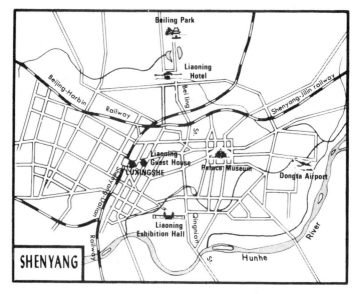

grandfather and father, respectively, of the Qing Emperor Shun Zhi.

Bei Ling (Northern Imperial Tomb)

This tomb, north of Shenyang, was built in 1643 A.D. Covering 1,112 acres (450 ha.), it is where Emperor Shun Zhi's father, Huang Tai Ji, and mother, Bo Er Ji Ji, were buried. Once the exclusive domain of the Imperial family of the Qing Dynasty, it is now a magnificent public park, open to all for rest and recreation.

Dong Ling (Eastern Imperial Tomb)

This scenic spot east of Shenyang is where the first emperor of the Qing Dynasty, Nu Er Ha Chi, and his wife were buried. The grounds are pleasant and attractive, with flowers, shrubs, and many ancient trees.

Shenzhen (SHUMCHUN)

Shenzhen is a city on the border between Guangdong Province and Kowloon, Hong Kong. Travelers to and from Hong Kong by road must pass over the Luoho Bridge here. It has

Shenyang Imperial Palace

now become China's first special economic region and approximately one-third of its total area can now be used for capital construction. By the end of last year, 490 industrial, commercial and other enterprises have been established with foreign investment or as joint venture companies, and most of them have already gone into business.

Tourism in the region has developed rapidly since the special economic region was set up. Hundreds of people come to Shenzhen everyday for a one-day trip from Hong Kong to have a glimpse of the scenery and life of this corner of the mainland. At the eastern end of Shenzhen, one can find a most beautiful beach where hotels, restaurants, swimming pools and other facilities for entertainment are to be built. Shenzhen will soon become a popular resort while at the same time developing its industry and commerce.

Shijiazhuang (SHIHCHIACHUANG)

Shijiazhuang in southern Hebei Province used to be a little village. It developed into a town at the turn of the century when it became a stopping place of two railways. It is an important hub of railway communications in North China. Shijiazhuang is the capital of Hebei Province with a population of 600,000.

PLACES OF INTEREST

Bethune International Peace Hospital of the Chinese People's Liberation Army

This name was officially given to the hospital in 1940 in commemoration of Dr. Norman Bethune, a Canadian physician and a great internationalist fighter who came to work in China in 1938. The first director was Dr. Kortis, an Indian friend of the Chinese people. The hospital, as it stands today, was developed on the base of a hospital founded in 1937 and includes the Bethune Memorial Hall and the Kortis Memorial Hall.

Mausoleum of Martyrs

Interred here are more than seven hundred army cadres and combat heroes of regimental level or above who laid down their lives in North China during the War of Resistance against Japan, the War of Liberation, and the Korean War. The tombs of Dr. Norman Bethune and Dr. Kortis are also here. Two beautiful bronze lions dating from 1185 A.D. can also be seen at this cemetery.

Zhaozhou Bridge

Zhaozhou is 25 mi. (40.2 km.) southeast of Shijianzhuang and the bridge is 2 mi. (3.2 km.) south of the town. It is also called Anji Bridge and the Great Stone Bridge. It was built in the Sui Dynasty around 600-610 A.D. by the famous mason Li Chun. This 168 ft. (50.82 m.) long, 30 ft. (9 m.) wide single-span vaulted bridge is made of twenty-eight separate rows of huge stones laid in parallel series, with a wide span and mild curve. The four small arches, which help reduce its weight and drain flood water, give the structure a lovely appearance.

Long Xing Temple, Zhengding

Zhengding is north of Shijiazhuang. Inside this ancient temple is a 79 ft. (24 m.) high bronze Buddha, cast in the fourth year of the Kaibo period of the Song Dynasty (971 A.D.). It is a testimony to the magnificent craftsmanship of the Song. The temple covers 2 sq. mi. (5.2 sq. km.) and has beautiful red and yellow galleries and roofs. There are marvelous stone and wood carvings as well as murals from different dynasties in the temple.

Shilin (STONE FOREST)

Shilin (Stone Forest) is 72 mi. (120 km.) southeast of Kunming. Winding about the forest is a well-worn trail 5,610 ft. (1,700 m.) long. Here stone pillars of strange shapes, some in solitary loftiness, some in clusters, seem to thrust straight out of the ground, the tallest towering 99 ft. (30 m.). But the most fascinating sights are found at Lianhuafeng (Lotus Blossom Peak), Jianfengchi (Sword Peak Pool), Wangfengting (Peak View Pavilion), and Shilinhu (Stone Forest Lake).

Shilin might be the place where Pan Gu stood when he created the universe by separating heaven from earth. Or the stone pillars might be those erected by the goddess Nu Wa to prop up the collapsing western firmament. Yet Shilin's rock formations are too strange even for such analogies from Chinese mythology. An ancient Chinese legend shows more convincingly how they were made.

Once upon a time one of the eight immmortals, Zhang Guolao, facing backward and riding a donkey, was driving over some northern mountains southward. On his way across a huge plain he came upon a young couple courting out in the open. "Why, young lovers don't even have a place where they can enjoy a little privacy" the kind-hearted old man mused. With a flourish of his hand he dumped all the mountains there in a heap. They tumbled every which way, forming a labyrinth in a stone forest. Since then loving hearts have always found it a perfect rendezvous.

At the back of Shilin is a lake which mirrors the strange stones. It is an ideal landscape for a beautiful painting. In the vicinity many other scenic splendors are tucked away in mountain forests. One is the Great Cataract. Water plunges down the ravine and is split in two halfway down by huge rocks. It resembles two enormous bolts of cloth unfolding in mid-air and pouring endlessly down into an unfathomable pool.

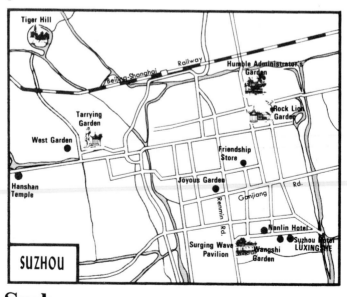

Suzhou (SOOCHOW)

Suzhou, an ancient city with a history of nearly 2,500 years, is

The leaning Pagoda at Tiger Hill

situated on the delta of the **Changjiang** (Yangtze River). It covers an area of 46 sq. mi. (119 sq. km.) and has a population of over half a million. Its suburbs and rural areas are studded with lakes and ponds which add beauty to the landscape. Both inside and outside the city there are exceptionally beautiful gardens representing the best landscape gardening south of

253

the Changjiang. High officials of the Song, Yuan, Ming, and Qing Dynasties had many parks and gardens built to serve as their exclusive resorts, among them Wang Shi Yuan (Garden of the Master of Nets), Shizi Lin (Lion Grove Garden), Liu Yuan (Tarrying Garden or Garden for Lingering), and Zhuo Zheng Yuan (Humble Administrator's Garden). Each is laid out in a style of its own and displays the characteristics of the special art of chinese landscaping.

PLACES OF INTEREST
Hu Qiu Shan (Tiger Hill)
In 518 B.C. Fu Chai, King of Wu, buried his father here. On top of this hill is an imposing structure — the pagoda of the Yun Yan (Cloud Rock) Temple built in 961 A.D. It is listed as one of the special historical sites under State protection. The temple courtyard is the highest point on the hill and commands a good view.The pagoda is one of the oldest in China and has over the years developed a pronounced inclination.

Xi Yuan (West Garden)
This garden, also known as Jie Chuang Lu Monastery, is famous for its hall of five hundred *arhats* (Buddhist statues of minor saints). To its west is a place to be appreciated in a hurry, since the scene over the lake changes before your eyes.

Cang Lang Ting
During the Song Dynasty this was the residence of Su Zimei, a man of letters. It was built in 1044 A.D. in an architectural style unique among the Suzhou gardens.

Suzhou Embroidery Research Institute
The school was set up in 1957 for the study of Suzhou embroidery, one of China's most applied arts. With a history of more than one thousand years, its hand embroidered silk has always been prized for exquisite workmanship, attractive designs, and bright colors.

Han Shan Temple
This is located in the West Feng Qiao Township of the city. The temple owes its fame to the poem "Overnight Stay at Feng Ziao," by Zhang Ji, a Tang Dynasty poet. Built in the sixth century it was later named after Han Shan and Shi De, two hermit monks of the Tang Dynasty who once lived there.

The Cold Mountain Temple

Lin Yan Hill

The hill, located 9 mi. (15 km.) west of the city, commands a bird's eye view of the picturesque Tai Hu Lake. It is not a place to be appreciated in a hurry, since the scene over the lake changes before your eyes.

North Temple Pagoda

The pagoda was built 1,700 years ago in the Three Kingdoms Dynasty (220-265 A.D.). It has recently been restored. Originally it was an eleven-story pagoda, today it has nine stories. This pagoda has a beautiful classic style, octagonal shape, and is 250 ft. (76 m.) high.

Tai Shan (TAISHAN MOUNTAIN)

Mount Taishan, more than 345 mi. (576 km.) in circumference, rises steeply and majestically in the middle of Shandong Province. Massive and awesome, it has been bound up with China's history throughout the ages and has been a rich source of inspiration for countless maxims, poetic allusions, and literary works of all kinds. To many people this mountain is a symbol of grandeur and stability as shown, for example, in the popular Chinese saying, "Stable as Mount Taishan."

The climb up is hard, but rewarding. The central path begins at Dai Zong Fang with a stone arch at the foot of the mountain. From here, a stone staircase winds its way up to Nan Tian Men (the Southern Celestial Gate), which shines in the blue sky like a ruby mounted on the green hills. From Dai Zong Fang to Nan Tian Men, the walking distance is about 6 mi. (10 km.), with eighteen flights of stone stairs to climb, totaling about seven thousand steps. Along both sides of the path peaks rise higher and higher and grotesque rock formations present interesting, ever-changing views. The higher one goes, the steeper the climb and the more wonderful the scenery. The last stretch to the top is so precipitous that, when one turns to look down, the footpath seems like a "staircase leading to the sky." When Li Bai, a Tang poet, ascended Nan Tian Men, he was so elated at the sight of the boundless expanse before him that he composed a poem. Two often quoted lines run:

> *"One long shrill cry from Nan Tian Men,*
> *Brings a cool breeze ten thousand li."*

China has many famous, high mountains. In the Himalayan area alone there are fourteen which rise to a height of over 26,400 ft. (8,000 m.). Some well known mountains, however, are really not very high. Tai Shan is only 4,950 ft. (1,500 m.) above sea level, but it is indisputably the greatest of the Five Sacred Mountains in China.

PLACES OF INTEREST
Tian Kuang (Celestial Gift) Hall
Tall and imposing, this main hall of the Dai Temple consists of nine rooms with double eaves, eight cornices and yellow glazed tile roofs. The frescoes (10 ft. high and 170 ft. long) of life-like figures, covering the east, west, and north walls are rare, outstanding works of art.

Jing Shi Yu Valley
Half a mile to the northeast of Dou Mu Palace is a huge wall of rock (one fifteenth of a hectare) bearing an engraving of the Diamond Sutra. Each character is more than a foot high. The forceful calligraphy of this ancient inscription is regarded as the prototype of the bank (placard) style.

Nan Tian Men Gate
This is opposite the Bei Tian Men Gate and can be reached by a steep, winding staircase. At the top is Mo Kong (Touching

the Sky) tower with a stone tablet bearing an inscription by Du Renjie, a poet of the Yuan Dynasty.

Bi Xia Temple

This is a magnificent cluster of finely decorated buildings. A statue of Bi Xia Yuan Jun (the Princess of the Colored Clouds) stands in the main hall which is roofed with bronze tiles. Its two wings and the main gates are covered with iron tiles.

Mo Ya Stele

The stele was put up in 726 A.D. by the reigning emperor. Engraved on it is an inscription, "Remembrances of Taishan" written by Emperor Xuan Zong (Li Longji) of the Tang Dynasty (618-907 A.D.).

Yu Huang Ding

Also known as the Tian Zhu (Celestial Pillar) Summit, it is the highest point of Mount Taishan and is marked by a stone, on which are the two characters "Ji Ding," meaning "the very top." Viewed from this summit, other far-off mountains seem like mounds.

Ri Guan Peak

Near the summit there is a huge stone protruding 20 ft. (6.1 m.) northward called Gong Bei (Push to the North) Stone or more commonly, Tan Hai (Probe the Sea) Stone. On a cloudless early morning the sunrise here is at its most spectacular.

He Ren Peak

On top of the Dong Shen Xiao Hill there stands a huge rock which looks like a menacing giant. It has come to be known as the He Ren Peak.

Hou Shi Wu

This is a unique, lovely, picturesque spot, with high peaks and ancient pines, located below Yao Guan Ting north of Mount Taishan.

Liu Chao Pines

So named because legend has it that these pines within the Pu Zhao (Universal Light) Temple enclosure were planted during the Six Dynasties Period (223-589 A.D.). The upper parts of the pines spread out like canopies and the twisted and intertwining branches resemble dragons in flight.

Tong Pavilion

This octagonal, double-eaved structure of gilded bronze patterned after the Imperial Palace, was built during the reign of Emperor Wan Li of the Ming Dynasty and later moved from the Bi Xia Temple to the Lin Ying Palace.

Taiyuan (TAIYUAN)

The city of Taiyuan, situated in central Shanxi Province, in the Fenhe River Valley, was originally called Jinyang. It has a history of twenty-five centuries. Destroyed by war in 979 A.D., it was rebuilt and renamed Taiyuan in 982 A.D. (Song Dynasty).

Taiyuan Basin has some of the richest coal and iron ore in the world. It is the capital of the province and one of China's heavy industrial centers with a population of over one million.

PLACES OF INTEREST

Jin Temples

At the foot of Xuanweng Mountain, 15 mi. (25 km.) to the southwest of Taiyuan, is an ancient park. The gardens were

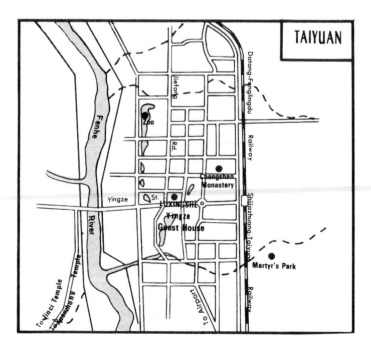

Jin Temple in Taiyuan

laid out in the midst of picturesque scenery and contain over one hundred temples, halls, pavilions, and bridges. These structures set off by the verdant growth of tall, ancient trees and other plants, with limpid brooks winding through, present an excellent combination of antiquity and natural beauty. This place is generally referred to as the Jin Temples. Frequently visitors are reluctant to leave when their tour of the gardens comes to an end.

Sheng Mu Dian (Temple of the Holy Mother)

This temple is the most magnificent of the Jin Temples. Built during the Tiansheng period (1023-32 A.D.), Northern Song Dynasty, it has a longer history than other temples here. It is surrounded by a veranda and the front of the hall is as wide as two rooms put together. This hall is the earliest existing example of such a design in ancient Chinese architecture. There are forty-three painted clay figures in the hall, all made in the

Song Dynasty, except for two smaller ones in a niche. These were added later. The Holy Mother, the most prominent statue, dressed in Imperial robes, is sitting sedately in the lotus position. The temple is also called Temple of the Holy Mother. Forty-two statues of ladies-in-waiting stand symmetrically on either side, life-like and graceful. They have well proportioned figures and are stylishly dressed. Life-sized and realistic, these statues portray some who are younger, some older, some slender, others more sturdy, even plump. Some look refined, some innocent, some sad. Each represents a particular type of character. Denoting an approach different from the conventional one that focuses on Buddha in temple art, the figures reflect the life and feelings of attendants bound in servitude at the Imperial Palace. They are masterpieces of ancient Chinese sculpture and occupy an important place in the history of the fine arts.

Pavilion of Nanlao Spring

To the south of the Temple of the Holy Mother is the octagonal Pavilion of Nanlao Spring built in the sixth century. The Nanlao Spring, which is the main source of the Jinshui River, gushes out of a stone cave under the pavilion, day and night, year after year. The water is crystal clear and the dark green duckweed and iridescent pebbles, glittering in the sun, are an attractive sight. The Tang poet, Li Bai, wrote, "Out of Jin Temple flows green jade." Located in a fault zone, the spring is 63° Fahrenheit (17° Celsius) all the year round. The water irrigates thousands of acres of paddy fields. Fan Zhongyan, a poet of the Northern Song Dynasty wrote the following lines in praise of the spring:

> *"Farmers are all watering their paddy,*
> *Same as in the Yangtze Valley."*

Tang Tablet

The famous Tang Tablet stands in the Zhen Guan Bao Han Pavilion. The inscription, in 1,203 characters, was written by Li Shimin, Emperor Taizong of the Tang Dynasty in 646 A.D. A great lover of the handwriting of the well-known Wang Xizhi, Li was himself a calligrapher of achievement. Executed with a flourish, the calligraphy is unconventional; each character embodies vigor, each stroke exhibits strength. With masterly skill, the engraver fully brought out the spirit of the original handwriting. Being the earliest tablet extant with an inscription written in the running hand, it is of great value in the study of the art of Chinese calligraphy.

Most impressive are the ancient trees in the temple yard including the famous cypress of the Western Zhou Dynasty (771 B.C.) and the scholar tree of the Sui Dynasty (581-618 A.D.). The cypress, inclining southward at a 40 degree angle to the ground, provides shelter for the Hall of the Holy Mother which is on its right. As Ouyang Xiu, a writer of the Song Dynasty wrote in a poem,

> *"The verdant, ancient, green cypress envelops a mist*
> > *heavy and dark,*
> *Nourishing all the grass and plants under*
> > *its shade."*

Over nine hundred years ago, it was already an object of interest because of its age. Today it is still full and sturdy. The ancient cypress, the ever-flowing spring, and the graceful ladies-in-waiting are the three most impressive treasures of the Jin Temples. Near the Temple of Guan Gong stands the scholar-tree, its aged branches intertwining and overlapping. Centuries have elapsed, but these trees are still full of life and reinforce the fascinating, timeless quality of the temples and brooks nearby.

Vineyards in Qingxu County

This county, under the jurisdiction of Taiyuan, is known for its grapes. Major producers are the Gaobai, Mayu, and Chengguan People's Communes. Viniculture began here about one thousand years ago and some of the vines are nearly one hundred years old. More than seventy varieties of grapes are grown here. The finer strains include Longyan (Dragon's Eye), Hei Ji Xin (Black Chicken Heart), Ma Nao (Amber), and Ping Er (Bottle).

Tianjin (TIENTSIN)

Tianjin is 74 mi. (120 km.) southeast of Beijing. It is on the coast of the Bo Hai. China's third largest city, it is a municipality directly under the Central Government (with Beijing and Shaghai). Its location at the convergence of five tributaries of the Hai He River, as well as at the juncture of the Beijing-Shanhaiguan and Tianjin-Pukou railroads, makes it a hub of convenient land and water transportation. Its population is over four million.

It was founded as a military station in 1404 A.D., and was designated as a treaty port in 1858. Since 1949, Tianjin has become an important industrial and commercial center as well as an international port.

It has several universities, colleges and medical schools. There is also an industrial exhibition hall here. Famous for its carpets (there are eight major factories), Tianjin is also known for various handicraft products such as clay figures and the woodblock New Year prints of Yangliuqing. Excellent seafood is to be found in the restaurants of Tianjin.

PLACES OF INTEREST
Terra Cotta Figurine Studio
The art of making clay figures, as practiced in the Tianjin locality, began in the nineteenth century. Its fame was established by the work of a craftsman of the town known as Ni Ren Zhang ("Master of Clay Figures") who used to make little figures representing characters from the theater, classical novels, and people from everyday life. Finely molded, these painted figures are both entertaining and artisitic.

Shui Shang Gong Yuan (Park on the Water)
This large park, laid out after 1949, occupies 494 acres (200 ha.) of which 230 acres (93 ha.) are water. A fine place for boating, it somewhat resembles the villages surrounded by water in areas south of the Changjiang (Yangtze River).

Art Museum
This is a regional museum built in 1957 for collecting, studying, and displaying ancient Chinese *objets d'art* of various dynasties. It has an excellent collection of Yuan, Ming, and Qing paintings.

Number One Carpet Factory
Fine quality carpets and carpet yarn have been produced here since 1958. Known for their lovely designs, well-matched colors, and national styles, the carpets are world famous.

Special Handicraft Workshop
Craftsmen here specialize in jade, stone, ivory, and wood carv-

ings of attractive designs, fine workmanship, and unique styles.

Applied Arts Factory

More than ten major items are produced, including shell mosaics, plumage pictures, traditional Chinese paintings, kites, and paper-cuts. The kites, designed by master craftsmen, are

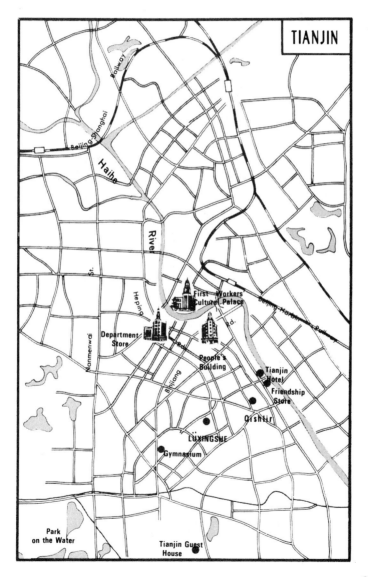

lively, brightly-colored representations of animals, insects, and birds.

Xingang (New Harbor)

This important center of foreign trade was built in 1952 and is the biggest artificial harbor in north China. The first two stages of construction, now completed, provided berths for eleven vessels of 10,000 tons and can also provide for ships of 30,000 and 40,000 tons. The third stage, started in 1972, is still under way. The wharves and harbor facilities are open to visitors.

Zhou Enlai Memorial Hall

In his youth, Zhou Enlai studied at Nankai School (1913-1917) and led the revolutionary movement in Tianjin. The hall was established on March 5, 1978, at the site of the former Nankai School (now Nankai Middle School).

Yangliuqing New Year Pictures

Block printing of New Year pictures is a popular form of Chinese folk art. Its beginnings can be traced back over three hundred years to the Chongzhen reign, Ming Dynasty. It evolved an artistic style of its own as it developed. Subject matter covers a wide range and includes the ways and customs of the common people, historical episodes, legends, folk tales, classical allusions, highlights from drama, children, landscape, flowers, and plants. Influenced by the traditional painting of the Song, Yuan, and Ming dynasties, the pictures are first printed with colored wood blocks and are then painted and retouched in color by hand. Chinese people hang them on their doors and walls on New Year's Day.

SHOPPING

There are a variety of shopping opportunities to be found in the following stores: Tianjin Department Store, Quan Ye Chang Market, Tianjin Friendship Store, and Yilin Pavilion Art Store.

Turpan County (TURFAN COUNTY)

The old town of Gaochang, located to the southeast of present-day Turpan County, was established in the first century B.C., flourished for about 1,500 years and was abandoned in the fourteenth century.

In ancient times it was one of the political, economic, and cultural centers in the Xinjiang area as well as an important town along the old "Silk Road." According to historical records, the master monk, Xuan Zang, of the Tang Dynasty passed Gaochang at the foot of Huoyan (Flame) Hill, in 627 A.D. on his way to India in search of Buddhist scriptures. He stayed at Gaochang for several months. A detailed report of the visit has come down to us in the "Biography of the Master Monk," This record is held in Daci'en Temple in Xi'an. According to this account, Qu Wentai, King of Gaochang, out of great respect for the monk, tried to make him stay on against his will. There was nothing Xuan Zang could do but go on a hunger strike. After some time it was obvious that he was declining. Qu Wentai was so moved that he agreed to let the monk resume his journey.

Ürümqi (ÜRÜMCHI)

Ürümqi is at the northern foot of the Tianshan Mountains in the northwest of China. It is the capital of the Xinjiang (Sinkiang) Uygur Autonomous Region and is its political, economic and cultural center. Since ancient times, people of all nationalities have lived here, pastured their herds, and developed this beautiful land. Ürümqi is now a flourishing industrial city.

Xinjiang is called the land of song and dance. Its population of eleven million consists of Han and thirteen national minorities, with the 5.4 million Uygur (Uighur) as the majority.

Most of Xinjiang was once dry and sparsely populated. Since 1949 great strides have been made to use the rich water resources from the year-round, snow-capped Tianshan Mountains. Underground irrigation canals have been rechanneled. The region's natural resources, including oil, iron, and phosphorus, are being developed. The People's Liberation Army has transformed thousands of acres of desert into fertile fields. Wheat is grown in large quantities along with rice, sorghum, maize and millet. Fruit is also grown in large quantities: delicious grapes, watermelons, the famous Hami melon, pears, apricots, and many others.

PLACES OF INTEREST
Tianchi (Lake of Heaven)
This beautiful lake lined with pines nestles high in the mountains southeast of Ürümqi. It is 6,435 ft. (1,950 m.) above sea level and covers an area of 1.9 sq. mi. (4.9 sq. km.). Beyond the southern end of Tianchi there is a small lake called Xiao Tianchi (Small Tianchi Lake). Water from the latter, at the northern side, gushes down from rifts between the rocks and forms a lovely waterfall. On the two-hour drive to Tianchi Lake, one can see the work being done to irrigate the area, build roads, and plant trees and vegetation.

Revolutionary Martyrs's Memorial Park
The park is situated in the scenic spot of Yan'erwo (Swallow's Nest) in the southern suburbs of Ürümqi. Construction started on July 1, 1956. Revolutionary martyrs buried in the park include Chen Tanqiu, one of the founders of the Communist Party of China, Mao Zemin, one of Chairman Mao's younger brothers, and Lin Jilu.

Museum of Xinjiang Uygur Autonomous Region
There are over two thousand ancient artifacts on display in the museum which was built in 1953. These artifacts are divided into eight periods: Stone Age; Warring States; Qin and Han Dynasties; Three Kingdoms; Eastern and Western Jin; Northern and Southern Dynasties; Sui and Tang; Song and Yuan Dynasties; Ming and Qing Dynasties. The historical relics on display show that Xinjiang has been an integral part of China since ancient times.

HOTELS
Peace Hotel
A large building, set behind a big courtyard, this hotel has some of the most comfortable rooms in China. The beds have blankets and quilts to ward off the cold nights; the bathrooms, provided with terry cloth robes, are large. The food in the dining room is delicious with mutton as its speciality. Breakfast consists of an omelet, sweet rolls, fried steam rolls with meat and onions, and good coffee.

SHOPPING

Ürümqi Friendship Store

This is a large building where you will find many of the local specialities including musical instruments, shoes, records, and ceramics.

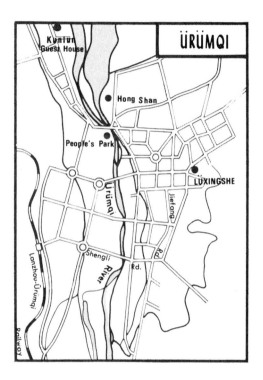

Wuhan (WUHAN)

Wuhan, on the Beijing-Guangzhou railway, is in reality three cities: Wuchang, Hankou, and Hanyang. Wuhan, situated in the middle reaches of the Changjiang (Yangtze River), is the capital of Hubei Province and an important junction of rail and water traffic.

The city has a long history rich in revolutionary tradition. It occupies a place of honor in China's annals for being closely associated with the 1911 Revolution and the February 7th General Strike of 1923. Its main revolutionary memorial places include the site of the Central Institute of the Peasant Movement, founded during the First Revolutionary Civil

War; Comrade Mao Zedong's former dwelling, and the Monument to the Martyrs of the 1923 General Strike.

East Lake, located in the eastern suburbs, is a much frequented scenic spot. To the west of the lake is the Hubei Provincial Museum where valuable historical relics are on display.

PLACES OF INTEREST

Comrade Mao Zedong's Former Dwelling
Located at 41 Du Fu Ti, in Wuchang, this is where Chairman Mao lived from the winter of 1926 to the autumn of 1927. He also founded the Central Institute of the Peasant Movement at 13 Hong Xiang Lane.

The Chang Jiang River Bridge at Wuhan
This steel bridge was the first to be built across the mighty Chiang Jiang (Yangtze River). Together with the approaches, it measures 5,511 ft. (1,670 m.) in length. Below the motorway on the bridge, there is a double-track railway. Construction of the bridge started on September 1, 1955 and was completed on September 25, 1957, providing a throughway for traffic between north and south China.

Wuhan Iron and Steel Company
One of the large iron and steel complexes built after the founding of New China, it includes ore mining, ore dressing, iron smelting, steel making and steel rolling plants backed up by ancillary enterprises. In addition, there are living quarters and welfare facilities covering a total floor space of over 10.7 million sq. ft. (1.0 million sq. m.).

Wuhan University
A comprehensive university for science and liberal arts, this university was erected on Luojia Hill, Wuchang, in 1913. The hill is one of the scenic spots of East Lake. The campus, with its many tall trees, is quiet and beautiful.

The Wuhan Acrobatic Troupe
The troupe was organized in 1953. Its large repertoire includes many unique and entertaining acts which have won tremendous acclaim at home and abroad. The acts include balancing on a pyramid of chairs, balancing a pagoda of bowls on the

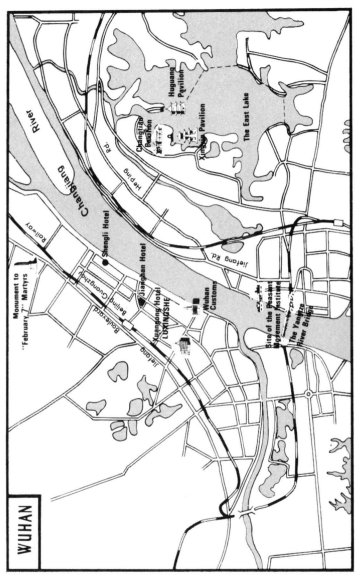

head, spinning plates, bicycle feats on a raised platform, trick riding on a bicycle, and many more.

East Lake

This is a vast lake so full of bays and gulfs that it has come to be called the "Lake of 99 Bays". The water is so clear one can see right to the bottom. Gazing into the distance, one finds that the water and the sky are the same color. The scenery along the lake is lovely, with its flowers and trees, pavilions and terraces. Chairman Zhu De once said when he visited this lake, "West Lake is at present lovelier than East Lake, but will one day give way to East Lake."

Gui Yuan Temple

This ancient Buddhist temple, an example of classic architecture commonly seen in south China, has a history of more than three hundred years. In it there is a huge hall containing five hundred Luohans (*arhats*) in different postures, each with an individual facial expression. Some may look experienced and astute, others jolly, angry, or complaisant. They are true to life and extremely well made.

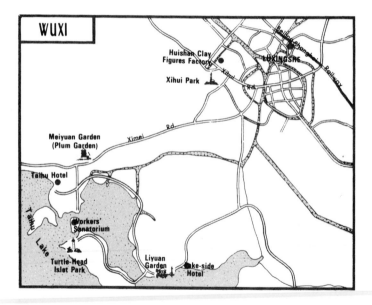

Wuxi (WUHSI)

Wuxi is on the north bank of Tai Hu Lake, with Hui Shan Hill to its west. With its mild climate, fertile soil, and richness in natural produce, it has been called "land of fish and rice." An attractive city with canals and cobbled streets, it is on the lower banks of the **Changjiang** (Yangtze River), in the southeast part of Jiangsu (Kiangsu) Province.

Wuxi, famous as a resort city, has an area of 78.7 sq. mi. (204 sq. km.) and a population of 650,000. One of the oldest cities in China, Wuxi has a history of over three thousand years going back to the last years of the Shang Dynasty (1766-1122 B.C.) and the beginning of the Zhou Dynasty. The Earl of Tai, who was the eldest son of Prince Tai and of the Zhou Dynasty, established the State of Juwu with its capital at Mei Village, east of the present city.

Wuxi is an important silk producing area. After 1949 the mulberry groves, which had previously been unattended, were restored and the silk and textile mills were expanded. There are more than 470 factories including bicycle construction, printing, enamelware, glassware, silk weaving and dyeing. Its industries include precision machine tools, diesel engines, air compressors, water pumps, textile machinery and electric cables and wires.

Three crops of rice are produced a year and the area produces wheat, numerous vegetables and fruit, and breeds pigs as well as fish. Wuxi has one university and 150 primary and middle schools. There are also twelve hospitals in the city.

Li Yuan Garden

PLACES OF INTEREST
Li Yuan Garden
Take a stroll in this park by Li Hu Lake on the southern outskirts of the city. The path winds by picturesque hills, quiet streams, arched bridges, pavilions, and towers. In the spring peach and willow trees lining the lakeside embankment

present dazzling views of pink and green, which make it nearly impossible to pass by without reaching for your camera.

Looking out over the lake from Yuan Tou Island, one can see Xiao Qi Hill all wrapped in greenery interspersed with glimpses of red walls. The Li Yuan Garden appears to be a mid-lake fairyland. Entirely surrounded by water, it gives the impression of a floating mirage. The attractive rock gardens and zigzag paths, typical of landscaping south of the Chang-jiang River, embody craftsmanship unsurpassed by nature herself.

Jiangsu Workers Sanatorium

This well equipped health resort was built in 1952 on Zhongdu Hill in Tai Hu Lake amidst pleasant, scenic surroundings. It has 140,000 sq. ft. (13,000 sq. m.) of floor space and over three hundred beds.

Mei Yuan (Plum Garden)

The garden spreads over a hill covered with 10,000 plum trees whose blossoms turn the landscape white and fill the air with fragrance. The top of the hill commands one of the best panoramic views of Tai Hu Lake.

Yuan Tou Park

This is actually an elongation of the western end of Chongshan Hill which juts into Tai Hu Lake to form a small peninsula. Its name comes from its shape, which is like the head of a turtle. This spot affords an excellent view of the surrounding landscape.

Yuan Tou Island

Covered with thickly wooded hills, it is best seen from the Wuxi shore. At sunrise and sunset clouds float over it in blazing glory, lighting up the white sails which move slowly over the lake. Pavilions and towers that fit in naturally with the landscape decorate the hills. The waves quietly lapping the rocks at the foot of the hills create a sense of serenity.

Xi Hui Park

The park lies between Xishan and Huishan Hills. Huishan is known for its springs, the most notable being "The Second Spring Under Heaven" consisting of a dozen Long Yan (Dragon's Eye) springs. Their clear sweet water is excellent for making tea. Xishan Hill is more than seven hundred feet high and was named Xi (Tin) because metal was discovered there during the first century A.D. At its crest is Long Guang (Dragon Light) Pagoda which commands a panoramic view of the city and the lake.

In the park is Ji Chang Yuan (Carefree Garden) built in 1506 A.D. during the reign of Emperor Zhengde of the Ming Dynasty. Its many tall, ancient trees and ingenious landscaping make it one of the finest examples of ancient landscape gardening in China.

Huishan Clay Figurine Studio

The Huishan painted clay figurines were first made in the Ming Dynasty and have enjoyed an uninterrupted history of over four hundred years. The figurines are characterized by rich folk artistry and unique national style, including bold exaggeration, striking contrast, bright colors, and simplicity of form. Most of the figures represent contemporary literary and political themes. They have vivid postures and bright colors. There is a small shop for visitors.

The Ancient Grand Canal

A trip for foreign guests on the ancient Grand Canal in Wuxi recently began operation. The Grand Canal from Beijing to Hangzhou is known as one of the longest canals in the world. It is more than 1300 years old and, like the Great Wall, is a great man-made project of ancient China. Many foreign guests say, "Being able to climb the Great Wall is something to be proud of." It is likewise something very special to take the one-and-a-half-hour trip along the Grand Canal. The scenery and the people and customs seen along the canal make the trip an enjoyable and rewarding one.

Xiamen (AMOY)

Xiamen was a nameless island one thousand years ago. In the Southern Song Dynasty (1127-1279 A.D.), it was named Jiahe Island. In 1387, Zhou Dexing built the city wall of Xiamen here to deter foreign invaders. In 1842, Xiamen became one of the five treaty ports. Now it is an important port for foreign trade, doing business with over 70 countries and regions. Xiamen is the terminal of the Yingtan-Xiamen Railway, and passenger ships sail between this port and Hong Kong. The island covers an area of 38 sq. mi. (100 sq. km.) with a population of

260,000. Situated in the subtropical zone, Xiamen has warm weather all year round. In the coldest month, the average temperature is above 53° Fahrenheit (12° Celsius) while in the hottest month it averages 82° Fahrenheit (28° Celsius).

The urban area is on the southwestern part of the island. The Culture Palace is in the downtown area. The port is always busy with ships coming and going.

PLACES OF INTEREST

Gulangyu

Gulangyu is a picturesque islet, separated from Xiamen by a .6 mi. (1 km.) wide strait.

Convenient ferry service is available to Gulangyu. The whole islet is covered by trees. Streets and houses have been built on the undulating terrain. The peak of the magnificent Dragon Head Hill is called Sunlight Rock, and is 290 ft. (90 m.) above sea level. Three hundred years ago Zheng Chenggong stationed his troops here. An exhibition hall was established in his memory. The Shuzhuang Park and the Gangzi Beach are very popular spots on Gulangyu and are frequented by many visitors.

Nanputuo Temple

Nanputuo is one of the famous ancient temples in south Fujian Province. Its history spans over 1,000 years and the splendid building with its ornamentation and fine Buddhist carvings is highly renowned. Nearby, there are the Xiamen University, the Luxun Museum and the Museum of Overseas Chinese. The vegetarian cuisine by Nanputuo Temple has enjoyed a high reputation for a long time.

Wanshishan Park

Wanshishan Park is not far from the city center. Inside the park, one may visit the Monument to the Martyrs, the Botanical Garden, the Wanshi Reservoir and many other places of interest.

Xiamen Zhonghan Park

The park is situated in the northeast side of the city near Shishan Hill and Yupingshan Hill. In the park there are natural streams, ancient temples, pavilions and a sports field. There is also a monument to Dr. Sun Yat-Sen.

Jimei Scenic Area

Jimei is the home town of the late Mr. Chen Jiageng and is also the location of the famous "Village of Schools." The Monument to the Liberation of Jimei was built in the center of Aoyuan Garden. To the south is the tomb of Mr. Chen Jiageng. The "Return Hall" was built to commemorate the patriotic deeds of Mr. Chen. On the southern part of the Jimei peninsula, there are miles of clustered school buildings. A pagoda-shaped, 15-story building, plus pavilions near three artificial lakes, make the area a very attractive one.

A long causeway built with white granite has linked Xiamen, Jimei and a new industrial area known as Xinglin. Thus Xiamen, the island, has become a peninsula.

Restaurants

The Green Island Restaurant and Overseas Chinese Hotel offer excellent food for visitors.

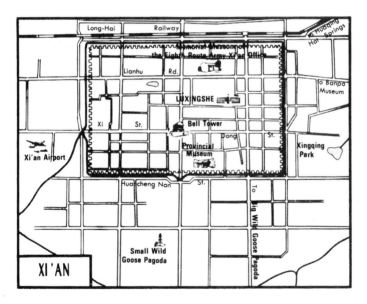

Xi'an (SIAN)

Xi'an, called Changan in ancient times, is the capital of Shaanxi Province and one of the principal cities in northwest China. It is a majestic city, situated between rivers and mountains in the center of the fertile Guanzhong Plain. It has a population of 2.5 million and covers an area exceeding 880 sq.

mi. (2,200 sq. km.).

Xi'an is one of the important cradles of Chinese civilization. The remains of the Banpo Village, first excavated in 1954, show that a complete matriarchal clan commune village existed here in the Neolithic age. Xi'an is also one of the famous ancient capitals of China. The city and towns nearby served intermittently as the capital of eleven dynasties from the eleventh century B.C. down to the early tenth century A.D.

Beginning in the Han Dynasty (206 B.C.-220 A.D.) Xi'an was already a center for international exchange between China and other countries. It was the starting point of the world famous "Silk Road" which promoted economic and cultural interchanges between Han and post-Han China with countries in West Asia and Europe. By the time of the Tang Dynasty (618-907 A.D.) contacts had become even closer between Xi'an and the neighboring countries of China to the east and south and countries in the Middle and Near East and Europe. Thousands of foreign diplomatic envoys, students, clergymen, and merchants lived there. Stories about their activities have been handed down to this day.

Having been the capital of so many dynasties, Xi'an has a host of historical sites. Among them are the Dayan (Big Wild Goose) Pagoda, the Xiaoyan (Small Wild Goose) Pagoda, the Forest of Steles, and the Bell Tower.

Xi'an also has a revolutionary tradition and was the capital for regimes established by two important peasant uprisings, one at the end of the Tang Dynasty and the other toward the end of the Ming (1368-1644 A.D.). Though of short duration, the regimes were of great historic significance.

The famous "Xi'an Incident" in modern Chinese history took place here in 1936. After it was settled peacefully, the Chinese Communist Party set up the Liaison Office of the Red Army, which later became the Xi'an Office of the Eighth Route Army.

Water conservation projects are important to this area. Wheat, rice, and cotton crops have benefited from the irrigation systems. Its industries include textiles, fertilizers, machinery, cement, electrical instruments, paper, and sewing machines. Coal, iron ore, manganese, and copper are mined. Xi'an has many universities, and the area has theatrical and opera troupes.

PLACES OF INTEREST

Shaanxi Provincial Museum

The museum, with a floor space of over 43,200 sq. ft. (4,000 sq. m.) was opened in 1952. There are more than two thousand ancient artifacts on display. They are divided into three sections: Forest of Steles (the oldest and richest collection of such stone tablets in China), Gallery of Stone Sculpture, and Historical Relics.

Dayan Pagoda

Banpo Museum

This neolithic site is a few miles from Xi'an. The Banpo people settled here some six thousands years ago. They cultivated their land, built houses, and lived as a primitive clan. Five excavations since 1954 have uncovered a village of forty-five houses, Stone Age pottery, tools, and bones. The site covers an area of 60,000 sq. yd. (50,000 sq. m.). It is divided into living quarters, a pottery making center, and a graveyard. The museum built to protect the site has a hall covering 23,400 sq. ft. (3,000 sq. m.) and two exhibition rooms.

Dayan (Big Wild Goose) Pagoda

This temple is on the grounds of the Temple of Good Will (Da Ci En) and is about 2 mi. (4 km.) south of Xi'an. It was built in 652 A.D. Xuan Zhuang, the famous master monk of the Tang Dynasty, here translated Buddhist texts that he had brought back from India. The pagoda, as it stands today has seven stories and is 211 ft. (64 m.) high. Spiraling staircases lead to the top where one is rewarded with a good view of Xi'an and the surrounding area.

Xiaoyan (Small Wild Goose) Pagoda

This temple is near the Big Wild Goose Pagoda and was built in 707 A.D. It has fifteen stories and is 148 ft. (45 m.) high. It has a fine and delicate style. On the north and south doors there are exquisitely carved ivory designs and Buddhist figures.

Bell Tower

Built in 1384 A.D. this tower is 119 ft. (36 m.) high. It is constructed of wood and brick with a superimposed ribbed roof and terraced eaves supported by brackets for each story. It is elegant and sturdy at the same time. On its first story is an impressive array of jewelry and wall hangings which are for sale.

Huaqing Hot Springs

The Springs are at the western foot of Lishan Hill east of Xi'an and have been known for more than five thousand years. The water with a temperature of 109° Fahrenheit (43° Celsius) contains many minerals and is good for bathing and treating various ailments.

Qin Shi Huang Mausoleum

This tomb, with its 132 ft. (40 m.) high tumulus, was built in

Life-size clay horses and warriors unearthed at the tomb of the First Sovereign Emperor of Qin, Xi'an

the third century B.C. for Qin Shi Huang, the first emperor of the Qin Dynasty (221-206 B.C.). In 1974 a huge pit with numerous Qin pottery figures was discovered to the east of the mausoleum. The unearthed clay warriors and horses are huge and life-like and provide valuable data for the study of the military weaponry and sculpture of the time. The excavation of this incredibly rich find is a continuing process and visitors can actually see the archaeologists at work revealing more and more of these remarkable statues. Nothing comparable to it has ever been uncovered in China before.

Qian Tomb
The tomb is on Mt. Liangshan to the northwest of Qianxian County 48 mi. (80 km.) from Xi'an. It is the joint tomb of Emperor Gao Zong and his consort, Empress Wu Zetian (624-705 A.D.).

Xing Qing Park
The park was built on the site of the Xing Qing Palace of the Tang Dynasty. Interesting buildings include the Chen Xiang (Garu Wood) Pavilion and the Hua E Xiang Hui (Flowers Shining Brightly) Gallery, both of which are built in the style of the Tang Dynasty.

Xingzi County (HSINGTSU COUNTY)

Xingzi County is situated by Boyang Lake at the southern foot of Lushan Mountain. It is said that the most beautiful places of Lushan are on the south side. These include the nine hundred year old Guan Yin Bridge, the terrace where Zhou Yu of the period of the Three Kingdoms (320-365 A.D.) selected his generals, and the rock on which Tao Yuanming, the well known poet of the Jin Dynasty, lay drunk. Also included are the famous Qing Yu Gorge, Xingzi Hot Springs, Yu Yuan Waterfall, and Yu Lian Spring.

PLACES OF INTEREST
Qing Yu Gorge

There are two waterfalls above Qing Yu Gorge: the Ma Wei (Pony Tail) Waterfall which gushes out of the narrow opening between Shuangjian and Wenshu Peaks, then bursts into dozens of watery wisps that resemble the tail of a pony; and the Lushan Waterfall, scores of feet high which sweeps down from between the Heming and Hangbao Peaks. The two waterfalls merge at Qing Yu Gorge presenting a magnificent view of "two white dragons flying out of the gorge."

On the rocks around the pool are inscriptions written by men of letters of past dynasties. The most valuable are "Qing Yu Gorge" and "Number One Mountain" written by Mi Fei of the Song Dynasty. East of the pool is Shu Yu Pavilion, to the west is Guan Pu Pavilion, both rebuilt after 1949. Beside the gorge are the ruins of Xiu Feng Temple, where there are still a number of stone tablets bearing ancient inscriptions.

Guan Yin Bridge, Yu Yuan Pool and the Sixth Spring Under Heaven

Across the San Xia Ravine in front of the Wu Lao Peak is the arched Guan Yin (Goddess of Mercy) Bridge built in 1014 A.D. The arch is made of 105 stone slabs, each weighing a ton. This 81 ft. (24.4 m.) long bridge is strong enough for present day trucks to pass over. The bridge is a clear demonstration of how early China's engineers mastered the mechanics of the arch.

Passing from the bridge up San Xia Ravine one reaches Yu Yuan Pool so named because a poet once wrote:

"*Unfathomable is the pool*
Where lies the white stone."

The white stone in the pool resembles a flock of sheep and therefore is called Marble Sheep. On the left of the pool are four pine trees resembling the pillars of a pavilion. This is the site of the Fei Lai Pavilion where it is said Governor Li Bo of the Tang Dynasty did his daily reading.

To the east of the bridge is a pavilion which houses a clear spring called the "Sixth Spring Under Heaven." As the story goes, Lu Yu of the Tang Dynasty sampled all the springs in China and decided that this one should rank number six. The water is pure, sweet, and invigorating.

Xingzi Hot Springs

Also called Lushan Hot Springs. The water at the mouth is 162° Fahrenheit (72° Celsius) and the average temperature of the water in the pool is 145° Fahrenheit (62.6° Celsius). As is recorded in the "Compendium of Materia Media" written by Li Shizhen, the well known pharmacologist of the Ming Dynasty (1368-1644 A.D.), "The Lushan Hot Springs have four openings. They are hot all the year round." The waters are good for treating rheumatism, spasms, paralysis, scabies, and tinea. After 1949 a completely equipped sanatorium was built on a site which at the time had been abandoned and had become overgrown with brambles. Hydrotherapy, supplemented by physiotherapy and traditional Chinese medicine, is producing good results.

Xuzhou (HSUCHOW)

The city of Xuzhou is at the junction of the railway lines running from Tianjin to Pukou and from Gansu to the Sea. It is a communications center for traffic between the four provinces of Jiangsu, Shangdong, Anhui, and Henan. Surrounding the city are hills with many scenic attractions.

PLACES OF INTEREST

Monument to the Martyrs of the Huai Hai Battle

A monument and memorial hall were opened here in 1965 in memory of those who died in the Huai Hai Battle, a decisive campaign waged by the Chinese People's Liberation Army from November 1948 to January 1949.

The monument, 126 ft. (38.5 m.) high, was built on the east

side of the Feng Huang (Phoenix) Hill, which is south of the city. It faces east, and on the front is an inscription in gold by Chairman Mao, "Monument to the Martyrs of the Huai Hai Battle." On the base in front there is another inscription and on each side, carvings in relief. Surrounding the monument are pavilions and a corridor. A flight of 129 steps leading to a spacious platform lends the edifice dignity and grandeur.

The memorial hall has inscriptions by the late Premier Zhou Enlai, and the late Chairman Zhu De; as well as inscriptions by CPC Vice-Chairman Deng Xiaoping, Chen Yun, and others. There are over 2,400 photos, relics, charts, and paintings. The grounds cover 100 acres (40 ha.) and are covered with pines and cypresses symbolic of the evergreen spirit of the revolutionary martyrs.

Yun Long Hill (Dragon in Clouds)

Its undulating shape, like that of a dragon weaving through mists and clouds, gives this promontory its name. It stands opposite Jiu Li Hill to the north and Zi Fang Hill to the east, with the city in between. A dense cover of old pines and cypresses screens off the sky while at its foot waves of Yun Long Lake ripple away into the distance. The lakeside is lined with willows. Many places of scenic beauty and historical interest are found here, including a stone carving from the Northern Wei Dynasty (386-534 A.D.) at the top of the hill, Xing Hua Temple, Fang He (Release the Crane) Pavilion, Zhao He (Call the Crane) Pavilion, Yin He (Water the Crane) Pavilion, Shi Yi (Try on a Garment) Pavilion, and Song Hui Pavilion.

Yan'an (YENAN)

Yan'an is on the northern Shaanxi (Shensi) Plateau by the Yanshui River. It is surrounded by hills with cave dwellings amidst the cliffs. An ancient mountain town, Yan'an received its name in the Sui Dynasty over 1,300 years ago. This is historically one of the most revered sites in China. It was the headquarters of the Communist Party from 1937 to 1947.

Led by Chairman Mao Zedong, the Red Army arrived at the town of Wuqi in northern Shaanxi in October, 1935, after completing the eight thousand mile Long March. They moved to Yan'an in 1937. During their more than ten years in Yan'an and northern Shaanxi, they led the Chinese people to victory in the war against Japan and the War of Liberation.

The main places to visit are the sites where the Chinese leaders, Chairman Mao, Liu Shaoqi, Zhou Enlai and Zhu De, lived and worked. There is the Museum Dedicated to Chairman Mao's Leadership. Other revolutionary sites are at the foot of Fenghuang Hill and at Yangjialing, Zaoyuan (Date Orchard), Wangjiaping, and Nanniwan.

There is a university, several factories, and some historical remains including Buddhist caves, the Yan'an Pagoda, a Ming tomb, a Taoist Hermitage and a Buddhist cemetery.

Yangshuo (YANGSHUO)

From Guilin to Yangshuo, the Li Jiang River winds among mountains and the scenery here is like a picture scroll 30 mi. (50 km.) long. On the six hour boat trip downstream to Yangshuo, one sees the "scroll" unfolding. On nearing the Erlang Gorge, a huge cliff comes into view. This is the famous "Picture Hill" which consists of horses of different colors caught in different positions.

On the right, after passing Picture Hill, there is Huangbu (Yellow Cloth) Beach. Here the river is wide and flows gently. Seven graceful peaks are likened to seven quiet young girls standing shoulder to shoulder. The fabled *Xingping Wonderland* starts here. With hills at its back and a river in the front, Xingping is a famous, ancient town. Caishi Hill looms high in front of the town while at the back the five peaks of the majestic Wuzhi Mountains vie with one another in beauty. The area is thick with bamboo groves. When a boat sails near, it disturbs the peace and makes egrets take wing, adding charm to the picturesque scene.

Around Yangshuo, there are dozens of peaks which form a ring and look like petals of a blooming lotus flower. The town of Yangshuo is right in the center of this green lotus. From the hilltops one has a wonderful view of the strange peaks and the new buildings and streets of the town. In the vicinity of Yangshuo, there are scenic spots like Page Boy Hill, the Tianjia River, the Ancient Ferry under a Banyan Tree, Chuan Yan Cave, and Moon Hill.

Ying Jiang Pavilion in Yangshuo

Yangzhou (YANGCHOW)

Yangzhou of Jiangsu (Kiangsu) Province is located on the bank of the Chang Jiang (Yangtze) River and the lower reaches of the Huai He River, with the Grand Canal running right through the city proper. It is an ancient city, built in Jiangsu-style architecture. Its origins go back to the Spring and Autumn Period (770-476 B.C.), about 2,400 years ago. Visitors often return home with a new concept of what "old" really is. For one who is used to thinking of his country's history in hundreds of years, it is undoubtedly interesting to find in China places which have continuous histories of more than two thousand years.

PLACES OF INTEREST
Shou Xi Hu (Slim West Lake)
The shape of the lake — long, narrow, and twisted — gives this scenic spot its name. The flowering plants along the banks are artistically spaced, giving the scene an aura of sustained elegance.

Fa Jing Temple
The temple, located to the northwest of the city, has several famous buildings in its precincts, such as the Memorial Hall of Monk Jian Zhen of the Tang Dynasty and Ping Shan Hall.

Ge Yuan Garden
There are luxuriant bamboo groves in the garden. Its rock gar-

Yangzhou

dens are constructed in an artistic style combining northern and southern methods of arrangement.

Ji Xiao Villa

The pavilions and towers are compactly laid out with great ingenuity giving it a picturesque and poetic quality.

Jiangdu Water Control Project

China's biggest project for diverting water from the Changjiang (Yangtze River) is in Jiangdu County near Yangzhou. All the work in designing, building, and installation of equipment was done without foreign assistance. Construction started in 1961 and was completed in 1975. A multi-purpose project for irrigation, drainage, navigation and power generation, it consists mainly of four large, modern electric pumping stations, six medium sized check gates, three navigation locks, and two trunk waterways.

SHOPPING

Yangzhou lacquerware is an attractive product of this area. It is inlaid with shells and mother-of-pearl and is produced in a variety of designs and patterns. Light passing over this lacquerware brings out a stunning variety of colors.

Yantai (YENTAI)

Yantai is a port city on the northern coast of the Jiaodong Peninsula. It is hemmed in by mountains opening on one side to face the Bo Hai Sea and the Liaodong Peninsula beyond. In southern Yantai there is a chain of undulating hills and the north has a number of off-shore islands such as Zhifu and Kongtong, forming a natural barrier. Yuhuang Peak, with an ancient edifice commanding an excellent view of the city, is a scenic spot so much like a fairyland in the Bo Hai Sea, that it is often referred to as the minor "Penglai" of Chinese mythology.

Civilization here can be traced back two thousand years. Qishan, a defense outpost, was set up in 1398 A.D., the 31st year of the reign of Hongwu in the Ming Dynasty. Beacon towers were built from Muping in the east to Penglai in the west, including one on top of the hill north of the city. They were popularly called "wolves' smoke towers" because wolves' dung was burnt to signal alarm. Hence the names Yantaishan (Smoke Tower Hill) for the peak and Yantai (Smoke Tower) for the city.

The area is famous for the cultivation of apple trees. Yantai apples are as famous at home and abroad as Laiyang pears. The Yantai winery built over eighty years ago as the Chang Yu Winery, produces twelve kinds of wine. They include three of the country's top quality alcoholic beverages.

Yantai is a deep-water, ice-free port. It has been repaired and expanded several times since 1949 and can accommodate seven passenger or cargo ships at the same time. Now open to foreign vessels, it is an important port for the country's maritime transport. It is also a fishing center.

Yichang (ICHANG)

Yichang (formerly known as Yilin), located on the north bank of the Changjiang (Yangtze River), is at the gateway of the Xiling Gorge. (See Changjiang Gorges p. 148). Yichang was known as a passage between Sichuan and Hubei Provinces, a trading and transportation port, and an important town for fairs as early as the Eastern Han Dynasty (25-220 A.D.). Now it has become the political and economic center of the western part of Hubei Province. Oranges, mushrooms, whitefungi walnuts, tea and lacquerware are among the local products.

PLACES OF INTEREST
Sanyou Cave (Three Friends Cave)
This cave lies at the foot of the Xiling Hill on the north bank of the Nanjin Pass. It is best known for the poetic inscriptions on its walls made by three writers of the Tang Dynasty (618-907 A.D.). There are also stone carvings in the cave and some inscriptions made during the Song Dynasty (960-1280 A.D.).

Gezhouba Dam Water Control Project

The Gezhouba Dam Water Control Project is the first giant dam project on the Changjiang. After the river rushes out of Nanjin Pass it abruptly turns south, slowing down and widening. Approximately 1.8 mi. (3 km.) past the turn, at Yichang, two islets — Gezhouba and Xiba — divide the river into three waterways. It is here that the giant project is under way. The massive dam includes a hydraulic power plant with 21 sets of turbo-generators, navigation locks, spillways and scouring sluices. The hydropower installations have a total generating capacity of 2.72 million kilowatts and an average annual output projected at 14.1 billion kilowatt hours. One spillway was completed and put into use on January 2, 1981. This 27-gate spillway can discharge a volume of over 2,808,000 cu. ft. (80,-000 cu. m.) of water per second.

Yixing (YIHSING)

Located in the southeastern part of Jiangsu Province, the city of Yixing has a mild climate. Its pottery is well known all over the country.

PLACES OF INTEREST

Dingshu Village of Yixing

With a setting similar to a traditional landscape painting, this picturesque town is quite secluded, with Tai Hu Lake on the east and hills on the other three sides. On entering one finds oneself literally in a world of pottery. Almost every family here is engaged in making ceramics. Kilns are found everywhere.

In ancient times it was known as the Pottery Capital. Archeological finds indicate that pottery was made here more than five thousand years ago. Pottery and primitive porcelains were made as early as the Shang and Zhou Dynasties. The manufacture of glazed pottery began in the Qin and Han Dynasties (221 B.C.-220 A.D.), and kilns were built in many widely scattered places. From the Wei Dynasty to the Northern and Southern Dynasties (220-581 A.D.), Qun Hill near Yixing was an important center for producing early ceramics in southern China. From the Sui to the Five Dynasties (581-

960 A.D.) ceramics were produced in great quantities, particularly after the introduction of an improved "Dragon" kiln. The Song and Yuan Dynasties (960-1368 A.D.) saw the creation of a dull brown or purplish stoneware known as boccaro in Dingshu. The production of pottery for civil and military use was expanded on an unprecedented scale, so that the town became a model for the whole country. Qun pottery and the dull brown stoneware rose in fame during the Ming and Qing Dynasties (1368-1911 A.D.). Its ceramic production rivaled the well known Jingdezhen porcelain.

The dull brown stoneware, a traditional product, is made from the local clay especially adaptable to pottery making. Known as the "clay of clays", it assumes a natural color of either purple, vermillion, or cream. Since the clay is sandy and no glaze is applied either inside or outside, it is slightly porous. A popular product is the dull brown teapot which is made in attractive shapes. These teapots have the capacity to retain for a long time the color, flavor, and fragrance of the tea brewed in them. Tea kept overnight will not deteriorate even on hot summer days. They do not crack when used to boil tea in winter and the outside does not become extremely hot. They serve not only as articles of daily use but as decorations or *objets d'art*. The longer the teapots are in use, the glossier they become. Thus they have earned the reputation of being "the best teapots in the world" and as such are cherished possessions both at home and abroad.

Flower pots made from this clay provide excellent conditions for growing plants since they tend to counteract root decay and keep the leaves from shedding. Large casseroles are also made suitable for steaming chicken, duck or other meat. The steamed meat usually turns out tender and the sauce well cooked and delicious. Today's pottery capital is flourishing more than ever before.

Shan Juan Cave

A cave formed more than a million years ago is in Luo Yan Hill 15 mi. (25 km.) southwest of Yixing. As the legend goes, some four thousand years ago a man called Shan Juan, for whom the cave is named, was reluctant to become involved in Yao's transfer of the crown to Shun and chose to live here in seclusion. The cave occupies an area of 54,000 sq. ft. (5,000 sq. m.) and looks like a magnificent three-storied marble building. All together there are four caves, which interconnect and have channels running through them on which boats can travel. It is often conceded to be the "biggest wonder south of Chang Jiang River."

At the opening of the middle cave stands the Pillar Peak, a 23 ft. (7 m.) stalagmite formed by water dripping from the stalactite above. The cave proper, spacious enough to hold a thousand people, is flanked by two huge rocks. One is in the shape of a lion and the other an elephant, which gives it its name, Lion-Elephant Hall.

From the middle cave one can ascend to the upper cave which is always filled with mist and is called Misty Realm. It is also known as the Warm Cave because it is warm in winter. Water trickling from the walls gathers into a crystal clear pool in which one can see "lotus flower reflections." Walking along the stone wall one encounters a pair of columns called Ancient Plum Tree Twins. The clear water and "plum trees" form a picture in translucent green, while above the overhanging rocks, like surging waves or huge clouds, shut out the sky. It is really a fantastic sight.

The middle cave leads to the lower through a man-made tunnel down 105 steps. The babbling sound of flowing water grows louder and louder as one descends. Finally it roars like wind and thunder or tossing surf on the shore. It may also beat like gongs and drums or pound like thousands of horses galloping. That is why the opening of the cave has been named "Billows Gateway" or "Gate of Gongs and Drums." There is a waterfall at the opening and the cave is also called "Cascade Cave." In it are numerous marvels of natural construction. Stone walls rising 66 ft. (20 m.) from the ground join to form the Arrow Gate. A towering stone pine with thick foliage spreading like a canopy looks utterly real whether seen at close hand or from a distance.

From the interior of the lower cave one enters the 396 ft. (120 m.) grotto with its rugged walls of grotesquely shaped rocks. Colored lights shining on the water give one the feeling of having arrived at the Crystal Palace of the Dragon King. One can also go downstream by boat to the outlet which opens on a broad view.

Once ashore, one passes around to the rear which is thickly wooded and has a network of small paths winding between the shade trees. A legend tells of Zhu Yingtai, a young lady in revolt against feudal conventions during the Jin Dynasty, who disguised herself as a male student in order to come here to study. Yingtai Tower remains and from it one can gaze out upon the lovely mountain scenery and the surrounding countryside.

Zhang Gong (The Revered Zhang) Grotto
The million-year-old grotto is in Mengfeng Mountain, 12 mi. (20 km.) southwest of the city. According to legend, a Han Dynasty priest, Zhang Daoling, lived a secluded religious life here. This 3,300 ft. (1,000 m.) long cave consists of seventy-two smaller caves linked by 1,500 man-made stone steps. It is like a fascinating fairy cave with winding paths and caves within caves. The climate is miraculously mild all the year round. It is sometimes referred to as a "Cave in Paradise."

Once inside the grotto the visitor encounters a spacious stone hall called Sea Mansion in front of which is a fathomless stone sea. The imposing vault is like the ridge of a high mountain. All around are strangely-shaped rocks and fantastic stalactites. Steps spiral up to the magnificent Hall of the Ocean King, overhung by jagged rock, enveloped in mist and cloud.

Two huge rocks make a pair of palace lanterns. Two others are like ancient pines standing straight and silent. Both sides of the hall open into clusters of smaller caves. They have metaphorical names such as Alimentary Canal Cave, Nostril Cave, Tunnel Cave, and Skylight Cave. From the grotto exit, it is only a short distance to the summit of the mountain. Far away to the east Tai Hu Lake meets the sky.

Yueyang (YOYANG)
Yueyang, located in northern Hunan Province by the Dongting Lake, is a city with over 2,000 years of history. It has a charming landscape and numerous historical relics.

PLACES OF INTEREST
Yueyang Tower
This tower lies on the west side of the city near the lake. It is considered to be one of the three most famous towers in South China. (The other two being Huanghe Tower in Wuchang and Tengwang Pavilion in Nanchang.) Built in 716 A.D. in the early Tang Dynasty (618-907 A.D.), renovated in 1045 A.D.

during the Song Dynasty (960-1280 A.D.) and rebuilt in 1867 during the Qing Dynasty (1644-1911 A.D.). It has preserved the artistic style of the Song Dynasty.

Dongting Lake
This large body of water stretches over an area of about 1,500 sq. mi. (3,900 sq. km.). It is the second largest fresh-water lake in China. To take a boatride in its clear and rippling water is indeed a treat.

Junshan
Junshan is a hilly isle in the Dongting Lake. Produced here is the rare "silver needle tea" (when the tea is infused, the tea leaves stand up like tiny needles and emit a delicate fragrance). This tea won a gold medal at the Leipzig International Fair (1956) and was called "Jade Inlaid with Gold."

Zhangzhou (CHANGCHOW)

Zhangzhou, an ancient city on Zhangzhou plain in Fujian Province, is famous for being a "city of flowers and fruits." The cultivation of narcissus in Zhangzhou has a history of over 500 years. Zhangzhou narcissus is characterized by its elegant style, translucent leaves, and straight stocks. Over a million bulbs of narcissus are cultivated annually, most of which are for export. The eight varieties of fruit produced in Zhangzhou are very famous. They are: Tianbao banana, Jiuhu litchi, longan, orange, pomelo, pineapple, carambola and mango.

PLACES OF INTEREST
Nanshan (Southern Hills) Temple
This temple was built in the early years of the Tang Dynasty (618-907 A.D.). It lies at the foot of the Nanshan Mountains beside the Jiulong River. Inside the temple is a 17 ft. (5.3 m.) stone statue of Buddha carved by celebrated Tang artisans. There is also an Indian Buddhist scripture from the Song Dynasty (1250-1265 A.D.), and camellia planted during the Ming Dynasty (1368-1644 A.D.). There is also a Ming Buddhist scripture (Huayan Jing) written by monks with their blood, and a two-ton, white jade Buddha and other interesting artifacts from the Qing Dynasty (1644-1911 A.D.).

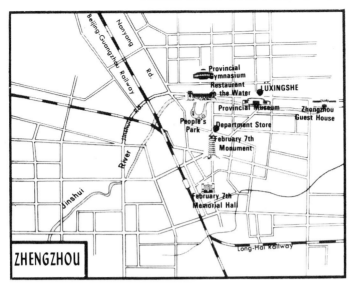

Zhengzhou (CHENGCHOU)

Zhengzhou is the capital of Henan (Honan) Province and is one of China's textile centers. It lies on the southern bank of the Huang He (Yellow River) at the junction of the Longhai and Beijing-Guangzhou Railways. A number of factories are open to visitors: the Zhengzhou No. 3 and No. 6 Cotton Textile Mills, the Zhengzhou Textile Machinery Plant, and the Zhengzhou Printing and Dyeing Works. The famous Shaolin Monastery is nearby. Visitors may reach there by 1.5 hours drive.

PLACES OF INTEREST

The February 7 Monument

Led by the Chinese Communist Party, a general strike of railway workers happened here on February 7, 1923. The monument was set up in 1971 to commemorate the struggle. It has twin towers rising 208 ft. (63 m.) and there is an exhibition of revolutionary relics of the general strike period.

The People's Park

The park occupies an area in the center of Zhengzhou on both banks of the meandering Jinshui (Golden Water) River. It is covered with evergreen trees and many varieties of flowers. The pavilions and winding corridors are artistically laid out. It

293

The February 7th Monument

is a pleasant experience to go boating on the river where the water reflects the surrounding scenery.

Henan Provincial Historical Museum

Many precious cultural artifacts unearthed and collected from all parts of the Province are on exhibition here. The exhibits illustrate the historical development of ancient societies and the great creativity of the people in China's central plains.

Prehistoric Site at Dahecun (Big River Village)

Excavations at Dahecun on the northern outskirts of Zhengzhou brought to light remains of the Yangshao "painted pottery" culture and the Longshan "black pottery" culture. Both of these cultures date back some five thousand years to the Neolithic age. The cultural layer is over 16 ft. (5 m.) thick and contains the foundations of many houses, tombs, and kilns. Numerous stone implements and bone tools were found, as well as pottery, lotus seeds, and grain.

Shang City Ruins

The ruins are located inside the city limits of Zhengzhou. The 4 mi. (7 km.) long wall of the ancient Shang city is still distinguishable. According to estimates, it goes back some 3,500 years and is the oldest site of an early Shang city to be discovered since 1949.

SHOPPING

There are a variety of shopping opportunities to be found in the following stores: Henan Provincial Arts & Crafts Company, Zhengzhou Municpal Arts and Crafts Service Department, Zhengzhou Municipal Friendship Store, and Zi Jing Store.

Zhenjiang (CHENCHIANG)

Zhenjiang is located in the central part of Jiangsu Province on the south bank of the Chang Jiang (Yangtze) River amidst picturesque hills. Here the east-west Shanghai-Nanjing Railway intersects the Grand Canal running north and south.

The city has a history of more than 2,500 years, its origins dating back to the twenty-seventh year (545 B.C.) of King Ling's reign in the Eastern Zhou Dynasty. Spots to visit include Jinshan and Beigushan Hills on the outskirts and also Jiaoshan Hill on an island in the river. The city is an important harbor and is known for its vinegar, pickled vegetables, and silk.

PLACES OF INTEREST

Jinshan Hill

This hill, northwest of the city, is 198 ft. (60 m.) high with a circumference of 1,716 ft. (520 m.) at its base. Halfway up is the Jinshan Temple. On the crest is the octagonal seven-story Ci Shou (Kindness and Longevity) Pagoda built of wood and bricks. There are four caves: Fa Hai (Buddhist Sea), Bai Long (White Dragon), Zhao Yang (Morning Sun) and Luo Han (The *Arhat*). West of the hill is a spring know in the Tang Dynasty (619-907 A.D.) as "The First Spring Under Heaven."

Jiaoshan Hill

Located in the middle of the river, this hill is named after Jiao Guang of the Eastern Han Dynasty (25-220 A.D.) who lived

Cishou Tower, Jinshan Temple

here in seclusion. It lies to the northeast of the city 495 ft. (150 m.) high with a base circumference of 5,600 ft. (2,000 m.). Clothed the year round in dark green, the color of jade, the hill is therefore also known as Fu Yu (Floating Jade) Hill. There are other scenic spots: Ding Hui Temple, Hua Yan Tower, Guan Lan (Viewing Billows) Tower, Bai Shou (Longevity) Pavilion, Zhuang Guan (Grand View) Pavilion, and Dong Sheng (Rising in the East) Tower. At the top of the hill is Xi Jiang Tower, a good place for watching the sunrise and observing river life.

Beigushan Hill

The hill, 158 ft. (48 m.) high, can be seen to the east of the city by the side of the river. Places of interest on it include Gan Lu (Sweet Dew) Temple, Duo Jing (Scenic) Tower, Ling Yun (Soar to the Clouds) Pavilion and an iron pagoda.

Scenic Areas in the Southern Suburbs

Dense woods, babbling streams, and quiet recesses are the attractions of the suburban wooded hills on the southern outskirts of the city. Hidden in the green foliage is Zhao Yin Temple. Here Xiao Tong, son of Emperor Wu of the Liang Dynasty (502-577 A.D.) studied and compiled the Zhao Ming Essays, the first anthology of essays ever collected in China. Zhu Lin (Bamboo Grove) Temple stands at the foot of Jiashan Hill, surrounded by thousands of young green bamboo plants as well as tall old trees. The tomb of Mi Fei, a famous painter of the Northern Song Dynasty (960-1127 A.D.) lies in front of He Lin Temple. The azaleas growing here in profusion are known far and wide.

Museum

This paradise for historians, archaeologists, and art lovers was built in 1958. Its collection boasts several rare editions of ancient books and includes paintings, calligraphy, rubbings, and bronzes.

Zhuoxian County (CHOHSIEN COUNTY)

Zhuoxian County is located 37 mi. (60 km.) southwest of Beijing. To the north of the county is Zhoukoudian where Peking Man once lived. To the south is Baiyangdian Lake where fish and crabs are abundant. Zhuoxian County was originally an ancient city and the magnificent Western Tombs of the Qing Dynasty were constructed here.

HOTELS

A newly built hotel in this old town has aroused special interest among tourists. Built in 1980, the hotel has two courtyards typical of Chinese traditional architecture. The setting is peaceful and delicate with bamboo, unusual rocks, stone lions and covered walkways, but the indoor facilities are completely modern. All of the 54 rooms have private bathrooms and are air conditioned.

Zunhua (TSUNHUA)

A large group of Imperial tombs of the Qing Dynasty (1644-1911 A.D.) is located at Zunhua (Tsunhua) County, Hebei Province, 76 mi. (125 km.) to the east of Beijing. Five of them are for emperors, fourteen for empresses. Concubines (136) and other women of the Imperial family were interred here as well.

At the center of this group of tombs is Xiao Ling, the tomb of Shunzhi, the first emperor of the Qing Dynasty. It is right before the main peak of the Changrui Mountains. From the stone arch which marks the entrance to the whole area, to the foot of the peak is a 3 mi. (5 km.) long axis. On both sides are dozens of structures of various designs linked by a 40 ft. (12 m.) wide path of brick and stone.

The extensive stone carving and numerous stone structures are characteristic of the advanced techniques in stone carving of the Qing Dynasty. The central path to the tombs is lined with stone figures and animals like those of the Ming Tombs near Beijing. They represent ministers, generals, horses, unicorns, elephants, camels and lions. The carvings are vivid and graceful, each complete in one piece of stone. The stately stone arch at the entrance, decorated with carved animals in various postures, is impressive.

The underground palaces are an important part of the tombs. The tomb of Yu Ling, which has been repaired, is different from that of Ding Ling near Beijing in that it is full of

Eastern Qing Tombs

Double Baboon Peak, Zhenjiang

stone carvings and inscriptions. The palace is 178 ft. (54 m.) underground with a total floor space of 3,528 sq. ft. (327 sq. m.). Entering, one passes through four stone doors and on each of them is a finely carved Bodhisattva posed in a different graceful standing position.

The arch of the first door has carvings of the four celestial kings, each seated and holding a symbolic object: a pipa (musical instrument), a sword, a flag, and a tower. All the huge stones used in the construction of the palace are carved and the vault overhead is covered with delicate designs.

Of all the tombs of the Qing Dynasty, the one for Dowager Empress Ci Xi has the best surface structure, indicating the advanced technology of the time. On the white marble balustrades around the Long En Dian (Hall of Great Kindness) are carvings of auspicious dragons and phoenixes, surging waves, and floating clouds. The dragon and phoenix stone in front of the hall is a unique work of art. Unlike similar dragon and phoenix motifs which appear in relief side by side on other tomb stones, this one has the phoenix above the dragon playing with a pearl.

The walls inside Long En Dian Hall and the two side halls are made of carved brick with patterns of plates and cups. In the middle there are five bats signifying longevity. The beams and ceilings are gilded, and the pillars have golden dragons coiling around them, creating an aura of splendor rarely found in other Imperial tombs.

5. Appendix

HELPFUL HINTS

Packing Recommendations. Bring those items for which there is no local substitution. Any special medicine that is required should be packed in sufficient supply. Envelopes purchased in China generally are not gummed. Adhesive tape would come in handy if you plan to mail letters during your stay. A small, pocket flashlight should be carried along if you anticipate outside activities in the evenings where street lights may not exist. A box of tissues will prove useful. If you wish to use an electric razor or hairdryer, bring a current adapter. China's basic current is 220 volts and it will ruin appliances designed for 110 volts unless used with an adapter. A shortwave radio is quite useful (battery or plug-in) because there are only a few publications available in English.

Clothing depends on the season. Refer to Temperature Charts on pages 322-323. In general, casual and comfortable clothes are best. Your visit to China will not require an evening dress or formal attire. It is more important to be prompt than to be elaborately dressed. Simple dresses, blouses and skirts or slacks for women, and trousers, open-necked shirts, or sports jackets for men are the norm. It would be wise to pack a light sweater for the evenings. A light-weight raincoat is recommended. In winter bring a warm coat and warm sleeping attire. In summer, having mosquito repellent available may be advisable, especially when traveling in the south. It is very important to have good, comfortable walking shoes.

Customs Procedures. When entering and leaving China you must have with you a valid passport and an official visa. (Your tour guide may keep the visas for the entire group.) Customs is a simple procedure and nothing to worry about. As long as all your documents are in order, going through customs will only take a few minutes.

Punctuality. In China it is considered bad manners to be late. Offices tend to open early and close promptly. Insofar as possible planes, trains, tours, meetings, and performances start on time. When attending a banquet be sure to allow sufficient traveling time to arrive at your destination early so as not to insult your host.

Cuisine. Be adventurous! Food in China is superb. Visitors are urged to sample the various local cuisines during their trip (although most hotel dining rooms have chefs skilled in the preparation of Western-style food). It is best to experiment freely and to eat in groups of four or more. The amount of food prepared for any given dish is the same no matter how many people are at the table. A good rule of thumb is to order one more dish than the number of guests at the table. Eating in a group enables you to try more dishes and maximize your familiarity with the various cuisines. There are no such things as chop suey, chow mein, or fortune cookies in China.

Chopsticks. You may or may not wish to experiment with chopsticks. There are always knives and forks available in the hotels and restaurants that you visit. Start out by using chopsticks and then, if you find it is too difficult, ask for a knife and fork. One of the most important aspects related to eating in China is to enjoy the experience.

Transportation. There is good, inexpensive public transport in the major cities and a large supply of taxicabs. Taxis can be easily contacted from your hotel. If you are going out for the evening, it is wise to retain the cab for after the theater or banquet. Just ask the cab driver to wait. The expense is not great, and it saves the visitor the difficulty of attempting to hire another cab. Be sure to mark down the number of your cab and the color. Although you think you'll remember, after several hours all cabs seem to look alike.

Souvenirs. There is a large variety of products one can purchase while in China ranging from very expensive to relatively inexpensive. Your tour will allow sufficient "shopping" time in the various cities visited. Army caps are a popular, inexpensive item to bring back for relatives and friends. Also tee shirts. Signature seals, popularly called chops, make a lovely gift and can be purchased in a wide range of prices. Signature seals are carved pieces of stone with symbols cut into the base which can be transferred to paper using an ink pad. If you buy a set of signature seals (eight in a box), you will save considerably over buying them individually. Unless you want a person's name carved on each, the characters for "long life" or "double happiness" are a nice substitute and only require the expense of carving one symbol. Ink pads in tin cases, as used by the people, may be bought inexpensively at the General Department Store. More expensive porcelain ink cases intended for gift giving are for sale at the chop stores.

Beverages. Don't drink the water. Every day a thermos of hot water and a carafe of cold water will be brought to your hotel room. Use this for washing your teeth, making instant coffee or tea, or mixing drinks. There are a wide variety of domestic beverages available from soft drinks to spirits. Some of them, such as Tsingtao Beer, you may already be familiar with. In the large hotels it is possible to purchase American whiskey, French champagne, and even California wines. Chinese coffee is quite good but some find it too strong. If you have your own favorite brand of instant coffee, pack a small jar for early mornings.

Valuables. There is no need to check valuables at your hotel since anything that might be misplaced and that is traceable will be returned to you. You can also depend on sales help and taxi drivers to give you the correct change.

Cigarettes. There are twenty brands of cigarettes produced locally and there are a few foreign brands (American, English, and Canadian) for sale. If you have developed a taste for a particular type, then it would be best to bring a supply of them with you for your stay.

Emergency. If there is an emergency and a traveler must be reached during his stay in China, the best places to call are the China Travel Service in Hong Kong (Telephone Number [5] 25 91 21) or the United States Embassy in Beijing (Peking) (Telephone Number 52 20 33). A security officer is on duty at the Embassy twenty-four hours a day.

Film Developing. While you will likely plan to have your exposed film developed once you return home, some brands of film can be processed with a high degree of quality reproduction if time allows. Film which can be developed: negative Kodacolor and Fuji Color, positive Ektachrome, and both negative and positive Agfa Color and Sakura.

Newspapers. As a special service to English speaking visitors, the Peoples Republic of China recently began publication of an English-language daily newspaper called the *China Daily*. In addition to international news, the paper plans to feature sections on world sporting events, finance and entertainment in Beijing.

CHINA INTERNATIONAL TRAVEL SERVICE (LÜXINGSHE)
Branches and Addresses

Head Office:	6 East Changan Street, Beijing Cable address: LÜXINGSHE BEIJING
Anshan	Anshan Hotel, Anshan
Beijing	Overseas Chinese Hotel, Beijing Cable address: 5861 Beijing
Changchun	No. 2 Stalin Blvd., Changchun Telephone: 91 19
Chengdu	Jingjiang Hotel, Chengdu Telephone: 59 14
Chongqing	People's Auditorium, Renmin Rd., Chongqing Telephone: 5 30 72
Dalian	No. 1 Stalin Square, Luda City Telephone: 3 55 14
Datong	2nd Floor, Revolutionary Comm., Datong Telephone: 27 04
Fushun	Fushun Guest House, Fushun Telephone: 65 50
Guangzhou	No. 179, Huanshi Road, Guangzhou Cable address: 1954 Guangzhou Telephone: 3 26 48
Guilin	Ronhu North Road, Guilin Telephone: 38 70
Harbin	No. 124 Dazhi St., Nangang District Telephone: 3 02 74
Hangzhou	North Huanhu Rd., Hangzhou Hotel, Hangzhou
Jilin	No. 223 Songjiang Road, Jilin Telephone: 35 55
Jinan	No. 372 Jingsan Road, Weiliu Road, Jinan Telephone: 3 53 51
Jiujiang	No. 77 Nansi Road, Jiujiang Telephone: 25 26

Kaifeng	No. 102 Ziyou Road, Kaifeng Telephone: 37 37
Kunming	East Dongfeng Road, Kunming Telephone: 52 86
Liuzhou	No. 1 Wenge Road, Liuzhou Hotel Telephone: 32 29
Nanchang	**Bayi Dadao, Jiangsi Hotel, Nanchan** **Telephone: 6 25 71**
Nanjing	No. 261 North Zhongshan Road, Nanjing Telephone: 8 51 53
Nanning	Fanxiu Road, Nanning Telephone: 47 93
Qingdao	No. 18 Longsan Road, Qingdao Telephone: 2 88 77
Shanghai	No. 66 East Nanjing Road, Shanghai Cable address: Luxingshe Shanghai
Suzhou	No. 115 Youyi Road, Suzhou Telephone: 46 41
Tianjin	No. 55 Chongqing Dao, Heping District Telephone: 3 48 31
Wuhan	Jianghanyi Road, Xuangong Hotel, Wuhan
Wuxi	No. 53 Dong Zhan Road, Wuxi Telephone: 56 72
Xi'an	Renmin Hotel, Xi'an Telephone: 2 38 58
Xuzhou	No. 20 Heping Road, Xuzhou Telephone: 48 42
Yantai	No. 10 Shuntai Street, Yantai Telephone: 36 15
Zhengzhou	No. 8 Jingshuihe Road, Zhengzhou Telephone: 55 78
Zibo	Zhongxin Road, Zhangdian District Telephone: 2 21 38

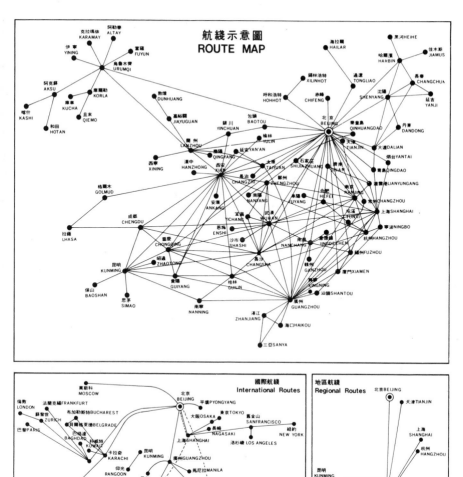

航綫示意圖
ROUTE MAP

萬科MOSCOW
法蘭克福FRANKFURT
布加勒斯特BUCHAREST
貝爾格萊德BELGRADE
倫敦LONDON
蘇黎世ZURICH
巴黎PARIS
巴格達BAGHDAD
科威特KUWAIT
卡拉奇KARACHI
仰光RANGOON
亞的斯亞貝巴ADDIS ABABA
北京BEIJING
平壤PYONGYANG
大阪OSAKA
東京TOKYO
長崎NAGASAKI
舊金山SANFRANCISCO
紐約NEW YORK
洛杉磯LOS ANGELES
上海SHANGHAI
昆明KUNMING
廣州GUANGZHOU
曼谷BANGKOK
新加坡SINGAPORE
馬尼拉MANILA
悉尼SYDNEY
墨爾本MELBOURNE

國際航綫
International Routes

--- 國際聯營航綫 International pool service

地區航綫
Regional Routes

北京BEIJING
天津TIANJIN
上海SHANGHAI
杭州HANGZHOU
昆明KUNMING
廣州GUANGZHOU
香港HONG KONG

309

RAILWAYS

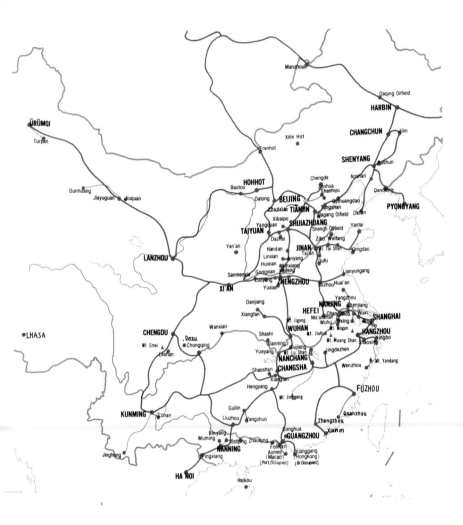

DISTANCES BETWEEN MAIN TOURIST CITIES

(Shortest distance between cities by rail in miles)

	Beijing	Shanghai	Tianjin	Guangzhou	Nanning	Changsha	Shaoshan	Wuhan	Nanjing	Wuxi	Suzhou	Hangzhou	Jinan	Qingdao	Xi'an	Kunming	Chengdu	Chongqing	Zhengzhou	Shijiazhuang	Dalian	Shenyang	Changchun	Harbin
Shanghai	908																							
Tianjin	85	823																						
Guangzhou	1436	1125	1521																					
Nanning	1593	1281	1678	828																				
Changsha	986	737	1071	451	607																			
Shaoshan	1067	755	1152	469	625	81																		
Wuhan	763	953	848	673	830	222	304																	
Nanjing	718	189	633	1314	1471	927	945	763																
Wuxi	828	79	743	1204	1361	817	835	873	110															
Suzhou	854	53	769	1178	1335	791	809	899	136	26														
Hangzhou	1025	117	940	1007	1164	620	638	842	307	197	171													
Jinan	307	601	222	1418	1575	968	1049	745	412	522	548	718												
Qingdao	551	845	466	1662	1819	1212	1293	989	656	766	792	963	244											
Xi'an	723	938	809	1322	1479	871	953	649	749	859	885	1056	731	975										
Kunming	1974	1662	2059	932	989	933	1014	1211	1852	1742	1716	1545	1937	2181	1206									
Chengdu	1272	1461	1357	1376	1136	989	1137	1172	1382	1272	1408	1579	1254	1498	523	683								
Chongqing	1585	1553	1670	1267	823	879	824	1102	1585	1695	1721	1436	1567	1811	836	684	313							
Zhengzhou	432	621	517	1005	1161	554	635	332	432	542	568	738	414	658	317	1523	840	1153						
Shijiazhuang	176	786	261	1261	1417	810	891	587	597	707	733	904	185	429	573	1779	1096	1409	256					
Dalian	769	1507	684	2205	2362	1754	1836	1532	1317	1427	1453	1624	905	1149	1492	2743	2041	2354	1200	945				
Shenyang	522	1260	437	1959	2115	1508	1589	1285	1071	1181	1207	1377	659	903	1246	2496	1794	2107	954	698	247			
Changchun	712	1449	627	2148	2305	1697	1779	1475	1260	1370	1396	1567	848	1092	1435	2686	1983	2296	1143	887	436	189		
Harbin	862	1600	777	2298	2455	1847	1929	1625	1410	1520	1546	1716	999	1243	1585	2836	2134	2447	1294	1038	586	340	150	

DISTANCES BETWEEN MAIN TOURIST CITIES

(Shortest distance between cities by rail in kilometers)

	Beijing	Shanghai	Tianjin	Guangzhou	Nanning	Changsha	Shaoshan	Wuhan	Nanjing	Wuxi	Suzhou	Hangzhou	Jinan	Qingdao	Xi'an	Kunming	Chengdu	Chongqing	Zhengzhou	Shijiazhuang	Dalian	Shenyang	Changchun
Beijing																							
Shanghai	1462																						
Tianjin	137	1325																					
Guangzhou	2313	1811	2450																				
Nanning	2565	2063	2702	1334																			
Changsha	1587	1187	1724	726	978																		
Shaoshan	1718	1216	1855	755	1007	131																	
Wuhan	1229	1534	1366	1084	1336	358	489																
Nanjing	1157	305	1020	2116	2368	1492	1521	1229															
Wuxi	1334	128	1197	1939	2191	1315	1344	1406	177														
Suzhou	1376	86	1239	1897	2149	1273	1302	1448	219	42													
Hangzhou	1651	189	1514	1622	1874	998	1027	1356	494	317	275												
Jinan	494	968	357	2284	2536	1689	1820	1200	663	840	882	1157											
Qingdao	887	1361	750	2677	2929	2082	2213	1593	1056	1233	1275	1550	393										
Xi'an	1165	1511	1302	2129	2381	1534	1665	1045	1206	1383	1425	1700	1177	1570									
Kunming	3179	2677	3316	2216	1501	1592	1621	1950	2982	2805	2763	2488	3119	3512	1942								
Chengdu	2048	2353	2185	2544	1829	1887	2018	1559	2048	2225	2267	2542	2019	2412	842	1100							
Chongqing	2552	2501	2689	2040	1325	1774	1905	1462	2552	2729	2771	2312	2523	2916	1346	1102	504						
Zhengzhou	695	1000	832	1618	1870	1023	1154	534	695	872	914	1189	666	1059	511	2453	1346	1353					
Shijiazhuang	283	1266	420	2030	2282	1435	1566	946	961	1138	1180	1455	298	691	923	2865	1765	1933	412				
Dalian	1238	2426	1101	3551	3803	2956	3087	2467	2121	2298	2340	2615	1458	1851	2403	3286	2006	2311	1759	1521			
Shenyang	841	2029	704	3154	3406	2559	2690	2070	1724	1901	1943	2218	1061	1454	2006	4020	2889	3393	1536	1124	397		
Changchun	1146	2334	1009	3459	3711	2864	2995	2375	2029	2206	2248	2523	1366	1759	2311	4325	3194	3698	1841	1429	702	305	
Harbin	1388	2576	1251	3701	3953	3106	3237	2617	2271	2448	2490	2763	1608	2001	2553	4567	3436	3940	2083	1671	944	547	242

TIME DIFFERENCES

Time is the same throughout China and it does not vary during the year. Chinese time is sixteen hours ahead of West Coast (Pacific) Time in the United States or thirteen hours ahead of Eastern Standard Time. When it is 12 Noon in Beijing (Peking), the standard time in different cities of the world is as follows:

City	Time	City	Time
Accra	4:00 AM	Manila	12:00 PM
Addis Ababa	7:00 AM	Melbourne	2:00 PM
Algiers	5:00 AM	Moscow	7:00 AM
Ankara	6:00 AM	Nairobi	7:00 AM
Baghdad	7:00 AM	New York	11:00 PM*
Bangkok	11:00 AM	Osaka	1:00 PM
Beijing	12:00 PM	Paris	5:00 AM
Belgrade	5:00 AM	Phnom Penh	11:00 AM
Bombay	9:00 AM	Pyongyang	1:00 PM
Bucharest	6:00 AM	Rangoon	10:30 AM
Buenos Aires	1:00 AM	Rome	5:00 AM
Cairo	6:00 AM	San Francisco	8:00 PM*
Colombo	9:30 AM	Singapore	11:30 AM
Damascus	6:00 AM	Stockholm	5:00 AM
Delhi	9:30 AM	Tehran	7:30 AM
Geneva	5:00 AM	Tokyo	1:00 PM
Hanoi	11:00 AM	Ulan Bator	12:00 PM
Karachi	9:00 AM	Vienna	5:00 AM
Lima	11:00 PM*	Warsaw	5:00 AM
London	4:00 AM	Washington, D.C.	11:00 PM*

denotes Previous Day

APPROXIMATE MONTHLY TEMPERATURES — JANUARY THROUGH JUNE

	BEIJING F	C	CHENGDU F	C	GUANGZHOU F	C	GUILIN F	C	HANGZHOU F	C	HARBIN F	C	KUNMING F	C	NANJING F	C	SHANGHAI F	C	WUHAN F	C	XI'AN F	C
January																						
Average	24	-4	42	6	57	14	46	8	38	3	3	-20	46	8	35	2	38	3	37	3	30	-3
High	51	11	64	18	82	28	82	28	75	24	40	4	72	22	67	20	68	20	70	21	61	16
Low	-9	-23	24	-4	32	0	23	-5	18	-8	-37	-39	22	-6	7	-14	15	-10	1	-17	-5	-21
February																						
Average	28	-2	46	8	58	15	48	9	41	5	4	-16	50	10	39	4	40	4	41	5	36	2
High	65	18	69	21	83	29	84	29	83	29	52	11	76	25	74	24	74	24	77	25	70	21
Low	-17	-27	26	-3	32	0	26	-3	15	-10	-27	-33	29	-2	9	-13	18	-8	5	-15	-2	-19
March																						
Average	40	4	54	12	64	18	56	13	49	10	23	-5	56	13	47	8	47	8	50	10	46	8
High	74	24	85	30	88	31	89	32	85	30	63	17	82	28	83	29	82	28	85	30	82	28
Low	10	-12	31	-1	38	3	32	0	26	-3	-20	-29	27	-3	19	-7	22	-6	23	-5	18	-8
April																						
Average	56	13	63	17	71	22	65	18	59	15	43	6	62	17	58	15	57	14	61	16	57	14
High	86	30	89	32	91	33	96	36	93	34	82	28	87	31	93	34	92	34	92	34	92	34
Low	27	-3	37	3	46	8	39	4	33	1	9	-13	33	1	32	0	32	0	31	-1	25	-4
May																						
Average	68	20	70	21	78	26	74	24	69	21	58	15	67	20	68	20	66	19	70	21	67	20
High	99	38	97	36	97	36	95	35	98	37	96	36	89	32	97	36	92	34	97	36	100	38
Low	37	3	48	9	58	15	52	11	45	7	26	-3	43	6	41	5	44	7	45	7	38	3
June																						
Average	76	25	75	24	81	27	79	26	76	25	68	20	67	20	76	25	74	24	78	26	78	26
High	103	40	96	36	98	37	99	38	103	40	97	36	88	31	101	39	98	37	100	38	107	42
Low	50	10	58	15	66	19	55	13	57	14	41	5	49	10	53	12	54	12	58	15	49	10

F = Fahrenheit; C = Celsius

APPROXIMATE MONTHLY TEMPERATURES — JULY THROUGH DECEMBER

	BEIJING		CHENGDU		GUANGZHOU		GUILIN		HANGZHOU		HARBIN		KUNMING		NANJING		SHANGHAI		WUHAN		XI'AN	
	F	C	F	C	F	C	F	C	F	C	F	C	F	C	F	C	F	C	F	C	F	C
July																						
Average	79	26	78	26	83	29	83	29	84	29	73	23	68	20	83	29	82	28	84	29	80	27
High	101	39	97	36	100	38	101	39	102	39	98	37	84	29	100	38	101	39	101	39	106	41
Low	60	16	63	17	71	22	70	21	67	20	52	11	54	12	62	17	66	19	63	17	59	15
August																						
Average	76	25	77	25	83	29	82	28	83	29	71	22	67	20	82	28	82	28	83	29	78	26
High	97	36	99	38	102	39	103	40	103	40	96	36	85	30	105	41	102	39	103	40	103	40
Low	54	12	60	16	72	22	65	18	65	18	47	8	48	9	63	17	67	20	64	18	54	12
September																						
Average	67	20	71	22	81	27	78	26	74	24	58	15	64	18	73	23	75	24	74	24	67	20
High	89	32	95	35	100	38	101	39	97	36	87	31	83	29	102	39	99	38	98	40	94	35
Low	39	4	53	12	60	16	55	13	54	12	30	-1	43	6	49	10	54	12	50	10	41	5
October																						
Average	55	13	62	17	75	24	69	21	63	17	43	6	59	15	62	17	64	18	64	18	56	13
High	85	32	86	30	92	34	95	35	90	32	80	27	79	26	92	34	88	31	94	35	91	33
Low	26	-3	43	6	52	11	46	8	34	1	10	-12	36	2	32	0	35	2	35	2	31	-1
November																						
Average	39	4	54	12	67	20	59	15	54	12	22	-6	53	12	51	11	55	13	51	11	44	7
High	76	25	75	24	90	32	87	31	88	31	59	15	77	25	80	27	83	29	83	29	71	22
Low	10	-12	33	1	42	6	37	3	26	-3	-15	-26	33	1	21	-6	25	4	23	-5	2	-17
December																						
Average	27	-3	45	7	59	15	50	10	43	6	4	-16	47	8	40	4	43	6	42	6	33	1
High	55	13	69	21	85	30	82	28	80	27	43	6	70	21	74	24	74	24	74	24	64	18
Low	-1	-18	27	-3	35	2	29	2	20	-7	-32	-36	24	4	11	-12	17	-8	16	-9	-3	-20

F = Fahrenheit; C = Celsius

AVERAGE ANNUAL RAINFALL CHART

(In Millimeters [mm.]/10 mm. = .3937 in./100mm. = 3.937 in.)

CITY	JAN	FEB	MAR	APR	MAY	JUN	JUL	AUG	SEP	OCT	NOV	DEC	YEAR
Harbin	4.3	3.9	12.5	25.3	33.8	77.7	176.5	107.0	72.7	26.6	7.5	5.9	553.7
Dalian	7.3	8.6	12.9	35.4	41.2	81.8	188.5	143.1	68.0	36.3	24.2	8.7	656.0
Hohhot	2.1	6.1	10.1	19.9	28.4	46.2	104.4	136.9	40.4	24.1	5.9	1.4	426.2
Beijing	2.6	7.7	9.1	22.4	36.1	70.4	196.6	243.5	63.9	21.1	7.9	1.6	682.9
Taiyuan	2.9	5.3	9.9	25.7	37.0	46.5	124.5	99.3	65.8	32.4	14.8	2.3	466.5
Jinan	6.2	10.4	16.1	36.1	36.8	73.7	214.0	147.9	60.9	33.0	28.9	8.2	672.2
Qingdao	7.6	11.4	12.5	33.3	48.7	92.2	209.7	155.2	108.2	15.5	34.8	9.7	768.8
Zhengzhou	8.8	12.6	29.2	50.8	46.4	68.3	134.8	135.2	67.2	40.6	34.4	7.8	636.1
Nanjing	31.8	52.9	78.6	98.3	97.3	140.2	181.7	121.7	101.2	44.1	53.1	30.2	1031.1
Shanghai	44.3	63.0	80.5	111.1	129.3	156.6	142.4	116.0	145.9	46.8	54.3	39.2	1129.4
Hangzhou	64.3	84.4	116.7	130.4	185.8	191.6	131.6	135.5	183.0	67.0	61.2	49.1	1400.6
Fuzhou	52.6	79.9	121.4	136.2	210.0	223.5	118.5	142.2	155.3	61.0	28.8	28.7	1328.1
Nanchang	59.1	93.8	170.2	221.1	306.5	277.3	127.0	93.8	85.1	57.2	62.2	44.9	1598.2
Wuhan	35.5	60.5	104.5	144.4	161.2	218.0	119.0	133.4	80.6	53.2	56.6	33.5	1200.4
Changsha	53.1	87.2	152.3	199.2	244.5	184.5	123.2	106.3	69.3	84.8	69.9	48.1	1422.5
Guangzhou	39.1	62.5	91.5	158.5	267.2	299.0	219.6	225.3	204.4	52.0	41.9	19.6	1680.6
Guilin	55.6	76.0	133.8	279.7	318.7	316.2	224.0	167.2	65.7	97.3	83.1	58.4	1875.7
Nanning	40.0	41.6	62.8	84.0	183.1	241.3	180.0	203.5	109.6	66.6	43.5	24.9	1280.9
Chongqing	18.8	20.9	43.2	72.3	155.4	165.4	156.7	141.0	132.3	99.2	51.2	24.7	1081.1
Chengdu	5.0	11.4	21.8	51.1	88.3	119.4	228.9	265.6	113.5	47.9	16.5	6.4	976.0
Kunming	10.0	9.8	13.6	19.6	78.0	181.7	216.4	195.2	122.9	94.9	33.7	15.9	991.7
Lhasa	0.2	0.1	1.5	4.4	20.6	72.1	141.7	149.1	57.3	4.8	0.8	0.3	453.9
Xi'an	7.6	10.3	24.7	53.0	62.3	57.6	105.9	80.1	100.2	61.5	34.0	7.1	604.3
Lanzhou	1.4	1.8	7.4	19.0	40.0	33.0	59.3	85.6	51.0	26.9	4.9	1.5	331.8
Urumqi	5.6	4.0	18.8	22.6	25.1	29.1	16.4	18.9	14.2	17.2	15.2	7.4	194.6
Turpan	1.0	0.1	1.7	0.4	0.6	3.6	2.5	3.1	0.9	0.5	0.5	1.1	16.6

CREDIT CARD ACCEPTANCE IN CHINA

1. Federal Card

Beijing: The Bank of China, Beijing Branch; Beijing Hotel; Friendship Hotel; Friendship Store; Marco Polo Shop and the Capital Airport.

Tianjin: The Bank of China, Tianjin Branch; Tiajin Hotel; Friendship Hotel; Friendship Store; Yilinge Art Store; Wenyuange Art Store; Yangliuqing Paintings Store; Applied Arts Factory; Carpet Factory No. 1; Carpet Factory No. 3; Xingang (New Harbor) Friendship Store; Special Handicraft Workshop and the People's Bank of Jixian County.

Guangzhou: The Bank of China, Guangzhou Branch; Guangzhou Foreign Trade Center; Baiyun Airport; Dongfang Hotel; Baiyun Guest House; Guangzhou Guest House; Friendship Store; Guangzhou Railway Station and Zhoutouzui Dock.

Hangzhou: The Bank of China, Hangzhou Branch; Overseas Chinese Hotel; Huagang Hotel; Friendship Store; Zhejiang Arts and Crafts Department Store; Hangzhou Municipal Arts and Crafts Department Store; Hangzhou Antique Store; Hangzhou Embroidery Factory; Jianqiao Airport and Hangzhou Hotel.

Nanjing: The Bank of China, Nanjing Branch and Nanjing Friendship Store.

Fuzhou: The Bank of China, Fuzhou Branch.

Hankou: The Bank of China, Hankou Branch.

Kunming: The Bank of China, Kunming Branch; Kunming Hotel; Cuihu Hotel.

Shanghai: The Bank of China, Shanghai Branch; Jinjiang Hotel; Heping (Peace) Hotel; Shanghai Mansions; Overseas Chinese Hotel; Guoji (International) Hotel; Hengshan Hotel; Jing'an Hotel; Dahua Hotel; Friendship Store; Arts and Crafts Department Store; Arts and Crafts Fair; Light Industry Management of Shanghai Exhibition Center; Sales Department of Carpet Factory; Sales Department of Jade Carving Factory and Carpet Showroom.

2. East Asia Americard-Visa

Beijing, Shanghai: (Same as Federal Card.)

Tianjin: The Bank of China, Tianjin Branch; Friendshp Store; Tianjin Hotel; Yilinge Art Store; Wenyuange Art Store; Yanliuqing Paintings Store; Applied Arts Factory; Carpet Factory No. 1 and Xingang (New Harbor) Friendship Store.

Guangzhou: (Same as Federal Card.)

Hangzhou: (Same as Federal Card.)

3. The Hongkong and Shanghai Banking Corp., Hongkong (Visa and MasterCard)

Beijing, Shanghai, Guangzhou, Hangzhou and Nanjing: (Same as Federal Card.)

Tianjin: The Bank of China, Tianjin Branch; Friendship Store; Tianjin Hotel; Friendship Hotel; Yilinge Art Store; Wenyuange Art Store; Yangliuqing Paintings Store; Applied Arts Factory and Carpet Factory No. 1.

Nanjing: The Bank of China Nanjing Branch; Friendship Store; Antique Store; Dingshan Guest House; Shuangmenlou Guest House; Nanjing Hotel and Shengli Hotel.

4. American Express

Guangzhou: The Bank of China, Guangzhou Branch; Guangzhou Foreign Trade Center; Baiyun Airport; Dongfang Hotel; Baiyun Hotel; Liuhua Hotel; Guangzhou Guest House; Friendship Store; Guangzhou Railway Station and Zhoutouzui Dock.

Shanghai: The Bank of China, Shanghai Branch.

NOTE: American Express has expanded its Emergency Check Service in China. Card holders may now cash personal checks for up to $1,500 per day at Bank of China locations in Beijing, Tianjin, Hangzhou, Guangzhou and Shanghai.

5. Diners Club

Guangzhou: (Same as American Express.)

Shanghai: (Same as Federal Card.)

HOTELS

CITY	HOTEL	TELEPHONE
BEIJING:	Beijing Hotel	(55 83 31) & (50 77 66)
	Youyl (Friendship) Hotel	(89 06 21)
	Jianguo Hotel	(50 22 33)
	Yanxiang Hotel	(50 66 66)
	Qianmen Hotel	(33 87 31)
	Diaoyutai Guest House	(86 61 52)
	Yanjing Hotel	(86 87 21)
	Huadu Hotel	(50 11 66)
CHANGCHUN:	Chunyi Hotel	(3 84 95)
	Changchun Guest House	(2 67 72)
	Nanhu Guest House	(5 35 51)
CHANGSHA:	Hunan Guest House	(2 63 31)
	Xiangjiang Guest House	(2 62 61)
CHENGDU:	Jinjiang Hotel	(2 44 81)
CHONGQING:	Chongqing Guest House	(37 71)
	Yuzhou Hotel	(5 14 86)
	Renmin Hotel	(5 34 21)
DALIAN:	Dalian Guest House	(2 31 11)
	Dalian Hotel	(2 31 71)
	Banchui (Ginseng) siet Guest House	(2 51 31)
	Nanshan Guest House	(2 51 03)
FUZHOU:	Overseas Chinese Guest House	(3 13 86)
	Minjiang Guest House	(3 34 92)
	Xihu Guest House	(3 22 27)
GUANGZHOU:	Dongfang Hotel	(6 99 00)
	Baiyun Guest House	(6 77 00)
	Nanhu Guest House	(7 80 52)
	Liuhua Guest House	(6 88 00)
	White Swan Hotel	(8 69 68)
GUILIN:	Ronghu Hotel	(38 11)
	Jiashan Hotel	(47 12)
	Lijiang Hotel	(28 81)
	Dangui Hotel	(35 76)
HANGZHOU:	Hangzhou Hotel	(2 29 21)
	Zhejiang Hotel	(2 44 83)
	Huagang Hotel	(2 40 01)
	Xiling Hotel	(2 29 21)
	Huajiashan Hotel	(2 64 50)
HARBIN:	International Hotel	(3 30 01)
	Beifang Mansion	(3 30 81)
	Hepingcun Hotel	(3 20 93)
JILIN:	Jilinshi Guest House	(35 55)
JINAN:	Jinan Hotel	(3 53 51)
	Nanjiao Guest House	(2 39 31)
KUNMING:	Kunming Hotel	(2 77 32)
	Cuihu Hotel	(2 21 92)
LANZHOU:	Youyi (Friendship) Hotel	(30 51)
	Lanzhou Hotel	(2 29 81)
	Ningwozhuang Hotel	(2 28 91)
LUOYANG:	Youyi (Friendship) Hotel	(21 59)
NANCHANG:	Jiangxi Guest House	(6 48 61)

CITY	HOTEL	TELEPHONE
NANJING:	Nanjing Hotel	(3 41 21)
	Shengli Hotel	(4 30 35)
	Dingshan Hotel	(8 59 31)
	Jinling Hotel	(4 11 21) & (4 25 25)
	Shuangmenlou Hotel	(8 59 31)
NANNING:	Mingyuan Hotel	(29 86)
	Yongjiang Hotel	(31 20)
	Xiyuan Hotel	(39 31)
	Yongzhou Hotel	(31 20)
QINGDAO:	Zhanqiao Hotel	(2 74 02)
	Huiquan Guest House	(2 52 16)
	Overseas Chinese Hotel	(2 77 38)
SHANGHAI:	Jinjiang Hotel	(53 42 42)
	Heping (Peace) Hotel	(21 12 44)
	Shanghai Mansions	(24 62 60)
	Jingan Guest House	(56 30 50)
	Guoji (International) Hotel	(22 52 25)
	Dahua Guest House	(52 30 79)
	Shanghai Guest House	(31 23 12)
SHENYANG:	Liaoning Guest House	(3 26 41)
	Liaoning Hotel	(6 25 46)
	Youyi (Friendship) Hotel	(6 28 22)
SHIJIAZHUANG:	Shijiazhuang Guest House	(63 51)
SUZHOU:	Suzhou Hotel	(22 98)
	Nanyuan Hotel	(46 41)
	Nanlin Hotel	(44 41)
TIANJIN:	Tianjin Hotel	(3 43 25)
	Tianjin Guest House	(3 96 13)
	Tianjin Friendship Guest House	(3 56 63)
	Tianjin Guest House	(2 40 10)
URUMQI:	Xinjiang Guest House	(2 22 33)
	Kunlun Guest House	(2 33 60)
	Tian Shan Mansion	(2 31 01)
	Urumqi Guest House	(2 45 76)
WUHAN:	Xuangong Hotel	(2 44 04)
	Jianghan Hotel	(2 39 98)
	Shengli Hotel	(2 25 31)
	Hongshan Guest House	(7 15 81)
WUXI:	Taihu Hotel	(2 30 01)
	Hubin Hotel	(2 67 12)
	Liangxi Hotel	(2 68 12)
	Shuixiu Hotel	(2 65 91)
XIAMEN:	Guinagyu Guest House	(20 52)
	Lujiang Mansion	(22 12)
	Overseas Chinese Mansion	(27 29)
	Xiamen Guest House	(24 46)
XI'AN:	Renmin Hotel	(2 51 11)
	Xi'an Guest House	(5 13 51)
	Shaanxi Guest House	(2 38 31)
	Xiaozhai Hotel	
ZHENGZHOU:	Zhengzhou Guest House	(2 49 37)

FRIENDSHIP STORES AND SAILOR'S CLUBS

Name	Address	Telephone
Beijing Friendship Store	Jianguomen Wai	59 35 31
Changchun Friendship Store	1 Xinfa Road	2 32 52
Changsha Friendship Store	Yingbin Road	2 63 31
Chongqing Friendship Store	Jiefangbei	4 19 55
Dalian Sailor's Club	137 Stalin Road	2 53 71
Guangzhou Friendship Store	Huanshi E. Road	3 59 78
Guangzhou Friendship Non-Staple Food Store	9 Jiaoyu S. Road	3 42 99
Guilin Friendship Store	107 Zhongshan Zhong Rd.	27 43
Hangzhou Friendship Store	302 Tiyuchang Road	2 64 80
Harbin Friendship Store	93 Nangang Dazhi St.	3 38 97
Nanchang Friendship Store	Bayi Avenue	6 32 68
Nanjing Friendship Store	3 Daqing Road	3 28 02
Qingdao Sailor's Club	Xinjiang Road	2 78 03
Shanghai Friendship Store	40 Beijing East Road	21 62 26
Shanghai Sailor's Club	20 Huang Pu Rd.	24 42 04
Shenyang Friendship Store	12 Zhongshan Rd., Sec. II	3 37 53
Shijiazhuang Friendship Store	Jiefang Rd., Qiaodong Dist.	67 70
Suzhou Friendship Store	92 Guanqian Street	48 24
Taiyuan Friendship Store	Southend of Wuyi Road	2 94 44
Tianjin Friendship Store	Jiefang N. Road	3 31 83
Tianjin Sailor's Club	Liu-mi, Xingan	35 36
Wuhan Friendship Store	Hongwei Rd., Qingshan	6 24 18
Wuxi Friendship Store	8 Zhongshan S. Road	25 13
Xi'an Friendship Store	Nanxin Street	2 15 51
Zhengzhou Friendship Store	E. Erqi Road	61 10

MAJOR ARTS AND CRAFTS DEPARTMENT STORES (ACDS)

Name (City)	Address	Telephone
Beijing ACDS	200 Wang Fu Jin	55 68 16
Beijing Painting Shop	289 Wang Fu Jin	55 34 09
Beijing, Museum of Chinese Arts	Inside the Museum	44 31 19
Beijing, Rong Bao Zhai Studio	W. Liu Li Chang	33 33 52
Changchun	13 Damalu Road	3 82 85
Chengdu	10 N. Section, Fandi Rd.	68 17
Chongqing	107 Zourong Road	4 27 97
Dunhuang	3 Dingcun Road	14
Foshan City	85 Dongfeng St.	8 71 80
Guangdong	Dongshanshuqian Road, Guangzhou	7 07 79
Guilin	126 Zhongshan Zhong Rd.	39 98
Hangzhou	519 Lixin Road	2 43 78
Hangzhou, Zhejiang	1 Jiefang Road	2 59 15
Jingdezhen	17 Zhushan Road	63
Jiuquan	23 E. Dajie	23 25
Kaifeng	57 Gulou Street	21 43
Kunming	Dongfeng W. Road	68 71
Nanchang	222 Zhongshan Road	5 11 19
Nanjing	168 Xinjiekou	4 26 19
Qingdao	212 Zhongshan Road	2 36 27
Shanghai	190 Nanjing W. Road	53 82 06
Shanghai Duoyunxuan	422 Nanjing E. Road	22 34 10
Suzhou	Ziyuanchang	63 13
Taiyuan	Wuyi Road, Southend	2 81 80
Wuhan	Zhongshan Da Dao, Minsheng Road	5 34 78
Wuxi	192 Renmin Road	37 78
Xi'an	18 Nansin Street	2 87 98
Yangzhou	240 Dukou Road	11 08
Zhengzhou	21 Jiefang W. Road	31 02

MAJOR ANTIQUE STORES

Name	Address	Telephone
BEIJING		
Baoguzhai Shop of Paintings and Calligraphy from Various Dynasties	63 E. Liu Li Chang	33 01 46
Chinese Museum of History Foreign Guest Service Dept.	Inside the Museum	55 42 09
Cuizhenzhai Shop of Modern Pottery and Porcelain	17 W. Liu Li Chang	
Guanfuzhai Shop of Chops, Inksticks and Inkstones	34A W. Liu Li Chang	33 12 09
Moyuange Shop of Contemporary Paintings and Calligraphy	58 E. Liu Li Chang	33 01 46
Palace Museum: Foreign Guest Service Dept.	Jiangzuexuan, Forbidden City	55 50 31
Qingyuntang Shop of Stone Rubbings	20 W. Liu Li Chang	33 12 09
Yunyuzhai Shop for Green Jades	108 E. Liu Li Chang	
Yunguzhai Shop of Pottery and Porcelain from from Various Dynasties	80 E. Liu Li Chang	33 66 82
Zhenahuan Shop of Metals and Stones	70 E. Liu Li Chang	33 19 51
CHANGCHUN	Jilin 7 Xi'an Dalu	2 25 37
CHENGDU, Sichuan Foreign Guest Service Department	Nanjiao Park	88 38
DALIAN	228 Tianjin Street	2 49 55
GUANGZHOU	Guanxiashi 575 Hongshu N. Road	8 76 00
GUANGZHOU-ART GALLERY	162 Wende Road	3 12 41
GUILIN	71 Zhongshan Road	25 94
HANGZHOU	31 Hubin Road	2 32 23
HARBIN	Heilongjiang 50 Hongjun Street Nangang	3 25 87

Name	Address	Telephone
JINAN		
Shandong General Antique Store	Quanchen Road	2 34 46
KUNMING	63 Dongfeng E. Road	6 54 48
NANCHANG		
Jiangzi Foreign Guest Service Department	28 Bayi Dadao	5 12 21
NANJING	7-11 Hanzhong Road	4 45 50
QUFU		
Shangdong Qufu County Shop	Kongfu	
SHANGHAI		
Shanghai Antique Store	218-226 Guangdong Rd.	21 22 92
Yufushi Branch Store	Anyuan Road	5 35 43
Yuyuan Branch Store	Yuyuan	28 91 09
SUZHOU Foreign Guest Service Department	344 Renmin Road	49 72
TIANJIN		
Yilinge Shop	175 Liaoning Rd.	2 03 08
Wenwange Shop	263 Heping Road	2 34 50
WUHAN	1039 Zhongshan Ave.	2 14 53
WUXI	466 Zhongshan Ave.	25 12
XI'AN	375 E. Dajie	2 71 87

FOREIGN CURRENCIES AND
TRAVELER'S CHECKS (T/C) ACCEPTED IN CHINA

Foreign Currencies

Australian dollar (A$), Austrian Schilling (Sch), Belgian Franc (BF), Canadian Dollar (Can$), Danish Krone (DKr), West German Mark (DM), French Franc (FF), Japanese Yen (Y), Malaysian Dollar (M$), Dutch Guilder (FL.), Norwegian Krone (NKr), Singapore Dollar (S$), Swedish Krona (SKr), Swiss Franc (SF), Pound Sterling (₤), US Dollar (US$), and Hong Kong Dollar (HK$).

Traveler's Checks and International Bank Drafts

Rafidain Bank, Baghdad, Iraq	US$, ₤	T/C
Arab Bank Limited, Amman, Jordan	US$, ₤	T/C
The National Bank of Australia Limited, Melbourne, Australia	A$	T/C
Bank of New South Wales, Sydney, Australia	A$	T/C
The Rural & Industries Bank of Western Australia, Perth, Australia	A$	T/C
Australia & New Zealand Banking Group Ltd.	₤, A$	T/C
Commonwealth Trading Bank of Australia, Sydney, Australia	₤, A$	T/C
The Mitsui Bank Limited, Tokyo	Yen	T/C
The Bank of Tokyo, Ltd., Tokyo	Yen, US$	T/C
The Sumitomo Bank, Ltd., Tokyo	Yen	T/C
The Fuji Bank, Ltd., Tokyo	Yen	T/C
Barclays Bank International Ltd., London	₤, US$	T/C
Lloyds Bank Limited, London	₤	T/C
Standard Chartered Bank Ltd., London	₤, US$	T/C
The Royal Bank of Scotland Ltd., London	₤	T/C
Grindlays Bank Ltd., London	₤	T/C
Midland Bank Ltd., London	₤	T/C
National Westminster Bank Ltd., London	₤	T/C
Thomas Cook & Son Ltd., London	L, US$, CAN$, A$	T/C
The Hongkong & Shanghai Banking Corp., Hongkong	HK$	T/C
Deutsche Genossenshcaftsbank Frankfurt, Berlin	Standard DM	T/C
Baden-Wurttembergische Bank, Stuttgart	Standard DM	T/C
Bankhaus H. Aufhauser, Munchen	Standard DM	T/C
Bank fur Gemeinwirtschaft, Frankfurt	Standard DM	T/C
Bayerische Hypotheken-und-Wechsel Bank, Muchen	Standard DM	T/C
Bayerische Vereinsbank, Muchen	Standard DM	T/C
Berliner Bank, Berlin	Standard DM	T/C
Berliner Handels-und-Frankfurter Bank, Frankfurt, Berlin	Standard DM	T/C
Bankhaus Burgardt & Brockelschen, . Dortmund	Standard DM	T/C
Commerzbank, Dusseldorf, Frankfurt, Hamburg	Standard DM	T/C

Deutsche Bank, Frankfurt, Dusseldorf	Standard DM	T/C
Deutsche Girozentrale-Deutsche Kommunalbank, Frankfurt, Berlin	Standard DM	T/C
Deutsche Verkenes-Kredit-Bank, Frankfurt	Standard DM	T/C
Deutsche Unionbank, Frankfurt	Standard DM	T/C
Dresdner Bank, Frankfurt	Standard DM	T/C
Bankhaus Hallbaum, Maier & Co., Hannover	Standard DM	T/C
Handels-und Privatbank, Koln	Standard DM	T/C
Lubeck Commerzbank, Lubeck	Standard DM	T/C
Hauck (Georg) & Sohn, Frankfurt	Standard DM	T/C
Bankhaus Martens & Weyhausen, Bremen	Standard DM	T/C
Merck, Finck & Co. Munchen, Dusseldorf, Frankfurt	Standard DM	T/C
National Bank, Essen	Standard DM	T/C
Bankhaus Neelmeyer, Bremen	Standard DM	T/C
Nikolaus Bank Hannover, Brunswick, (Braunschweig), Gotingen	Standard DM	T/C
Oldenburgische Landesbank, Oldenburg	Standard DM	T/C
Reuschel & Co., Munchen	Standard DM	T/C
Karl Schmidt Bankgeschaft, Hof	Standard DM	T/C
Vereins-und Westbank, Hamburg	Standard DM	T/C
M.M. Warburg-Brinckmann, Wirtz & Co., Hamburg	Standard DM	T/C
Westfalenbank, Bochum	Standard DM	T/C
Banque Nationale de Paris, Paris	F. Fr.	T/C
Societe Generale, Paris	F. Fr.	T/C
Credit Lyonnais, Paris	F. Fr.	T/C
Swiss Bankers Travellers Cheque Centre, Borne	S. Fr.	T/C
Banque de Bruxelles, Brussels	B. Fr	T/C
Societe Generale de Banque, Bruxelles	B. Fr	T/C
Algemene Bank Nederland N.V., Amsterdam	FL	T/C
Amsterdam-Rotterdam Bank N.V., Amsterdam	FL	T/C
Nederlandsche Middenstandsbank N.V., Amsterdam	FL	T/C
Den Norske Creditbank, Oslo	N. Kr.	T/C
Bank of America, San Francisco	US$	T/C
Manufacturers Hanover Trust Co., New York	US Int. Money Order	T/C
Chase Manhattan Bank, New York	US$	T/C
American Express Co., New York	US$, Can$, S.Fr., Ł, DM, F.Fr., Yen	T/C
Citicorp, New York	US$	T/C
First National Bank of Chicago, Illinois	US$	T/C
Republic National Bank of Dallas, Texas	US$	T/C
The Royal Bank of Canada, Montreal	Can$, US$, World Money Order	T/C

MONEY CONVERSION CHART

Exchange Rate at time of publication: 1 Yuan = $ .50

1 Dollar = RMB 2.00

U.S. Dollars	RMB	RMB	U.S. Dollars
$ .10	.2 Yuan	10 Fen	$ .05
	(2 Jiao or 20 Fen)	(1 Jiao)	
$ .50	1 Yuan	50 Fen	$ .25
	(10 Jiao or 100 Fen)	(5 Jiao)	
$ 1.00	2 Yuan	1 Yuan	$ .50
$ 2.00	4 Yuan	2 Yuan	$ 1.00
$ 3.00	6 Yuan	3 Yuan	$ 1.50
$ 4.00	8 Yuan	4 Yuan	$ 2.00
$ 5.00	10 Yuan	5 Yuan	$ 2.50
$ 6.00	12 Yuan	6 Yuan	$ 3.00
$ 7.00	14 Yuan	7 Yuan	$ 3.50
$ 8.00	16 Yuan	8 Yuan	$ 4.00
$ 9.00	18 Yuan	9 Yuan	$ 4.50
$ 10.00	20 Yuan	10 Yuan	$ 5.00
$ 11.00	22 Yuan	11 Yuan	$ 5.50
$ 12.00	24 Yuan	12 Yuan	$ 6.00
$ 13.00	26 Yuan	13 Yuan	$ 6.50
$ 14.00	28 Yuan	14 Yuan	$ 7.00
$ 15.00	30 Yuan	15 Yuan	$ 7.50
$ 20.00	40 Yuan	20 Yuan	$ 10.00
$ 25.00	50 Yuan	25 Yuan	$ 12.50
$ 30.00	60 Yuan	30 Yuan	$ 15.00
$ 40.00	80 Yuan	40 Yuan	$ 20.00
$ 50.00	100 Yuan	50 Yuan	$ 25.00
$ 75.00	125 Yuan	75 Yuan	$ 37.50
$100.00	200 Yuan	100 Yuan	$ 50.00

POSTAL RATES (IN RMB YUAN)

	Weight	Rates			
		Domestic		**Hong Kong**	
		Local	Out of Town	and Macao	**International**
Letters	up to 20 grams	0.04	0.08	0.08	0.40
Post Cards	each	0.02	0.04	0.04	0.30
Registered letters	each	0.12	0.12	0.12	0.50
Air mail	for each 10 grams or less		0.02	0.02	0.30

WEIGHTS AND MEASURES

Below is a simple conversion chart showing the standard units of weight, length, and volume in the Metric System, the Chinese Market System and the American System.

meter	shichi	foot
1	3	3.28
0.33	1	1.09
0.30	0.91	1
kilometer	**shili**	**mile**
1	2	0.62
0.5	1	0.31
1.61	3.22	1
hectare	**mu**	**acre**
1	15	2.47
0.07	1	0.16
0.40	6.07	1
liter	**sheng**	**gallong**
1	1	0.22
4.55	4.55	1
kilogram	**jin**	**pound**
1	2	2.20
0.5	1	1.10
0.45	0.91	1
50	1dan (= 100 jin)	110

THE CHINESE DYNASTIES

Pinyin Spelling	Wade-Giles Spelling	Dates
XIA	HSIA	B.C. 2205-1766
SHANG	SHANG	B.C. 1766-1122
ZHOU	CHOW	B.C. 1122-770
SPRING AND AUTUMN PERIOD	SPRING AND AUTUMN PERIOD	B.C. 770-476
WARRING STATES	WARRING STATES	B.C. 476-221
QIN	CHIN	B.C. 221-206
HAN	HAN	B.C. 206-A.D. 220
THREE KINGDOMS	THREE KINGDOMS	A.D. 220-265
JIN	TSIN	A.D. 265-420
SOUTHERN AND NORTHERN	SOUTHERN AND NORTHERN	A.D. 420-589
SUI	SUI	A.D. 589-618
TANG	TANG	A.D. 618-907
FIVE DYNASTIES AND TEN KINGDOMS	FIVE DYNASTIES AND TEN KINGDOMS	A.D. 907-960
SONG	SUNG	A.D. 960-1280
YUAN	YUAN	A.D. 1280-1368
MING	MING	A.D. 1368-1644
QING	CHING	A.D. 1644-1911

SPECIFIC EMPERORS OF MING AND
QING DYNASTIES

Pinyin Spelling	Wade-Giles Spelling	Dates
MING	**MING**	**A.D. 1368-1644**
Hong Wu	Hung Wu	1368-1399
Jian Wen	Chien Wen	1399-1403
Yong Le	Yung Lo	1403-1425
Hong Xi	Hung Hsi	1425-1426
Xuan De	Hsuan Teh	1426-1436
Zheng Tong	Cheng Tung	1436-1450
Jing Tai	Ching Tai	1450-1457
Tian Shun	Tien Shun	1457-1465
Cheng Hua	Cheng Hua	1465-1488
Hong Zhi	Hung Chih	1488-1506
Zheng De	Cheng Teh	1506-1522
Jia Jing	Chia Ching	1522-1567
Long Qing	Lung Ching	1567-1573
Wan Li	Wan Li	1573-1620
Tai Chang	Tai Chang	1620-1621
Tian Qi	Tien Chi	1621-1628
Chong Zhen	Chung Cheng	1628-1644
QING	**CHING**	**A.D. 1644-1911**
Shun Zhi	Shun Chih	1644-1662
Kang Xi	Kang Hsi	1662-1723
Yong Zheng	Yung Cheng	1723-1736
Qian Long	Chien Lung	1736-1796
Jia Qing	Chia Ching	1796-1821
Dao Guang	Tao Kuang	1821-1851
Xian Feng	Hsien Feng	1851-1862
Tong Zhi	Tung Chih	1862-1875
Guang Xu	Kuang Hsu	1875-1908
Xuan Tong	Hsuan Tung	1908-1911

MAJOR HOLIDAYS

There are nine national holidays celebrated in the People's Republic of China during the year. All are marked by a variety of public and private celebrations.

New Year's Day, January 1st.

Spring Festival, China's only three-day holiday, is celebrated starting on the first day of the old lunar calendar (known in the West as Chinese New Year). The Spring Festival usually occurs in February and is marked by family reunions.

International Working Women's Day, March 8th, commemorates the struggle of working women all over the world.

International Labor Day, May 1st, celebrates working people throughout the world.

May 4th, "Youth Day," recalls the demonstration on May 4, 1919, by thousands of patriotic students in Beijing's Tian An Men Square to protest imperialist aggression in China.

Children's Day, June 1st.

Anniversary of the Founding of the Communist Party of China, July 1st.

Anniversary of the Founding of the Chinese People's Liberation Army, August 1st.

National Day, October 1st, celebrates the occasion of the founding in 1949 of the People's Republic of China.

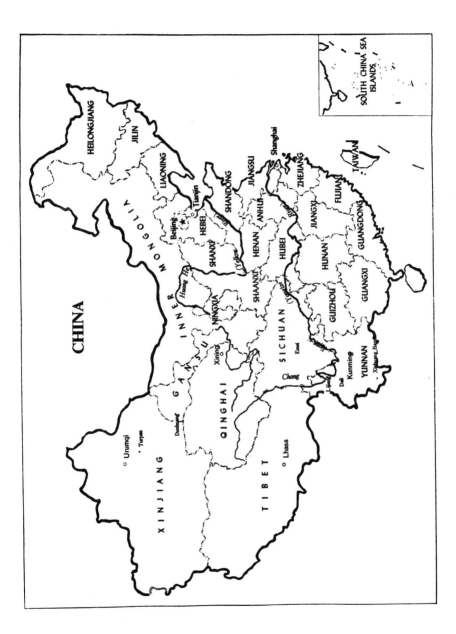

USEFUL PHRASES

The selection that follows offers some common phrases in four matched colums. The first column gives the word or phrase in English, the second column express the phonetic Pinyin, the third is the older Wade-Giles spelling, and the last column represents the word or phrase in Chinese characters.

English	Pinyin	Wade-Giles	Chinese
GENERAL PHRASES			
Welcome.	Huānyíng.	(Huanying.)	欢迎。
Hello.	Nǐ hǎo.	(Ni hao.)	你好。
How do you do?	Nǐ hǎo ma?	(Ni hao ma?)	你好吗?
I am very well,	hěn hǎo.	hen hao.)	很好。
thank you.	Xièxie nǐ,	(Hsiehhsieh ni,	谢谢你,
What's your name?	Guìxìng?	(Kuei hsing?)	贵姓?
My name is...	Wǒ xìng...	(Wo hsing...)	我姓······
Good morning.	Zǎo.	(Tsao.)	早。
Good evening.	Wǎnshàng hǎo.	(Wanshang hao.)	晚上好。
Please. (only at beginning of a sentence.)	Qing	(Ching.)	请。
Please.../come in/sit down/.	Qing.../jìn/zùo/.	(Ching.../chin/tso/.)	请······/进/坐/。
Pardon. (Excuse me.)	Duì bù qǐ.	(Tui pu chi.)	对不起。
See you tomorrow.	Míngtiān jiàn.	(Mingtien chien.)	明天见。
Good-bye.	Zàijiàn.	(Tsaichien.)	再见。
What's.../this/that/?	Zhè shì/nà shì/...shénme?	(Che shi/na shi/...shih mo?)	/这是/那是/······什么?
It's...	Zhè shì...	(Che shi...)	这是···
Where are you from?	Nǐ cóng nǎli lái?	(Ni tsung nali lai?)	你从那里来?
Do you speak English?	Nǐ huì jiǎng yīngyǔ ma?	(Ni hui chiang yingyu ma?)	你会讲英语吗?
Is there an interpreter?	Yǒu fānyi ma?	(Yu fanyi ma?)	有翻译吗?
I don't understand.	Wǒ tīng bù dǒng.	(Wo ting pu tung.)	我听不懂。
Excellent.	Hǎo jíle.	(Hao chile.)	好极了。

English	Pinyin	Wade-Giles	Chinese

DINING

English	Pinyin	Wade-Giles	Chinese
Please give me the menu.	Qǐng bǎ càidān gěi wǒ.	(Ching pa tsai-tan kei wo.)	请把菜单给我。
What dish is this?	Zhè shì shéme cài?	(Che shi shih-mo tsai?)	这是什么菜？
I like... /Chinese food/ European food/.	Wǒ xǐhuān... /zhōngcān/ /xīcān/.	(Wo hsihuan... /chungtsan/ /hsitsan/.)	我喜欢… …/中餐/ 西餐/。
I don't like hot food.	Wǒ bù chī là de.	(Wo pu chi la te.)	我不吃辣的。
I don't want too much food.	Cài bú yào tài duó.	(Tsai pu yao tai tuo.)	菜不要太多。
Do you like it?	Hǎochī ma?	(Haochih ma?)	好吃吗？
This is delicious.	Hǎochī jíle.	(Haochih chile.)	好吃极了。
Help yourselves.	Qǐng chī ba.	(Ching chih pa.)	请吃吧。
We would like... /beer/white wine/...please.	Wǒmen yào... /píjiǔ/báijiǔ/.	(Women yao... /pichiu/pai-chiu/.)	我们要… …/啤酒/ 白酒/。
Please make up the bill.	Qǐng suàn-zhàng.	(Ching suan-chang.)	请算帐。
Bottoms up.	Gānbēi.	(Kanpei.)	干杯！
To our friendship.	Wèi wǒmende yǒuyì gān bēi.	(Wei womente yuyi kanpei.)	为我们 的友谊干 杯！

SHOPPING

English	Pinyin	Wade-Giles	Chinese
I want to buy... /this/that/.	Wǒ yào mǎi... /zhège/nàge/.	(Wo yao mai... /cheke/nake/.)	我要买… …/这个/ 那个/。
How much is it?	Duōshǎo qián?	(Tuoshao chien?)	多少钱？
How much all together?	Yígòng duōshǎo qián?	(Yikung tuoshao chien?)	一共多少钱？
How much is... /a catty/one ounce/a pack-et/a bottle/?	Duōshǎo qián... /yī jīn/yī liǎng/ yī bāo/yī píng/?	(Tuoshao chien .../yi chin/ yi liang/yi pao yi ping/?)	多少钱… /一斤/一 两/一包/ 一瓶/？
Have you chea-per ones?	Yóu piányīde ma?	(Yu pienyide ma?)	有便宜的吗？
Have you better ones?	Yóu hǎode ma?	(Yu haode ma?)	有好的吗？
Have you... /larger/smaller/ longer/shorter/ ...ones?	Yóuméiyóu... /dàde/xiǎode/ chángde/ duǎnde/?	(Yumeiyu... /date/hsiaote/ changte/ tuante/?)	有没有… …/大的/ 小的/长 的/短的/？
No, thank you.	Bú yào, xièxie.	(Pu yao, hsieh-hsieh.)	不要，谢谢。
Yes, please, I will take it.	Hǎo, wó yào zhège.	(Hao, wo yao cheke.)	好，我要这个。
Please make out a bill.	Qǐng kāi fāpiào.	(Ching kai fa-piao.)	请开发票。

English	Pinyin	Wade-Giles	Chinese
NUMBERS			
One	Yī	(Yi)	一
Two	Èr	(Erh)	二
Three	Sān	(San)	三
Four	Sì	(Szu)	四
Five	Wǔ	(Wu)	五
Six	Liù	(Liu)	六
Seven	Qī	(Chi)	七
Eight	Bā	(Pa)	八
Nine	Jiǔ	(Chiu)	九
Ten	Shí	(Shih)	十
Hundred	Bǎi	(Pai)	百
Thousand	Qiān	(Chien)	千
Ten thousand	Wàn	(Wan)	万
OTHERS			
I, me	Wǒ	(Wo)	我
You	Ni	(Ni)	你
He (him), She (her)	Tā	(Ta)	他，她
Man	Nánrén	(Nanjen)	男人
Woman	Nǔrén	(Nujen)	女人
Comrade	Tóngzhì	(Tungchih)	同志
Interpreter	Fānyì	(Fanyi)	窈译
Friendship	Yǒuyī	(Yuyi)	友谊
Shop, store	Shǎngdiàn	(Shangtien)	商店
Toilet (Men)	Nán cèsǔo.	(Nan tsesuo.)	男厕所
Toilet (Ladies)	Nǔ cèsuǒ.	(Nu tsesuo.)	女厕所
Yesterday	Zuótiān	(Tsotien)	昨天
Today	Jīntiān	(Chintien)	今天
Tomorrow	Míngtiān	(Mingtien)	明天
East	Dōng	(Tung)	东
South	Nán	(Nan)	南
West	Xī	(Hsi)	西
North	Běi	(Pei)	北
Spring	Chūn	(Chun)	春
Summer	Xià	(Hsia)	夏
Autumn	Qiū	(Chiu)	秋
Winter	Dōng	(Tung)	冬

THE EIGHTEEN MOST APPRECIATED
DRINKS OF CHINA

The following are the eighteen drinks which were chosen in 1979 by China's National Wine Tasting Committee as "The Eighteen Most Appreciated Drinks of China." A brief description of each follows the listing.

Cheng Gang Chiew
Chu Yeh Ching
Chuang Hsing Da Chu Chiew
Fen Chiew
Gu Jing Gong Jiu
Hsi Feng Chiew
Jin Jiang Bai Lan Di
Lu Chow Lao Jiao Te Chu Chiew
Mao Tai Chiew

Muscatel
Qingdao Bai Putao Jiu
Shaohsing Chia Fan Chiew
Te Zhi Bai Lan Di
Tsingtao Beer
Tung Chiew
Vermouth
Wu Liang Ye
Zhongguo Hong Putao Jiu

Cheng Gang Chiew
Cheng Gang Chiew is a sweet rice wine made in Longyen County, Fujian. It contains a balanced amount of amino acid and occasional drinking can help the circulation, build up vital energy, and nourish the blood.

Chu Yeh Ching
Also called Green Bamboo Leaf Liquor, it is a gold colored drink, slightly bitter but soft with a unique bouquet derived from its blend of spirits and medicinal herbs. Among its ingredients are bamboo leaves, orange peel, cloves, angelica root, sandalwood, and costus root. In summer a glass of Chu Yeh Ching mixed with ice water or soda water plus sugar and cherries makes a lovely, refreshing, cool drink.

Chuang Hsing Da Chu Chiew
Among white liquors it belongs in the light, fragrant category. It is a product of the Chengdu Distillery in Sichuan, formerly the Chuang Hsing Lao Hao Wine Mills, which was founded in 1824. The liquor has a fermentation period of sixty days which enables it to become mellow before it is distilled. It is then aged for one year before being bottled and shipped.

Fen Chiew
Transparently clear, Fen Chiew has a light bouquet and a lingering sweet taste. It is made by a unique traditional method in which yeast is added to the already steamed ingredients which are then placed in an earthenware vat and buried underground to ferment. After fermentation it is distilled into wine. Yeast is added again for a second

fermentation and distillation. Results from the two separate distillations are then blended together to form the final product.

Gu Jing Gong Jiu

Gu Jing Gong Jiu is fermented by using water from an ancient well. Legend tells us that the well was built in the fifth century. The water from the bottom is mellow and sweet, giving the wine a distinctly pure and pleasing taste. It was a tributary item for the emperor in the Ming Dynasty thus the name, Gu Jing Gong Jiu — Tribute Wine from the Ancient Well. Production ceased until 1959 when the government built a new distillery. An old fermenting pond, however, built at the beginning of the Ming Dynasty, is still being used.

Hsi Feng Chiew

This wine can be described as sour but not tart, bitter but not sticky, fragrant but not pungent, peppery but not irritating, with a lingering sweet taste. According to historical documents, Hsi Feng Chiew was known and praised as early as the Tang Dynasty (618-907 A.D.). With a fermentation period of only fourteen to fifteen days, it is then aged from two to three years so its quality can become ever more fragrant and rich.

Jin Jiang Bai Lan Di

This brandy has a golden color with a heavy grape fragrance. Its taste is slightly bitter yet still refreshing. Jin Jiang Bai Lan Di is the oldest brandy made in China. It won a Gold Quality Award and a Certificate for Superior Product at the International Exposition in Panama in 1915. Smooth but not strong, it is described as "the fine drink that leaves one refreshed but not drunk."

Lu Chow Lao Jiao Te Chu Chiew

Rich aroma and a smooth, sweet, lingering taste are the characteristics of this fine Chinese wine. According to written records, the oldest cellar of Lu Chow Lao Jiao Te Chu Chiew Distillery was built around 1650. Its excellent quality is in part due to the meticulous selection of the choicest ingredients coupled with adoption of traditional crafts. After distillation the wine is stored in a special ceramic jar and aged from one to two years.

Mao Tai Chiew

Mao Tai is a famous banquet drink. It is a crystal clear liquor with a luscious scent, smooth and mellow to the taste. The making of Mao Tai is a technique unique to China with repeated fermentation, multiple distillation, meticulous mixing, and cellar aging before it is bottled and shipped. Mao Tai Chiew has been made for over 270 years. At the Panama World's Fair in 1917 it was ranked as one of the foremost wines in the world and won the Most Famous Wine award at that fair.

Muscatel

Muscatel is a sweet grape wine with a rich, but slightly tart taste. Amber colored, it is made by separately using the methods of fermentation for sweet and dry wine and then aged for over two years, thus attaining a more perfect color, aroma, and taste.

Qingdao Bai Putao Jiu

Also called Chefoo White Wine, this is a sweet grape wine, light golden in color, with a fruity flavor. Other distinctive qualities of Qingdao Bai Putao Jiu are its mellow and refreshing taste. The wine is made from the choice Longyan grapes. Advanced scientific fermenting technqiues and rich production experiences are used coupled with a long-aging period to produce Qingdao Bai Putao Jiu.

Shaohsing Chia Fan Chiew

Also called Shaoxing Rice wine, it is the oldest rice wine in China. Brewed from choice glutinous rice, the method uses a specific process of fermentation and low temperature pressing. Golden in color, it is rich in nutritional value. It has a long aging period which creates its rich bouquet and a mellow flavor distinctly its own. Shaohsing Chia Fan Chiew had its beginnings over two thousand years ago. Down through the centuries, its popularity has never declined.

Te Zhi Bai Lan Di

This brandy has a golden color with a rich bouquet. In addition to the long-term aging necessary for all brandies, during the aging process Te Zhi Bai Lan Di is also put through a cold treatment. As a result this brandy is sweet and smooth with a flavor which is neither too strong nor too pungent.

Tsingtao Beer

Tsingtao Beer is a crystal-clear, fully carbonated drink which is light in color. It is brewed from the unadulterated spring water of Laoshan. The superior quality of the water is most important to its special taste. The beer was first produced in 1903 and is exported to over thirty countries and regions.

Tung Chiew

Clear in color, with a heavy bouquet, Tung Chiew is a sweet drink. Its unique flavor comes from uniting two medicinal herbs, one which is rich and aromatic, and the other which has a mellow, lingering taste. Tung Chiew was first produced eighty years ago. In the fifties a new distillery was built on the same spot for its production.

Vermouth

Vermouth is a dark, amber colored drink. Made from a mixture of medicinal herbs and aging wines, it is a sweet, enriched tonic with a slightly dry and bitter taste. It is brewed from a selection of Longyan grapes and choice white grapes from the Dazhe region. In the long aging process juices from more than ten medicinal herbs are used such as saffron, crocus, round cardamon, lilia clove, the meat from the Chinese cassia fruit, and Chinese alpine leaf.

Wu Liang Ye

This liquor is crystal clear with a mellow bouquet and an aroma that lingers long after one has finished drinking it. Wu Liang Ye, or five grain liquid, derives its name from the five grains used as its ingredients: sorghum, rice, glutinous rice, corn, and wheat. It is meticulously fermented by a distinctive technique, drawing from the essence of the five grains, then stored until the taste reaches a pure state of fragrance, mellowness, sweetness, and clearness.

Zhongguo Hong Putao Jiu

Zhongguo Hong Putao Jiu is also known as Chinese Red Wine. It is a dark amber colored drink having a distinct grape flavor and a heavy bouquet. Slightly tart, it is fermented by selecting grapes of superior quality. Newly distilled wine is blended with wine which has already been aged for at least two years. This process produces a wine of exceptional quality.

SAMPLE BANQUET MENUS

Eating in China

On the following pages we have provided sample banquet menus from several restaurants in the main tourist cities. For those with gourmet tastes, we also include a list of the most popular dishes in China and the restaurants where they are served. As you travel through China it is possible that you will be able to order similar dishes in different cities and different restaurants than are shown here. Eating in China and sampling the many, varied, exotic dishes available there is a unique, memorable experience to be long remembered.

BEIJING

Feng Ze Yuan Restaurant
Telephone 33 28 28

Reasonable in Price (RMB 20-RMB 30 per person)

冷盘	Assorted Cold Hors d'Oeuvres
鸡蓉鱼翅	Chicken Puffs with Sharksfin
油爆大虾	Deep Fried Prawns
香酥鸡	Crisp Chicken
扒鲍龙须菜	Asparagus with Dried Abalone
红烧鱼	Braised Fish in Brown Sauce
杏仁豆腐菠萝	Almond Beancurd with Pineapple

Moderate in Price (RMB 30-RMB 40 per person)

五样冷盘	Five Cold Dishes
磨茹汤	White Fungus Soup
芝麻炒鸡	Fried Sesame Chicken
绿豆芽炒肉丝	Deep Fried Pork Slices with Bean Sprouts
兰片炒鲍鱼	Abalone and Cane Shoots
雪花大虾	Prawn with Snow Flakes
炒三鲜	Three Delicacy Combination
月饼	Moon Cake

BEIJING

Peking Hotel Restaurant
Telephone 55 22 31

Northern Chinese Cuisine (RMB 20-RMB 30 per person)

翅黄公鸭	Braised Golden Shark's Fin
京式海参	Sea Cucumber Beijing Style
一品[illegible]	Duck Rolls in Pot with Mixed Vegetable
酱汁鲤鱼	Carp Cooked with Soy Paste
干贝炒虾球	Shrimp Ball and Scallops
蟹卷扒白菜	Chinese Cabbage Braised with Crab Paste
杏仁豆腐	Almond Flavored Gelatin

Sichuan Cuisine (RMB 20-RMB 30 per person)

兰片豌豆苗汤	Bamboo Shoots with Tender Pea Leaves Soup
糖醋鱿鱼	Sweet and Sour Squid
樟茶鸭子	Smoked Duck flavored with Tea
叉烧	Roast Pig
干烧桂鱼	Braised Mandarin Fish
炸虾	Fried Whole Shrimp
糖香桃汤	Sweet Walnut Soup

BEIJING

Sichuan Restaurant
Telephone 33 63 56

Reasonable in Price (RMB 20-RMB 30 per person)

红烧鱼翅	Sharksfin in Brown Sauce
锅巴海参	Crisp Rice with Sea Cucumber
蜀酱大虾	Prawn in Sichuan Sauce
干煸牛肉絲	Beef Shreds Sichuan Style
大让竹笋	Bamboo Sprouts
鱼香茄子	Eggplant with Fishy Flavor
雪花桃泥	Snowy Mashed Walnut

Moderate in Price (RMB 20-RMB 30 per person)

干烧青鱼	Fish in Hot Sauce
樟茶鸭子	Duck Smoked with Tea Leaves
熏鸡	Smoked Chicken
回鍋肉	Twice-Cooked Pork Slices
小笼牛肉	Beef in Small Bamboo Steamer
三絲鱼翅	Sharksfin with Three Shreds
摇蛀时菜	Fresh Vegetables with Dried Scallops
麻婆豆腐	Beancurd with Pepper and Chili
酒糟果子羹	Fruit in Rice Wine

GUANGZHOU

Ban Xi Restaurant
Telephone 8 56 55

Reasonable in Price (RMB 20-RMB 30 per person)

三蛇�虎烩	Three Kinds of Stewed Snake
脆皮炸子鹅	Fried Chicken
玉簪田鸡腿	Fried Frogs' Legs with Vegetables
酥炸竹节虾	Fried Prawns
红烧鲍脯	Abalone Fillet with Brown Sauce
清蒸嘉鱼	Steamed Fish
干烧伊扇	Braised Noodles
四种咸点	Dim Sum: Four Kinds of Salty Pastry
二种甜点	Dim Sum: Two Kinds of Sweet Pastry

Moderate in Price (RMB 30-RMB 40 per person)

像生冷拼盘	Assorted Cold Hors d'Oeuvres Platter
蟹肉烩鱼翅	Braised Crab with Sharksfin
金华玉树鸡	Chicken with Ham and Broccoli
挂炉烤鹅	Roasted Goose
油泡鲜虾肉	Sauteed Shrimp
红玉熊掌	Braised Bear's Paw with Brown Sauce
清蒸桂鱼	Steamed Mandarin Fish
广州炒饭	Fried Rice Guangzhou Style
四种咸点	Dim Sum: Four Kinds of Salty Pastry
二种甜点	Dim Sum: Two Kinds of Sweet Pastry

GUANGZHOU

Bei-Yuan Restaurant (North Garden Restaurant)
Telephone 3 24 71

Reasonable in price (RMB 20-RMB 30 per person)

桂花乌扎	Delicacies with Cinnamon Blooms
甘花鸡脯	Fried Chicken Cutlet
菊花炒蛇羹	Braised Snake Soup with Chrysanthemum
杏油脆皮虾	Crispy Prawns Marinated in Sesame Oil
双闷琵琶翅	Crab with Sharksfin
玉簪田鸡腿	Fried Frogs Legs with Vegetables
糖醋秘方鱼	Deep Fried Fish with Sweet and Sour Sauce
炒山水河粉	Fried Broad Noodles
双甜美	Dim Sum: Two Kinds of Sweet Pastry
双咸美	Dim Sum: Two kinds of Salty Pastry

Moderate in Price (RMB 30-RMB 40 per person)

七彩冷拼盘	Assorted Cold Hors d'Oeuvres Platter
四宝炒牛奶	Sauteed Milk with Four Delicacies
名牌花雕鸡	Chicken Flavored in Shao-xing Wine
油泡鲜虾仁	Sauteed Shrimp
翡翠鲈鱼球	Perch Balls with Green Vegetables
月影龙凤燕（高）	Bird's Nest with Lobster and Pigeon Eggs
金钱酿蟹盒	Stuffed Crab
杏油炒饭	Fried Rice
双甜美	Dim Sum: Two Kinds of Sweet Pastry
双咸美	Dim Sum: Two Kinds of Salty Pastry

SHANGHAI

Luyang Tswun Restaurant
Telephone 53 97 87

Reasonable in Price (RMB 20-RMB 30 per person)

花色冷盘　　Assorted Cold Hors d'Oeuvres Platter
排南虾仁　　Beinen Shrimps
奥香鸡丝　　Sliced Chicken with Hot Sauce
鸽蛋吐司　　Pigeon Egg with Toast
锦杨刺参　　Mandarin Fish with Lychee
荔枝桂鱼　　Sliced Pork Hochuan Style
合川肉片　　Egg White Puffs with Assorted Delicacies
一品芙蓉　　Two Kinds of Pastry
双色点心　　Fresh Fruits (in Season)
应时鲜菓

Moderate in Price (RMB 30-RMB 40 per person)

小花篮冷盘(以人支)　Hors d'Oeuvres in Small Basket
罗汉虾仁　　Lo Han Shrimps
锦锈鱼练　　Fried Sliced Fish
透明鸡脯　　Crystal Chicken Slices
陈庆牛肉　　Beef with Seasoned Orange Peel
明珠酥鲍　　Abalone Fillet
叉烧桂鱼　　Mandarin Fish with Roast Pork
锦杨酥鸡　　Crispy Chicken Luyang Style
什锦干丝　　Assorted Dry Beancurd Shreds
一品南施　　Assorted Delicacies
花色点心　　Assorted Snacks
应时鲜菓　　Fresh Fruits (in Season)

SHANGHAI

Shanghai Mansions
Telephone 24 62 69

Reasonable in Price (RMB 20-RMB 30 per person)

荷花冷盆　　Assorted Cold Hors d'Oeuvres Platter
六　小　碟　　Six Small Side Dishes
苹果虾仁　　Shrimps with Apple
金钱牛仔　　Veal and Mushrooms
蟹黄拆烩鱼肚　Fish Head with Crab Spawns
黄桥烧饼　　Sesame Cake
鸭茸鸽粥　　Chicken Congee
三花草炖　　Stewed Mixed Vegetables
芦须桂鱼　　Mandarin Fish with Asparagus
雪菜野鸭汤　Wild Duck Soup with Pickled Vegetables
翡翠烧卖　　Steamed Dumplings with Vegetables
核桃酪　　　Walnut Cream

Moderate in Price (RMB 30-RMB 40 per person)

金奥冷盆　　Assorted Cold Hors d'Oeuvres Platter
六　小　碟　　Six Small Side Dishes
烩虎尾　　　Stewed Oxen Tails
佛手鸽　　　Chicken with Chinese fruit
葱拨海参　　Sea Cucumber with Scallion
贾氏丝并　　Shredded Turnip Cake
煮干丝　　　Boiled Dry Beancurd Shreads
红焖甲鱼　　Stewed Turtle with Brown Sauce
荷叶包鸭腿　Duck's Leg Wrapped in Lotus Leaf
火腿斑鸠汤　Ham and Pigeon Soup
千层油糕　　Thousand Layer Cake

SHANGHAI

Xin Ya Cantonese Restaurant
Telephone 22 36 36

Reasonable in Price (RMB 20-RMB 30 per person)

花式冷盘	Assorted Cold Hors d'Oeuvres Platter
清炒虾仁	Sauteed Shrimps
肉茸戈渣	Fried Mashed Meat
植物四宝	Four Delicacies from Assorted Vegetables
鸳鸯明虾	Prawns in Two Styles
茅台白鸡	Chicken Flavored in Mao-tai Wine
古老肉	Sweet and Sour Boneless Pork
八珍鱼翅	Sharksfin with Eight Delicacies
双色点心	Dim Sum: Two Kinds of Pastry
应时鲜果	Fresh Fruits (in Season)

Moderate in Price (RMB 30-RMB 40 per person)

金鸡冷盘	Decorated Cold Chicken Platter
四小碟	Four Small Side Dishes
双色虾仁	Shrimps in Two Flavors
红罗雪衣	Turnip with Snow Peas
玉树鸡	Chicken with Broccoli
鸡牛柳	Chicken Cutlets and Beef Fillets
三色明虾	Prawns with Three Kinds of Sauce
片皮填鸡	Roasted Stuffed Duck
鲍鱼四宝	Abalone with Four Delicacies
火腿鱼翅	Ham with Sharksfin
银耳奶露	White Custard Cream
四色点心	Dim Sum: Four Kinds of Pastry
应时鲜果	Fresh Fruits (in Season)

100 MOST POPULAR CHINESE DISHES

1. Beijing Roast Duck — Quanjude Roast Duck Restaurant, Bianyifang Roast Duck Restaurant, Beijing Roast Duck Restaurant — 北京烤鸭

2. Beijing Instant-Boiled Mutton Slices — Donglaishun Moslem Restaurant, Hongbinlou Restaurant, Beijing Hotel Restaurant, Beijing — 北京涮羊肉

3. Toad-Like Ablone — Fangshan Restaurant, Beijing — 蛤蟆鲍鱼

4. Brooding Phoenix (hen or duck) — Fangshan Restaurant, Beijing — 凤凰趴窝

5. Stewed Sea Cucumber with Scallion — Fengzeyuan Restaurant, Cuihualou Restaurant, Beijing — 葱烧海参

6. Stewed Shark's Fin in Casserole — Fengzeyuan Restaurant, Cuihualou Restaurant, Beijing — 砂锅鱼翅

7. Carp Served Alive — Tingliguan (Oriole Hall) Restaurant of Summer Palace, Beijing — 活吃鲤鱼

8. Fried Prawn Croquettes — Minzu (Nationalities) Hotel, Beijing — 水晶虾饼

9. Rice Crust with Three Delicacies (chicken breast meat, ham and tender bamboo shoots — Sichuan Restaurant, Beijing — 锅巴三鲜

10. Spring Chicken "Lanterns" — Sichuan Restaurant, Beijing — 闵油灯笼鸡

11. Pilose Antler with Three Sea Delicacies shark's fin, scallop meat, sea cucumbers and hen mash — Zinqiao Hotel, Beijing — 鹿茸三海凤

12. Mutton Shashlicks — Restaurant of Beijing Cultural Palace of Nationalities — 烤羊肉串

13. Peach-Blossom Pigeon Eggs — Donglaishun Restaurant, Beijing; Jinyang Restaurant, Beijing — 桃花鸽蛋

14. Braized Beef Tendons in Brown Sauce — Hongbinlou Restaurant, Beijing — 红扒蹄筋

15. Crunchies Rice Crust with Delicacies Juice — Cuihualou Restaurant, Kangle Restaurant, Beijing — 桃花泛

16. Dong'an Chicken — Quyuan Restaurant, Beijing — 东安鸡

17. Chrysanthemum-Blossom Silver Fungus — Tongchunyuan Restaurant, Beijing — 菊花银耳

18. Assorted Slices and White Fungus in Chafing Dish — Yuhuatai Restaurant, Beijing — 什锦银耳鱼锅

19. Roast Goose — Jianguo Hotel Restaurant, Beijing — 烤鹅

20. Roast Pigling — Beijing Hotel Restaurant and Dasanyuan Restaurant, Beijing — 明炉片皮猪

21. Rape Hearts with Champignons — Beijing Hotel Restaurant — 鲜蘑酿菜心

347

22. Simmered Shark's Fin in Brown Sauce	Beijing Hotel Restaurant	黄燜鱼翅
23. Bird's Nest in Clear Soup	Beijing Hotel Restaurant	清汤燕菜
24. Chrysanthemum-Blossom with Snake, Cat and Chicken	Snake Food Restaurant, Guangzhou	菊花龙虎凤
25. Stir-Fried Shredded Snakes	Snake Food Restaurant, Guangzhou	五彩炒蛇丝
26. Fried Squirrel	Yeweiziang Restaurant, Guangzhou	百花酿松鼠
27. Stewed Lynx Meat	Yeweiziang Restaurant, Guangzhou	红烧果子狸
28. Roast Pork Rolls	Beiyuan Restaurant, Guangzhou	桂花香扎
29. Fried Duck Webs with Oyster Sauce	Beiyuan Restaurant, Guangzhou	蚝油鸭脚
30. Quails with Multi-Layer Shortbread	Panxi Restaurant, Guangzhou	鹌鹑千层酥
31. Steamed Chicken with Delicacies Juice	Panxi Restaurant, Guangzhou	香汁油气鸡
32. Tea-Smoked Chicken	Dasanyuan Restaurants, Guangzhou and Beijing	茶香鸡
33. Hot Oil with Peeled Fresh Shrimps	Yuyuan Restaurant, Guangzhou	油泡鲜虾仁
34. Crispy Chicken	Datong Restaurant, Guangzhou	脆皮鸡
35. Peony-Blossom Duck with Bean-Curd	Datong Restaurant, Guangzhou	牡丹西施鸡
36. Wenchang Chicken	Guangzhou Restaurant, Guangzhou	文昌鸡
37. Stewed Muntjac	Overseas Chinese Mansion, Guangzhou	花胶拆烩黄猄
38. Sunned-Chicken	Tingyauxuan Restaurant, Guangzhou	太阳鸡
39. Fried Pork Shred with Virmicelli	Shahe Restaurant, Guangzhou	滑炒肉丝河
40. Camphor and Tea Smoked Duck	Chengdu Restaurant, Sichuan; Beijing Hotel Restaurant, Beijing	樟茶鸭子
41. Stir-Fried Pork Cubelets with Peanuts	Chengdu Restaurant, Sichuan; Sichuan Restaurant, Beijing	宫保鸡丁
42. Colourful Bean-Curd	Chengdu Rongleyuan Restaurant, Sichuan	五彩豆腐
43. Stuffed-Glutinous-Rice Chicken with Assorted Delicacies	Chengdu Rongleyuan Restaurant, Sichuan	八宝糯米鸡
44. Stuffed-Assorted-Delicacies Duck	Yizhishi Restaurant, Chonqing	八宝全鸭
45. Leaf-Smoked Spareribs	Yizhishi Restaurant, Chongqing	烟熏排骨
46. Steamed Bighead Fish	Yizhishi Restaurant, Chongqing	清蒸肥头鱼
47. Sweet and Hot Pork Shred	Chongqing Restaurant	鱼香肉丝
48. Boiled Beef	Chongqing Restaurant	水煮牛肉

49.	Sweet and Sour Pork	Xinya Restaurant, Shanghai; Main Restaurants and Hotels in Guangzhou	古老肉
50.	Fried Fresh Milk	Xinya Restaurant, Shanghai	戈渣鲜奶
51.	Smoked Pomfret	Xinya Restaurant, Shanghai	烟鲳鱼
52.	Lonyuan Bean-Curd	Meilongzhen Restaurant, Shanghai	龙园豆腐
53.	Egg-White Tomatoes	Meilongzhen Restaurant, Shanghai	芙蓉蕃茄
54.	Steamed Giant Salamander	Xinghualou Restaurant, Shanghai	清炖海狗鱼
55.	Stewed Mixture of Snake, Wild Cat and Hen Meat	Xinghualou Restaurant, Shanghai	龙虎斗
56.	Peeled Fresh Shrimps with Bean-Curd	Xinghualou Restaurant, Shanghai	西施虾仁
57.	Steamed Minced Crab and Pork Meat Balls	Yangzhou Restaurant, Shanghai	清炖蟹粉狮子头
58.	Soft-Shelled Turtle Stewed in Soy	Laozhengxing Restaurant, Shanghai	红烧甲鱼
59.	Asparagus in White Sauce	Gongdelin Vegetarian Restaurant, Shanghai	奶油芦笋
60.	Fried Pigeon Eggs	Dasanyuan Restaurant, Nanjing	煎酿百花鸽
61.	Stewed Mandarin Fish	Dasanyuan Restaurant, Nanjing	麒麟桂鱼
62.	Duck and Shark's Fin	Jiangsu Restaurant, Nanjing	鸭包鱼翅
63.	Yangzhou Hairtails	Caigenxiang Restaurant, Yangzhou	扬州刀鱼
64.	Salted Chicken	Caigenxiang Restaurant, Yangzhou	卤鸡
65.	Multi-Flower Wine Simmered Pork	Yanchuan Restaurant, Zhenjiang	百花酒焖肉
66.	Jingxiang Bean-Curd	China Restaurant, Wuxi	镜箱豆腐
67.	West Lake Vinegar Fish	Louwailou Restaurant, Hangzhou	西湖醋鱼
68.	Jiaohua (Beggar) Chicken	Zhiweiguan Restaurant, Hangzhou	叫化童鸡
69.	West Lake Water Shield Soup	Zhiweiguan Restaurant, Hangzhou	西湖莼菜汤
70.	Shelled Shrimps with Dragon-Well Tea	Hangzhou Restaurant, Hangzhou; Beijing Hotel Restaurant, Beijing	龙井虾仁
71.	Dongo Pork	Hangzhou Restaurant	东坡肉
72.	Stewed Intestines	Jufengde Restaurant, Jinan	九转大肠
73.	Stir-Fried Pig Maw with Chicken Gizzard	Jufengde Restaurant, Jinan	油爆双脆
74.	Fried Crucian Carp	Jufengde Restaurant, Jinan	干烧鲫鱼
75.	Fried Oyster	Main Restaurants and Hotels in Beijing Chunhelou Restaurant, Qingdao	炸蛎黄

76.	Rose-Like Rice Crust	Chunhelou Restaurant, Qingdao	玫瑰锅炸
77.	Steamed Porgy	Chunhelou Restaurant, Qingdao	清蒸加吉鱼
78.	Stir-Fried Conches	Chunhelou Restaurant, Qingdao	油爆海螺
79.	"Gourd" Chicken	Xi'an Restaurant	葫芦鸡
80.	Fresh Fish in Chafing Dish	Xi'an Restaurant	奶汤锅子鱼
81.	Simmered Pine Nut with Pork Cubelets	Wuyi Restaurant, Xi'an	松子酿方肉
82.	Colourful Fillet	Wuyi Restaurant, Xi'an	彩云里脊
83.	Chrysanthemum, Scallop	Wuyi Restaurant, Xi'an	菊花干贝
84.	Strong-Smelling-Preserved Bean-Curd	Huogongdian Restaurant, Chansha	臭豆腐
85.	Fotiaoqiang (Assorted Delicacies from Sea and Land)	Juchunyuan Restaurant, Fuzhou	佛跳墙
86.	Stewed Spareribs	Hubin Hotel and Taihu Hotel, Wuxi Xinnanxuan Restaurant, Xiamen	烧排骨
87.	Crab with Assorted-Delicacies	Xinnanxuan Restaurant, Xiamen	八宝芙蓉蟹
88.	Salted Stir-Fried Pig Maw	Dengyinglou Restaurant, Tianjin	盐爆肚仁
89.	Fried Prawns	Grand Hotel, Tianjin	煎烹对虾
90.	Stewed Steamed Crabs	Friendship Hotel, Tianjin	清蒸蟹
91.	Steamed Bream	Wuchang Restaurant, Wuhan	清蒸鳊鱼
92.	Peony-Like Mandarin Fish	Wuchang Restaurant, Wuhan	牡丹桂鱼
93.	Stewed Black Carp's Fin	Wuchang Restaurant, Wuhan	烧鲭鱼划水
94.	Wuchang Fish	Wuchang Restaurant, Wuhan	武昌鱼
95.	Stewed Bear's Paw	Beijing Hotel Restaurant, Beijing; Lumingchun Restaurant, Shenyang	红扒熊掌
96.	Peach-Blossom Prawns	Lumingchun Restaurant, Shenyang	燕尾桃花虾
97.	Stewed Gecko (Gejie) with Mountain Tortoise	Nanning Restaurant, Nanning	蛤蚧炖鹰龟
98.	Stewed Silver Fungus with Pangolin	Nanning Restaurant, Nanning	雪耳炖穿山甲
99.	Squirrel-Shaped Mandarin Fish	Songhelou Restaurant, Suzhou	松鼠桂鱼
100.	Cherry Pork	Songhelou Restaurant, Suzhou	樱桃肉

INDEX

A

Agriculture 25
Air Service 47-50, 309
Alphabet, Chinese Phonetic 28-30
Amoy, see Xiamen
Ancestral Temple, Foshan 172
Ancient Grand Canal, The, Wuxi 273
Animals of China 66-8
Anningwenquan, Kunming 214
Anshan (Anshan) 149
Antiques, Stores, 53, 322-3
Applied Arts Factory, Tianjin 263
Art Museum, Tianjin 262
Arhats 254
Arts and Crafts, Chinese 57-60
Arts and Crafts Department Stores 52,
  333
Arts and Crafts Factory, Fuzhou 176
  Harbin 186
Arts and Crafts Gallery of Jiangxi
  Province, Nanchang 227
Arts and Crafts Research Institute,
  Shanghai 135
Avenue of the Animals, Ming Tombs
  98

B

Badaling 93, 95
Baggage, Allowance 49-50
Baggage Declaration for Passengers,
  facsimile 37
Bai Causeway, Hangzhou 182
Bai Hua Zhou Island, Nanchang
  227-8
Bai Ta, Lanzhou 215
Bai Yun Hotel, Guangzhou 125
Bai Yun Shan Park 123
Baimasi, Luoyang 221-2
Ballet 61
Ban Xi Restaurant, Guangzhou 127
Banpo Museum, Xi'an 278
Banquets, Sample Menus 339-46
Bao Gong Temple, Hefei 189
Bao Guo Temple, Ningbo 237-8
Baotou (Paotow) 150
Bao Tu Springs, Jinan 200
Baoguangsi, Chengdu 161
Bei Hai Park, Beijing 84-7
  Site Plan of 85

Bei Ling, Shenyang 248
Bei Yuan Restaurant, Guangzhou 128
Beidaihe 241
Beigushan Hill, Zhenjiang 297
Beijing (Peking) 22, 71-112
  City Map of 73
  Hotels 105-9
  Places of Interest 74-102
  Restaurants 109-12
  Shopping 102-5
Beijing Hotel, Beijing 105
Beijing Hotel Restaurant, Beijing 109
Beijing Roast Duck Restaurant,
  Beijing 110
Beishan Park, Jilin 198
Beiwenquan Park, Chongqing 163
Bell Tower, Xi'an 278
Bethune International Peace Hospital
  of the Chinese People's Liberation
  Army, Shijiazhuang 250
Beverages 305
Bi Shu Shan Zhuang, Chengde 158
Bi Xia Temple, Tai Shan 257
Bian Yi Fang Roast Duck Restaurant,
  Beijing 110
Birds of China 66-8
Bo Hai (Pohai Sea) 22, 23
Bund, Shanghai 134

C

CAAC 47-9
Cables 42-3
Cang Lang Ting, Suzhou 254
Canton, see Guangzhou
Canton Trade Fair 121
Capital, of China 22
Carpet Works, Hohhot 191
Chang Ling, Ming Tombs 100
Changchun (Changchun) 151-2
  City Map of 151
Changjiang Bridge, Nanjing 231
Changjiang Gorges
  (Yangtze River Gorges) 152-4
Changjiang River Bridge at Wuhan
  268
Changsha (Changsha) 154-8
  City Map of 155
Chenchiang, see Zhenjiang
Chenchow, see Zhengzhou or
  Zhangzhou

Chengde (Chengteh) 158-9
Chengdu (Chengtu) 159-61
  City Map of 159
Chengteh, see Chengde
Chengtu, see Chengdu
Chiayukuan Pass, see Jiayuguan Pass
Children's Palace, Shanghai 137
Children's Railway, Harbin 187
China Hotel, Guanzhou 125
China International Travel Service
  (Lüxingshe) 32, 33
  Branches and Addresses 307-8
Chinghung, see Jinghong
Chingkang Shan, see Jinggang Shan
Chingtehchen, see Jingdezhen
Chinhuangtao, see Qinhuangdao
Chongqing (Chungking) 161-4
Chopsticks, how to use 56-7, 304
Chiuchiang, see Jiujiang
Chufu, see Qufu
Chungking, see Chongqing
Cigarettes 305
CITS, see China International Travel
  Service
Civil Aviation Administration of
  China, see CAAC
Climate, of China 22
Clothing 38-9, 303
Coal Hill (Jing Shan), Beijing 84
Communist Party of China 28
Comrade Mao Zedong's Former
  Dwelling, Wuhan 268
Cong Terrace, The, Handan 179
Conghua Hot Springs, Guangzhou
  123
Credit Cards 46-7
  List of Types Accepted and
  Locations of Acceptance 317
Crime Exhibition Halls, Chongqing
  164
Cui Hua Lou Restaurant, Beijing 112
Cuisine, Chinese 53-6, 304, 335ff.
  Banquets, Sample Menus 339-46
  100 Most Popular Dishes, 337-40
Currency, Chinese see Renminbi
Currency, Foreign 46
  List of Types Accepted 324-5
Customs 36-8, 304

Daguanlou, Kunming 212-3
Dahecun, Prehistoric Site at,
  Zhengzhou 294
Dahua Guesthouse, Shanghai 141
Dalian (Talien) 164-5
  City Map of 164
Dalian Harbor 165
Datong (Tatung) 166-7
Datong Restaurant, Guangzhou 128
Dayan Pagoda, Xi'an 278
Dazu County (Tatzu County) 167
Department Stores 52
Dian Chi Lake, Kunming 212
Diaoyutai State Guest House 105
Diner's Club 47, 329
Ding Ling, Ming Tombs 98-100
Dingshu Village, Yixing 288-9
Dong Fang Hotel, Guangzhou 125
Dong Fang Restaurant, Guangzhou
  129
Dong Hai (East China Sea) 22-3
Dong Ling, Shenyang 248
Donghu Guest House, Shanghai 141
Donglaishun Restaurant, Beijing 112
Dongting Lake, Yueyang 292
Drink see Cuisine, Chinese
Drum Hill, see Gushan
Drum Tower, Jiuquan 208
Du Fu Caotang, Chengdu 160
Du Xiu Feng, Guilin 178
Dynasties, Chinese 328

D

Da Huo Fang Reservoir, Fushun 174
Da Long Qiu Cataract, Shaoxing 246
Da Ming Lake, Jinan 200
Dachengdian, Qufu 243

E

East China Sea, see Dong Hai
East Lake, Wuhan 269
East Outer Section, Imperial Palace,
  Beijing 83-4
Embroidery 59
Emei Shan (Mount Omei) 167-8
Emergency 306
Entertainment, in China 60-2
Entry, into China 36-8
Exit, from China 38

F

Fa Jing Temple, Yangzhou 285
Fang Shan Restaurant, Beijing 87,
  111
February 7 Monument, The,
  Zhengzhou 293
Fei Lai Shi, Lu Shan 224

Fen 43
Feng Ze Yuan Restaurant, Beijing 111
Film 40
  Developing 306
First National Congress, Chinese
  Communist Party, Site of,
  Shanghai 139
First Normal School of Hunan,
  Changsha 155
Fish, Freshwater 66
Folk Arts Research Society, Foshan
  171-2
Foochow, see Fuzhou
Food see Cuisine, Chinese
Forbidden City, Beijing 76, 77-9
  Site Plan of 78-9
Foreign Currency, see Currency
Foreign Exchange Certificates 44-5
Foshan (Foshan) 169-73
Fragrant Hill Hotel 106
Friendship Stores 51-2
  List of Names and Addresses 320
Fruit, Beijing Preserved 65
Fu Liang Cheng Pagoda, Jingdezhen
  203
Fushun (Fushun) 173-4
Fushun Exhibition Hall 174
Fuzhou (Foochow) 174-6
Fuzhou West Lake, Fuzhou 175

G

Gantang Lake, Jiujiang 207
Garden Hotel, Guanghou 126
Garden of the Purple Clouds of
  Autumn, Shanghai 140
Gate of Heavenly Peace, see Tian
  Men Gate
Gate of Heavenly Purity, Beijing 82
Ge Yuan Garden, Yangzhou 285
Gezhouba Dam Water Control
  Project, Yichang 288
Ginseng 64
Glass Works, Dalian 165
Golden Top Temple, Emei Shan 169
Government, China 30
Grand Level Land Temple, Emei
  Shan 168
Grapes 65-6
Great Hall of the People, Beijing 75
Great Wall, The 71, 93-5, 196, 240
Great Wall Sheraton Hotel, Beijing
  106
Gu Lou, Nanjing 233

Gu Shan, Hangzhou 183
Guan Yin Bridge, Xingzi County 280
Gushan (Drum Hill) Fuzhou 175
Guang Xiao Si Temple, Guangzhou
  120
Guangzhou 112-30
  City Map of 113
  Hotels 124-26
  Places of Interest 115-23
  Restaurants 127-30
  Shopping 123-4
  Guangzhou Antique Shop,
    Guangzhou 124
  Guangzhou Cultural Park 122
  Guangzhou, Day Trips from 123
  Guangzhou Foreign Trade Center
    121
  Guangzhou Restaurant, Guangzhou
    128
  Guangzhou Zoo, Guangzhou 122
Guanyin Cave, Shaoxing 247
Gui Yuan Temple, Wuhan 270
Guilin (Kweilin) 176-79
  City Map of 177
Gulangyu, Xiamen 274

H

Hai He (Haiho River) 23
Haiho River, see Hai He
Hall of Complete Harmony, Beijing
  81
Hall of Mental Cultivation, Beijing
  82-3
Hall of Preserving Harmony, Beijing
  81-2
Hall of Supreme Harmony, Beijing
  80-1
Hall of Union, Beijing 82
Han Shan Temple, Suzhou 254
Han Tombs, Luoyang 222
Handan (Hantan) 179
Hangchow, see Hangzhou
Hangzhou (Hangchow) 180-5
  City Map of 181
Harbin (Harbin) 185-7
  City Map of 185
Harbin Zoo 187
Harbors 24
He Ren Peak, Tai Shan 257
Hefei (Hofei) 188-9
  City Map of 188
Hei Hu Springs, Jinan 200
Heilong Jiang (Heilung River) 23
Heilongjiang Provincial Museum,
  Harbin 186

Heilung River, see Heilong Jiang
Henan Provincial Museum,
  Zhengzhou 294
Hengshan Hotel, Shanghai 142
Heping Hotel
  Beijing 106
  Shanghai 142
Hints, Helpful 303-6
History, Chinese 25-8
Hofei, see Hefei
Hohhot (Huhehot) 189-92
  City Map of 190
Holidays, Chinese 330
Hongyancun, Chongqing 163
Hot Springs, Huang Shan 194
Hotels, General Information 39-40
  Beijing 105-9
  Guangzhou 124-6
  Hangzhou 185
  Hohhot 192
  Shanghai 141-5
  Ürümqi 266
  Zhuoxian County 297
Hotels, Names and Addresses 318-9
Hou Shi Wu, Tai Shan 257
Hsingtzu, see Xingzi
Hu Qiu Shan, Suzhou 254
Hua Lin Si Temple, Guangzhou 121
Hua Lin Temple, Fuzhou 175
Hua Shan (Huashan Mountain)
  195-6
Huadu Hotel 107
Huai He (Huaiho River) 23
Huaiho River, see Huai He
Huagang Guan Yu, Hangzhou 182
Huang Hai (Yellow Sea) 22
Huang He (Yellow River) 23
Huang Hua Gang Mausoleum of
  Martyrs, Guangzhou 117
Huang Long Dong, Hangzhou 183
Huang Shan (Yellow Mountain) 193
Huangpu (Whampoa), Guangzhou
  112
Huaqing Hot Springs, Xi'an 278
Huashan Mountain, see Hua Shan
Huayan Monastery, Datong 167
Huhehot, see Hohhot
Huishan Clay Figurine Studio, Wuxi
  273
Hunan Ceramics, Changsha 156

Imperial City 76
Imperial Garden, Beijing 82
Imperial Palace 76, 77, 79-84
Imperial Palace Museum of
  Shenyang, Shenyang 247
Importing, Restrictions 36-8
Inoculation 36
Inventions, Chinese 21
Islands, 23
Ivory, Restrictions 38

J

Ji Xiao Villa, Yangzhou 286
Jiangdu Water Control Project,
  Yangzhou 286
Jiangsu Workers Sanatorium, Wuxi
  272
Jianguo Hotel 107
Jiangxi Provincial Museum,
  Nanchang 227
Jiao 43, 45
Jiaoshan Hill, Zhengjiang 295-6
Jiayuguan Pass (Chiayukuan Pass)
  196-7
Jiayuguan Pass (castle) 208-9
Jilin (Kirin) 197
Jimei Scenic Area, Xiamen 275
Jin Jiang Club, Shanghai 140
Jin Temples, Taiyuan 258-9
Jinan (Tsinan) 199-201
Jinglun Hotel, Beijing 107
Jing Shan (Coal Hill), Beijing 84
Jing Shi Yu Valley, Tai Shan 256
Jing'an Hotel, Shanghai 142
Jinjiang Hotel, Shanghai 142
Jingdezhen (Chingtehchen) 202-3
Jingdezhen Museum 203
Jinggang Shan (Chingkang Mountain)
  198-9
Jinghong (Chinghung) 203-5
Jinling Hotel 234
Jinshan Hill, Zhenjiang 295
Jinyun Shan, Chongqing 163
Jiuhua Shan (Nine Flowers Mountain)
  206
Jiuquan (Chiuchuan) 208
Jiuquan Spring, Jiuquan 208
Jokhang Temple, Lhasa 218
Junshan, Yueyang 292
Juzi Dao, Changsha 155

I

Imperial Ancestral Temple, Beijing
  79

K

Kaifeng (Kaifeng) 209-11

Kaiyuan Temple, Quanzhou 242
Kirin, see Jilin
Kubla Khan 71, 86
Kunming (Kunming) 211-14
    City Map of 211
Kweilin, see Guilin

L

Lakes 23
Lanchow, see Lanzhou
Language, Chinese 28
Lanzhou (Lanchow) 214-16
    City Map of 214
Lao Shan, Mt. Qingdao 240
Laodong Park, Changchun 152
Leshan 216-7
Lhasa 217-8
Lido Hotel, Beijing 107
Li Yuan Garden, Wuxi 271-2
Lian Hua Feng, Huang Shan 194
Lianyun Gang (Lienyun Harbor) 218
Lienyun Harbor, see Lianyun Gang
Lin Yan Hill, Suzhou 255
Ling Feng Peak, Shaoxing 246-7
Ling Gu Pagoda, Nanjing 234
Ling Yan Monastery, Shaoxing 246
Ling Yin Monastery, Hangzhou 183
Lingyun Hill, Leshan 216
Liquors 57, 335-36
Litchi (Lychee) 66
Liu Bu, Jinan 200
Liu Chao Pines, Tai Shan 257
Liu Li Chang Jie, Beijing 100-2, 104
Liuchow, see Liuzhou
Liuhe Pagoda, Hangzhou 183-4
Liuzhou (Liuchow) 219-20
Lixin Vegetarian Restaurant,
    Shanghai 147
Longbai Hotel, Shanghai 143
Long Hua Temple, Shanghai 140
Long Shou Yan, Lu Shan 224
Long Xing Temple, Zhengding 251
Longmen Grottoes, Luoyang 220
Longting, Kaifeng 210
Loyang, see Luoyang
Lu Shan (Lushan Mountains) 222-5
Lu Shan Botanical Garden, Lu Shan
    224
Lu Xun Memorial Hall, Shaoxing 245
Lu Xun's Museum and Tomb,
    Shanghai 134
Ludiyan, Guilin 178
Luohans, see Arhats
Luoyang (Loyang) 220-2

City Map of 220
Luoyang Bridge, Quanzhou 242
Luoyang Museum, Luoyang 222
Lushan Mountains, see Lu Shan
Lüxingshe, see China International
    Travel Service
Lychee, see Litchi

M

Marco Polo 27, 86
Master Card 46, 140, 317
Mausoleum of Martyrs, Shijiazhuang
    251
Mawangdui Tombs, Changsha 157
Mawei Port, Fuzhou 175
Medical Services 40
Mei Yuan, Wuxi 272
Melons, Hami 65
Memorial Hall of Chairman Mao,
    Beijing 75-6
Memorial Hall of the C.P.C.
    Delegation at Plum Tree Village,
    Nanjing 232
Memorial Park for the Martyrs of the
    Guangzhou Uprising, Guangzhou
    115
Meng Bi Sheng Hua, Huang Shan 194
Meghai Temple, Jinghong 205
Menghai Temple, Jinghong 205
Menus, Banquets 339-46
Meridian Gate, Beijing 80
Ming Jiao Si Temple, Hefei 189
Ming Tombs 95-100
    Site Plan of 97
Ming Xiao Tomb, Nanjing 230
Mink 65
Minzu Hotel, Beijing 108
Mo Ya Stele, Tai Shan 257
Mogan Shan (Mogan Mountain) 225
Mogao Grottoes (Mokao Grottoes)
    225
Mokao Grottoes, see Mogao Grottoes
Money Conversion Chart 326
Monument to the Martyrs of the Huai
    Hai Battle, Xuzhou, 281-2
Monument to the People's Heroes,
    Beijing 75
Moslem Restaurant, Shanghai 147
Mosque Dedicated to the Saint,
    Guangzhou 120
Mount Everest, see Qomolangma
Mount Jolmo Lungma, see
    Qomolangma

Mount Omei, see Emei Shan
Mount Lushan, see Lu Shan
Mountains 24
Municipalities of China
  Beijing 71-112
  Shanghai 130-47
  Tianjin 261-4
Museum, Zhenjiang 297
Mural Paintings of the East Jin
  Dynasty, Jiuquan 209
Museum of Chinese History, Beijing
  75
Museum of Chinese Revolution,
  Beijing 75
Museum of Natural Science, Dalian
  165
Museum of Natural Sciences,
  Shanghai 136
Museum of Xinjiang Uygur
  Autonomous Region, Ürümqi 266

N

Nan Hai (South China Sea) 22-3
Nan Tian Men Gate, Tai Shan 256
Nan Yuan Restaurant, Guangzhou 129
Nanchang (Nanchang) 226-8
  City Map of 227
Nanhua Yanyun Restaurant, Shanghai
  146
Nanjing (Nanking) 228-34
  City Map of 229
Nanjing Lu (Nanjing Road), Shanghai
  134, 141
Nanjing Museum, Nanjing 231
Nanking. see Nanjing
Nanning (Nanning) 234-7
  City Map of 235
Nanputuo Temple, Xiamen 274
Nanshan Temple, Zhangzhou 292
Nanwenquan Park, Chongqing 163
National Institute of the Peasant
  Movement, Guangzhou 115
National People's Congress 30, 75
Nationalities, in China 22
Natural Resources 25
Newspapers 306
Ningbo (Ningpo) 237-8
Ningpo, see Ningbo
Nine Dragon Screen,
  Beijing 85, 87
  Datong 166
Nine Flowers Mountain, see Jiuhua

Shan
Norbulingka, Lhasa 218
North Temple Pagoda, Suzhou 255
Northern Yan Dang Shan, Shaoxing
  245
Number One Carpet Factory, Tianjin
  262

O

Oceans 22-3
Old Palace, Beijing, see Imperial
  Palace, Beijing
Opera 60-1

P

Packing recommendations 303
Pagoda of Six Harmonies, see Liuhe
  Pagoda
Pai Yun Ting, Huang Shan 194
Painting 58
Palace of Earthly Tranquility, Beijing
  82
Palace of Heavenly Purity, Beijing 82
Palace Museum, Beijing, see Imperial
  Palace
Pandas 67-8, 90
Paper-cuts 59-60, 172
Passport 36
Pavilion of Nanlao Spring, Taiyuan
  260
Peace Hotel, Ürümqi 266
Pearl River, see Zhu Jiang
Pier, The, Qingdao 239
Peking, see Beijing
Peking Hotel, see Beijing Hotel
Peking Hotel Restaurant, see Beijing
  Hotel Restaurant
Peking Man 25, 71
Peony Gardens, Luoyang 222
People's Park
  Hohhot 190
  Zhengzhou 293
People's Park, Shanghai, see Renmin
  Park, Shanghai
People's Restaurant, Shanghai 147
Phrases, Useful 332-3
Pilose (Deer) Antler 64-5
Pinyin 28-30
Pohai Sea, see Bo Hai

Population, of China 21
Potala Palace, The, Lhasa 217
Postal rates 327
Postal Services 43
Pottery 59
Products, Native 62-6
Punctuality 304

Q

Qi Xing Yan, Guangzhou 123
Qian Duo Lian Hua, Anshan 150
Qian Fo Shan, Jinan 200
Qian Men Gate, Beijing 76
Qian Men Hotel, Beijing 108
Qian Tomb, Xi'an 279
Qin Shi Huang Mausoleum, Xi'an 278-9
Qingjing Temple, Quanzhou 242
Qing Shui Tang, Changsha 154
Qing Yu Gorge, Xingzi County 280
Qing Yun Pu, Nanchang 228
Qingcheng Shan, Chengdu 161
Qingdao (Tsingtao) 238-40
Qingdao Aquarium, Qingdao 239
Qingdao Harbor, Qingdao 239
Qinhuangdao (Chinhuangtao) 240-1
Qiong Hua Island, Beijing 86-7
Qiongzhusi Temple, Kunming 213
Qomolangma Feng 22, 24
Quarantine 36
Quanzhou (Chuanchow) 241-2
Qufu (Chüfu) 242-3
Qutang Gorge, Changjiang Gorges 152

R

Railroads 50-1
Railway Map 310
    Distances Between Main Tourist Cities 311-12
Rainfall Chart, Annual 316
Ren Shou Si Temple, Foshan 171, 172
Renmin Park, Shanghai 136
Renminbi (RMB) 43
Resources, Natural 25
Restaurants
    Beijing 109-12
    Changsha 157
    Chengdu 161
    Guangzhou 127-30

Guilin 179
Hangzhou 185
Jinan 201
Kunming 214
Nanjing 234
Nanning 237
Shanghai 145-7
Revolutionary Martyrs' Memorial Park, Urümqi 266
Ri Guan Peak, Tai Shan 257
Rivers 23
Roman Catholic Cathedral, Guangzhou 121
Rong Bao Zhai Studio, Beijing 102
Round Town, Beijing 86-7
Ruijin Guest House, Shanghai 143

S

Sacred Way, Ming Tombs 96, 98
Sailor's Clubs 51-2
    Names and Addresses 320
Sanyou Cave, Yichang 287
Sea Gull Hotel, Shanghai 144
Sculpture 58
Sha Mian Isle, Guangzhou 116
Shaanxi Provincial Museum, Xi'an 277
Shahe Restaurant, Guangzhou 129
Shan Juan Cave, Yixing 289-90
Shandong Provincial Museum, Jinan 201
Shang City Ruins, Zhengzhou 294
Shanghai (Shanghai) 130-45
    City Map of 132
    Hotels 141-5
    Places of Interest 134-41
    Restaurants 145-7
    Shopping 141
Shanghai Hotel, Shanghai 144
Shanghai Industrial Exhibition 134
Shanghai Mansions Hotel, Shanghai 143
Shanghai Museum, Shanghai 135
Shanghai Zoo, Shanghai 140
Shanhaiguan, Qinhuangdao 240
Shaohsing, see Shaoxing
Shaoshan (Shaoshan) 243
Shaoxing (Shaohsing) 244-7
Shell Mosaics Workshop, Dalian 165
Sheng Mu Dian, Taiyuan 259
Shenzhen (Shumchun) 248-9
Shenyang (Shenyang) 247-8
    City Map of 248
Shiwan Ceramics Factory, Foshan 170

Shi Xin Feng, Huang Shan 194
Shihchiachuang, see Shijiazhuang
Shijiazhuang (Shihchiachuang) 250-1
    City Map of 250
Shilin (Stone Forest) 251-2
Shopping, General 51-3
    Beijing 102-3
    Changsha 157
    Chengdu 161
    Guangzhou 123-4
    Guilin 178
    Hangzhou 184
    Hohhot 192
    Jinan 201
    Kunming 214
    Nanjing 234
    Nanning 237
    Shanghai 141
    Tianjin 264
    Urümqi 267
    Yangzhou 286
Shou Xi Hu, Yangzhou 285
Shui Shang Gong Yuan, Tianjin 262
Sian, see Xi'an
Sichuan Restaurant, Beijing 111
Sichuan Restaurant, Shanghai 146
Silk 62
Silk Dyeing and Printing Mill, Foshan
    170
Six Eastern Palaces, Imperial Palace,
    Beijing 83
Six Western Palaces, Imperial Palace,
    Beijing 83
Sixth Spring Under Heaven, Xingzi
    County 280-1
Snake Restaurant, Guangzhou 130
Solitary Hill, see Gu Shan
Song Jiang Xian, Shanghai 141
Songhua Lake, Jilin 197
Songhua River, Jilin 198
Soochow, see Suzhou
South China Botanical Garden,
    Guangzhou 122
South China Sea, see Nan Hai
Souvenirs 305
Stalin Park, Harbin 187
Special Handicraft Workshop, Tianjin
    262
Stamps 40
    Cost of 327
State Council, of China 30
Stone Forest, see Shilin
Su Causeway, Hangzhou 182
Su Dongpo 119
Summer Palace, Beijing 91-3
Sun Yat-Sen Mausoleum, Nanjing
    229-30

Sun Yat-Sen Memorial Hall,
    Guangzhou 118
Sun Yat-Sen Memorial Park, Beijing
    79
Sun Yat-Sen Park, Qingdao 239
Suzhou (Soochow) 252-5
Suzhou Embroidery Research
    Institute, Suzhou 254

T

Tai Shan (Taishan Mountain) 255-8
Taiyang Dao, Harbin 187
Taiwan Province 23
Taiyuan (Taiyuan) 258-61
    City Map of 258
Talien, see Dalian
Tang Gang Zi Spring, Anshan 149-50
Tang Tablet, Taiyuan 260-1
Tatung, see Datong
Tea 62-4
Telegrams 42-3
Telephones 40-2
Temperatures, in China 38-9, 314-5
Temple Dedicated to Service to the
    Country, Emei Shan 168
Temple of Heaven, Beijing 87-90
    Site Plan of 88
Temple of the Chen Family
    Ancestors, Guangzhou 121
Temple of the Jade Buddha, Shanghai
    136
Temple of the Six Banyan Trees,
    Guangzhou 119
Temple to the Town Gods, Shanghai
    139
Temple of Yu, Shaoxing 245
Ten Thousand Years Temple, Emei
    Shan 168-9
Terra Cotta Figurine Studio, Tianjin
    262
Theater 61
Thunderclap Temple, Emei Shan 168
Tian An Men Gate, Beijing 76-7, 79
Tian An Men Square, Beijing 74-5
Tian Kuang Hall, Tai Shan 256
Tian Tan Park, Beijing, see Temple of
    Heaven Park
Tianchi, Urümqi 266
Tianjin (Tientsin) 261-4
    City Map of 263
Tianyige Library, Ningbo 238
Tientsin, see Tianjin
Tieta, Kaifeng 209
Tiger Taming Temple, Emei Shan 168

Time Differences 325
Ting Li Guan Restaurant, Beijing 112
Tong Pavilion, Tai Shan 258
Topography 24
Trains, see Railroads/Railways
Transportation, Inter-city 50-1, 304
Transportation, Intra-city 51
Traveler's Checks, Chinese 45
Traveler's Checks, Foreign 46
　List of Types Accepted 324-5
Tsinan, see Jinan
Tsingtao, see Qingdao
Tsunhua, see Zunhua
Turfan, see Turpan
Turpan County (Turfan County) 264-5

U

Ürümchi, see Ürümqi
Ürümqi (Ürümchi) 265-7
　City Map of 267
Ürümqi Friendship Store, Ürümqi 267

V

Valuables 305
Vegetarian Restaurant, Guangzhou
　130
Vineyards in Qingxu County, Taiyuan
　261
Visa, for China 36
Visa, Application for, facsimile 34-5
Visa Credit Card 46, 317

W

Wai Ba Temples, Chengde 158-9
Wan Jiang Park, Chengdu 160
Wang Fu Jing, Beijing 104
Wanshishan Park, Xiamen 274
Weights and Measures, Chart 327
West Lake, see Xi Hu
Whampoa, see Huangpu
White Dagoba, Beijing 85, 86, 87
White Swan Hotel 126
Wild Game Restaurant, Guangzhou
　130
Wines 57, 335-38
Workers' Cultural Palace, Lanzhou
　216

Working People's Park, Luoyang 222
Wu Dang Zhao Monastery, Hohhot
　190
Wu Gorge, Changjiang Gorges 152-3
Wu Lao Feng, Lu Shan 224
Wu Quan Hill, Lanzhou 215
Wu Ta Pavilion, Hohhot 191
Wudangzhao Temple, Baotou 150
Wuhan (Wuhan) 267-70
　City Map of 269
Wuhan Acrobatic Troupe, The,
　Wuhan 268
Wuhan Iron and Steel Company,
　Wuhan 268
Wuhan University, Wuhan 268
Wuhsi, see Wuxi
Wuli Bridge, Quanzhou 242
Wulong Hill, Leshan 216-7
Wuxi (Wuhsi) 270-3
　City Map of 270

X

Xi Hu (West Lake), Hangzhou 181
Xi Hui Park, Wuxi 272
Xi Jiao Park, see Shanghai Zoo
Xi Yuan, Suzhou 254
Xi'an (Sian) 275-9
　City Map of 275
Xiamen (Amoy) 273-5
Xiamen Park, Xiamen 274
Xian Ren Dong, Lu Shan 223
Xiangbishan, Guilin 178
Xiangguosi, Kaifeng, 211
Xiangtangshan Grottoes, Handan 180
Xiao Tian Chi, Lu Shan 224
Xiao Yao Jin, Hefei 188
Xiao Ying Zhou Island, Hangzhou
　181
Xijiao Guest House, Shanghai 145
Xiling Gorge, Changjiang Gorges 153
Xin Qiao Hotel, Beijing 108
Xin Ya Restaurant, Shanghai 146
Xing Qing Park, Xi'an 279
Xingang, Tianjin 264
Xingguo Guest House, Shanghai 145
Xingzi County (Hsingtsu County)
　280-1
Xingzi Hot Springs, Xingzi County
　281
Xinlicheng Reservoir, Changchun 152
Xishan, Kunming 212
Xuan Wu Lake, Nanjing 230
Xuzhou (Hsuchow) 281-2

Y

Yalu Tsangpo River, see Yarlung
  Zangbo Jiang
Yan Hu, Shaoxing 246
Yan Tan Park, Lanzhou 216
Yan'an (Yenan) 282-3
Yang Kai Hui's Home, Changsha 156
Yangchow, see Yangzhou
Yangliuqing New Year Pictures 264
Yangshou (Yangshuo) 283
Yangtze River Gorges, see
  Changjiang Gorges
Yangzhou (Yangchow) 284-6
Yangzhou Restaurant, Shanghai 146
Yanjing Hotel, Beijing 108
Yanshui Pavilion, Jiujiang 207-8
Yantai (Yentai) 286-7
Yanxiang Hotel 108
Yarlung Zangbo Jiang (Yalu Tsangpo
  River) 23
Yellow Mountain, see Huang Shan
Yellow River, see Huang He
Yellow Sea, see Huang Hai
Yenan, see Yan'an
Yentai, see Yantai
Yichang (Ichang) 287-8
Yihsing, see Yixing
Yiling Cave, Nanning 235-7
Yinzhi Aqueduct, Shaoshan 243
Yixing (Yihsing) 288-91
Youyi Hotel, Beijing 109
Yu, the Mandarin's Garden, Shanghai
  138-9
Yu Hua Terrace, Nanjing 229
Yu Huang Ding, Tai Shan 257
Yu Yuan, Shanghai 138-9
Yu Yuan Pool, Xingzi County 280
Yuan 43, 44
Yuan Tou Island, Wuxi 272
Yuan Tou Park, Wuxi 272
Yuantong Park, Kunming 213
Yue Lu Hill, Changsha 156
Yue Xiu Park, Guangzhou 117

Yueyang (Yoyang) 291-2
Yueyang Tower 291
Yueyashen, Guilin 178
Yun Long Hill, Xuzhou 282
Yun Tai, Lianyun Gang 218
Yungang Grottoes, Datong 166
Yunsun Steamboat, Shanghai 138
Yuwangtai, Kaifeng 211

Z

Zengjiayan, No. 40, Chongqing 164
Zhang Gong Grotto, Yixing 291
Zhangzhou (Changchow) 292
Zhao Jun Tomb, Hohhot 191
Zhaolong Hotel, Beijing 109
Zhaozhou Bridge, Shijiazhuang 251
Zhen Hai Tower, The, Guangzhou
  118-9
Zhengzhou (Chengchou) 293-5
  City Map of 293
Zhenjiang (Chenchiang) 295-7
Zhenjiang, Scenic Areas, Southern
  Suburbs 297
Zhong Shan Lu, Shanghai 134
Zhongshan (Dr. Sun Yat-Sen) Park,
  Qingdao 239
Zhou Enlai Memorial Hall, Tianjin
  264
Zhu Jiang (Pearl River) 23
Zhuoxian County (Chohsien County)
  297
Zijin Shan Observatory, Nanjing 232
Zoo
  Beijing 90-1
  Guangzhou 122
  Harbin 187
Zu Ci Miao Taoist Temple, Foshan
  173
Zunhua (Tsunhua) 298-9